PAUL
BOWLES

_____ *A Study of the Short Fiction* ___

Also available in Twayne's Studies in Short Fiction Series

Twayne's Studies in Short Fiction

Gordon Weaver, General Editor
Oklahoma State University

PAUL
BOWLES

_____ *A Study of the Short Fiction* ___

Allen Hibbard
Middle Tennessee State University

TWAYNE PUBLISHERS · *NEW YORK*
Maxwell Macmillan Canada · *Toronto*
Maxwell Macmillan International · *New York Oxford Singapore Sydney*

Twayne's Studies in Short Fiction Series, No. 46

Twayne Publishers
Macmillan Publishing Company
866 Third Avenue
New York, New York 10022

Maxwell Macmillan Canada, Inc.
1200 Eglinton Avenue East
Suite 200
Don Mills, Ontario M3C 3N1

Macmillan Publishing Company is part of the Maxwell Communication Group of Companies.

Library of Congress Cataloging-in-Publication Data

Hibbard, Allen.
    Paul Bowles : a study of the short fiction / Allen Hibbard.
        p.   cm. — (Twayne's studies in short fiction series ; no. 46)
    Includes bibliographical references and index.
    ISBN 0-8057-8318-0 (alk. paper)
    1. Bowles, Paul, 1910–   —Criticism and interpretation.   2. Short story.   I. Title.   II. Series: Twayne's studies in short fiction ; no. 46.
    PS3552.O874Z66   1993
    813'.54—dc20   92-46049
                                                                              CIP

The paper used in this publication meets the minimum requirements of American National Standard for Information Sciences—Permanence of Paper for Printed Library Materials. ANSI Z3948-1984.∞™

10 9 8 7 6 5 4 3 2 1

Printed in the United States of America

Contents

Contents

PART 3. THE CRITICS

Preface

Hear the other side, see the other side.
—St. Augustine

Frightfulness is never more than an unfamiliar pattern.
—Paul Bowles, "Call at Corazón"

Paul Bowles has been widely recognized as one of this century's most masterful storytellers. Gore Vidal, for example, has boldly claimed that "his stories are among the best ever written by an American" and that "as a short story writer, he has had few equals in the second half of the twentieth century."[1] Yet surprisingly, despite this sort of acclaim Bowles is seldom found in the surveys and anthologies of contemporary American short stories.[2] Even in literary circles many have only a vague notion of who Bowles is and what he has written.

As Vidal suggests, part of the reason Bowles has largely remained a cult figure, not enjoying the popular reputation he justly deserves, lies in his extended residence in Morocco; he simply has not been much in the public eye here. Vidal's explanation, however, does not go far enough. There is, in a good many of these stories, something quite unsettling, potentially subversive, that many would probably just as soon keep at arm's length. Bowles's vision of America certainly does not jibe well with the omnipresent, nearly oppressive middle-class ethos of com-placency—a fierce clinging to the efficacy of private property, neatly trimmed lawns, moral uprightness, and mechanistic routine. For much of his early life, Bowles was a vagabond, metaphysically and physically, in a way calling to mind Deleuze and Guattari's discussions of the nomadic stance.[3] (*Without Stopping*, he appropriately titled his autobiography.) His fiction attests to the horror and exhilaration lying ominously on the periphery of our lives, piercing the illusory calm, at times, with a sudden violence.

Despite his many years of expatriation and the undeniable influence of continental ideas and Moroccan landscapes on his writing, Bowles, like Henry James, is unquestionably an American author, writing very much in the American grain. (He has, all these years, never seriously considered giving up his American passport.) "Beneath the violent surfaces of the novels and many of the stories," Steven Olson writes, "lies a persistent anti-patriarchal stratum that is characteristically American."[4] The subversive intent of Bowles's work is entirely consistent with visions expressed in the best of American literature, by Melville, Thoreau, and so many others. And the often violent encounter with the "other" has been at the core of the American experience since the landing of Christopher Columbus and the initiation of the slave trade.

Like a great many American writers, Bowles has had considerable success with short and long fiction. Yet while Bowles's artistry has taken many shapes—poems, musical compositions, novels, translations—the form of the short story has clearly suited him best. To this form he has shown the most enduring commitment. During a period of more than 50 years, Bowles has written and published in excess of 60 stories, a surprising proportion of which are truly excellent and memorable.

While there were many imaginable approaches to this study of Bowles's short fiction, the one I have adopted here is essentially chronological. Once I began to think of an organizational scheme, it soon became apparent that this method would not only preserve the integrity of individual stories but display the development of the writer's themes and style over the course of a long career. Thus, I have divided the study into six chapters, each devoted to the first American volumes of Bowles's stories.[5]

My purpose here is severalfold: to introduce readers to Bowles's short story oeuvre; to map out the territory so that the reader might find one's way about it; to supply, inasmuch as possible, biographical material relevant to the creative process; to distill from the analysis of his stories a "Bowlesian aesthetic" (what it is that makes for the Bowles story); and, in a limited way, to contextualize Bowles's work within the broader cultural currents of the twentieth century.

Any criticism must recognize the primacy of the texts it addresses. My hope is that this discussion will engage readers. Those who already have some acquaintance with Bowles's fiction will, I hope, pleasurably recall those stories; those who have not yet read Bowles will, I hope, be moved to sample them.

Poets and artists, Proust tells us, have the power to create and render "some marvelous site, different from the rest of the world."[6] The stories formed in the mind of a particular writer all bear, in some way, that writer's special imprint. We immediately recognize the Chekhov story, the Maupassant or Henry James or Katherine Mansfield story, when we come on it, if we have been familiar with the author's work. What, then, distinguishes the Bowles story?

One of the most distinguishing characteristics of Bowles's fiction is his use of foreign settings. The remarks of Eudora Welty in her landmark essay "Place in Fiction" apply well to Bowles. "Place," she writes, "absorbs our earliest notice and attention, it bestows on us our original awareness; and our critical powers spring up from the study of it and the growth of experience inside it." Welty calls setting "the ground conductor of all the currents of emotion and belief and moral conviction that charge out from the story in its course."[7] "Place undoubtedly works upon genius," she notes (Welty, 123). Further, "every story would be another story, and unrecognizable as art, if it took up its characters and plot and happened somewhere else" (Welty, 122).

Bowles himself has spoken of the importance of place in the making of his stories. In the preface to *A Distant Episode: The Selected Stories of Paul Bowles*, he writes, "It seems a practical procedure to let the place determine the characters who will inhabit it."[8] His extensive travels have brought Bowles in contact with a prodigious range of tropical and exotic places, many of which he has appropriated as backdrops for stories. While his use of Latin American settings, as we shall see, is extraordinarily evocative, it is North Africa that has had the most sustained influence on his work, since he first glimpsed the port of Tangier in 1931, a destination suggested by Alice B. Toklas and Gertrude Stein. The Tangier Bowles has known in the twentieth century has been subject to the same types of cultural and geographic influences felt by Ibn Battuta, the famous fourteenth-century traveler who set out from Tangier. The city was then "a converging point of four geographical worlds—African and European, Atlantic and Mediterranean. It was an international town whose character was determined by the shifting flow of maritime traffic in the strait—merchants and warriors, craftsmen and scholars shuttling back and forth between the pillars or gliding under them between the ocean and the sea."[9]

Tangier in particular, and North Africa more generally, has given Bowles the subject matter of a large proportion of his fiction. The experience of Morocco, felt in Bowles's fiction, was aptly described by Edith Wharton, whose visit there preceded Bowles's by just a decade or so. "If one loses one's way in Morocco," she writes, "civilization vanishes as though it were a magic carpet rolled up by a djinn."[10] This is precisely the feeling Bowles's fiction leaves us with. Charges of neocolonialism—that he has represented Morocco and Moroccans in a manner most suitable to his own psychological and economic needs—should not detract from the dazzling quality of the stories themselves.

Bowles's thematic concerns rise from the experiences his characters have in these foreign landscapes. Most stories in some way involve a kind of transgression, or crossing of boundaries: crime ("Doña Faustina," "Julian Vreden,"); transformation from human to animal ("By the Water," "Allal," "Kitty"); moral transgressions ("The Echo," "Pages from Cold Point"); insanity ("You Are Not I," "If I Should Open My Mouth"); experiences with drugs ("Tapiama," "He of the Assembly"); death ("The Delicate Prey," "In the Red Room"); and the cultural encounter ("Tea on the Mountain," "The Time of Friendship," "Pastor Dowe at Tacaté," and so many others). Dostoyevsky's assertion that Poe "almost always chooses the rarest reality and places his hero in the most unaccustomed circumstance or psychological situation" suits Bowles just as well, if not better.[11]

Bowles is, moreover, known for the sense of terror to which he often subjects his characters and readers. Referring to "A Distant Episode," one of his most gruesome stories, Bowles has said, "Shock is a *sine qua non* to the story. You don't teach a thing like that unless you are able, in some way, to make the reader understand what the situation would be like to *him*. And that involves shock."[12]

Bowles's depiction of violence and terror is just one of the things that make him distinctly modern. Like so many modernist writers, Bowles's view of modern life is thoroughly pessimistic. Like Joseph Conrad, he has sought his identity in relation to cultures most wholly foreign to his own. Like Lawrence, he has sought more lively, natural human behavior in primitive societies. Like Kafka, he has found modern mechanistic and bureaucratic practices absurd, if not deeply pernicious. Like Camus and Sartre, he has subscribed to existentialist views of human action and belief. Expatriation to a traditional culture such as Morocco, then, must be seen as a logical response to his disgust with a modern world both morally and aesthetically bankrupt.

If Bowles's thematic concerns are unmistakeably modern, he is formally (at least until his later stories) more conservative, sharing more affinities with nineteenth-century masters such as Flaubert, Turgenev, James, and even Tolstoy (who were all attentive to the aesthetic shapes their tales took) than with postmodern experimenters such as William Gass and Robert Coover, or with K mart realists such as Raymond Carver and Bobbie Ann Mason.

While there is, in the Bowles story, an almost obsessive fascination with life on the edge, it is tempered or offset by the very narrative strategies by which the stories are told. Transgressive acts, as shocking as they may be, are contained within traditionally crafted forms. Generally, the Bowles story is told in a fairly straightforward, linear manner, yielding a hard, smooth surface that supports no moral comment on the actions that take place. The power of his stories, we may feel, comes from the stance of the storyteller. The teller's presence is intensely felt, yet at the same time he is distant, coy, cold, or simply out of reach. In this space the writer/teller captivates his audience, creating the desire to listen, to follow the line, with the expectation that he will, despite the snares, derive some pleasure. Jane Bowles's description of one of her characters, Andrew Mclean—"Reticence enhanced his charm"—nicely captures that quality which gives Bowles's fiction its power.[13] The storyteller builds suspense by giving things out in small doses, in holding back as long as he possibly can, in releasing at just the right moment.

The Bowles story is as deliberately crafted as his short musical compositions, with the same attention to tone, balance, structural integrity, and harmony. "The good storyteller," Bowles wrote in the introduction to Larbi Layachi's *A Life Full of Holes*, "keeps the thread of his narrative almost equally taut at all points."[14] Bowles's means of composition and aesthetic principles greatly resemble those described by Poe:

> A skilful literary artist has constructed a tale. If wise, he has not fashioned his thoughts to accommodate his incidents; but having conceived, with deliberate care, a certain unique or single *effect* to be wrought out, he then invents such incidents—he then combines such events as may best aid him in establishing this preconceived effect. If his very initial sentence tend not to the outbringing of this effect, then he has failed in his first step. In the whole composition there should be no word written, of which the tendency, direct or indirect, is not to the one preestablished design.[15]

There is, then, a causal rigor, a kind of formal determinism in shaping the story. The writer does not so much *force* the story as let it enter his consciousness and give birth to itself, sui generis, on its own terms.

Bowles's stories, finally, often call our attention to the very act of storytelling. Stories are sometimes embedded within other stories, and narrators at times seem themselves to be involved in the act of piecing together whatever has happened in a particular instance. In his book on Bowles, Richard F. Patteson has amply illustrated how the fiction-making enterprise can be thought of as an attempt to provide shelter, as well as order, in a world fraught with potential terror and chaos.[16] Walter Benjamin offers yet another perspective on the status of storytelling in the modern world, extremely relevant to the case of Bowles. In "The Storyteller" (subtitled "Reflections on the Works of Nicolai Leskov"), Benjamin makes a sharp distinction between the art of the novel and that of the story, suggesting that the novel has been dependent on a book culture, while the story has had its origins in societies with thriving oral traditions. Novels are necessarily products of prolonged isolation. "The storyteller," on the other hand, "takes what he tells from experience— his own or that reported by others. And he in turn makes it the experience of those who are listening to his tale."[17] Benjamin's views, like those of many with Marxist sympathies, contain a nostalgic yearning for a more organic, traditional social order. This is the kind of world Bowles has embraced, and sought to hold onto. In Tangier he has been open to stories, whether they be transformed from what others have told or wholly imagined. He has, likewise, taken a lively interest in local, semiliterate Maghrebi storytellers, recording their tales and translating them into English. All this has doubtless affected his own work.

In his essay "The Geography of the Imagination," Guy Davenport isolates three essential stylistic and thematic components of Poe's poetry—"grotesque, or Gothic; arabesque, or Islamic; classical, or Graeco-Roman."[18] All these elements certainly coalesce in the typical Bowles story.

All told, Bowles has been an explorer of unknown or unfamiliar spaces. In his stories rich and unfamiliar experiences are marvelously related. As such, his work exists on the margins of our common experience. Fortunately, we have begun to realize the value of that which occurs on the periphery. It infuses art with vitality. It helps define what the center is. It sounds its cries of warning.

For more than 12 years, I have been collecting and reading everything I could find by or about Paul Bowles. I still remember walking into the Left Bank Bookstore in Seattle's Pike Place Market and buying a copy of Bowles's *Collected Stories*. The arabesque design on the cover of the Black Sparrow paperback caught my eye and sparked my curiosity. I cannot remember anyone having recommended the writer, though Brian Kiteley has often claimed credit for bringing Bowles to my attention. My first impression of Bowles—the originality of his voice, the allure of his settings, and the bristling incidents in his tales—is today even more deeply confirmed.

My interest in Bowles may in part have led me to Egypt, where I taught for four years at the American University in Cairo, and, at long last, to pilgrimages I made from Cairo to Tangier. There in Morocco I experienced firsthand the land Bowles had written about, and frequently found myself wondering to what extent the Morocco I knew was really there and to what extent it had been created by my sustained imaginative engagement with Bowles's fiction.

This book will seem a very modest venture, I am afraid, given the extent of support it has enjoyed. Many individuals and institutions have generously nourished this intellectual quest. Ewing Campbell first suggested that I contact Gordon Weaver about the possibility of doing the book. With friend and novelist Brian Kiteley, I have been involved in a sustained dialogue concerning the meaning and place of Bowles. While in Cairo I met Dr. Leslie Croxford, who had himself spent time writing in Tangier and knew Bowles. It was Dr. Croxford who suggested that I go to Morocco, which I did, for two consecutive summers, 1987 and 1988, thanks to travel and research grants from the American University in Cairo. In Morocco Bowles gave generously of his time, saying on one occasion, not terribly confidently, "I'm sure you know what you are doing." Conversations with Phillip Ramey, Rodrigo Rey Rosa, and Gavin Lambert also shed light on my subject.

On this side of the Atlantic as well, many have willingly aided with the project. John Murphy and Ron Messier, as friends and colleagues, have blindly believed in the value of this pursuit. A research grant from the Harry Ransom Humanities Research Center (HRC) at the University of Texas, in the summer of 1991, gave me a chance to pour over Bowles manuscripts, letters, and notebooks and to glean material that has enriched the book. Among the fine staff there I wish to single out and thank publicly Dr. Thomas Staley, Cathy Henderson, and Patricia Fox. Virginia Spencer Carr, whom I met there at the HRC, kindly recommended the photo I chose to use. Of help also have been Bernard R. Crystal, of the Rare Book and Manuscript Library at the Butler Library, and Timothy D. Murray, at the University of Delaware. At Middle Tennessee State University, I have relied on the fine services of Betty McFall, of interlibrary loan, who has diligently tracked down material for me. Anthony Tate collected articles and typed in portions of the manuscript, always with his natural good cheer. Heather Uffelman helped me at key stages by reading and offering criticisms on the manuscript, keeping track of permissions, printing out the book, and doing countless other things; something of her fine spirit lives in this book. Michael Wolfe of Tombouctou Press, a writer in his own right, has been of more help than he perhaps has realized. And my brother-in-law, Allan Nettleton, answered a frantic plea for computer software to convert material from one system to another.

From the beginning Gordon Weaver has had faith in this book and has encouraged me to seize every opportunity I could. His fine editing has saved me much embarrassment.

Finally, my wife, Nora, and two children—Dashiell and Alexandra—have sacrificed much for this long-elusive book. At the age of two, Dashiell explained my absence by saying, "Baba. 'Rocco. Later."

Part 1

THE SHORT FICTION

The Delicate Prey and Other Stories

Early Tales

In November 1950 Random House brought out *The Delicate Prey and Other Stories*.[19] Even when considered forty-odd years after its publication, this first collection of Paul Bowles stories is astonishing. Among the volume's 17 stories are some of the writer's finest, representing one of his most productive periods, the late 1940s. The collection established a range of themes Bowles subsequently continued to explore and, along with his first novel, *The Sheltering Sky* (1949), helped secure Bowles's literary reputation. These early works were responsible in large part for creating the image most readers and critics have of the author today.

Only two of the stories in this volume are set in the United States. Five are set in North Africa, and the rest in various parts of Latin America. Place, usually vastly foreign, has always been for Bowles the condition prerequisite for telling a story. The reader is invited to enter strange, sometimes uncomfortable worlds made luminous by the light of fiction. The stories in *The Delicate Prey*, written in a sure and natural style, bear the stamp of an imagination drawn to the exotic, the genuinely bizarre, and Gothic horror.

A writer's early work, while usually not his best, often announces themes and obsessions, tells us something about original impulses, and reveals something about how he approaches his work. With this in mind, we should look at three of Bowles's earliest stories, all of which appeared in his first volume. These stories are important because they mark a juncture at which Bowles began to direct more of his talents and energies, then involved with his thriving musical pursuits, toward literary ventures. Their successful completion most likely rekindled writerly ambitions first ignited by the acceptance of a poem at the Paris-based literary journal *transition* when Bowles was 16.

When Bowles wrote "Tea on the Mountain," which heads the *Collected Stories* and must be thought of as the earliest work the writer considered worth preserving, he viewed the story as "a thing by itself." "I didn't intend to write any more," he has said, recollecting the time of writing. "I just felt like writing it that day. I suppose it was snowing out. I just remember shutting myself in and writing this story."[20] Lawrence

Stewart's recounting of the conditions surrounding the story's genesis in 1939, when Bowles was nearly 30, tells us a great deal about the psychological motivations driving Bowles's writing: "Five years had passed since Bowles had last seen Morocco. Then, one winter afternoon in his apartment on Brooklyn's Columbia Heights he began thinking of Tangier, of the taboos and rituals of the Arab culture, of the situation of an American novelist, living off publisher's advances, of a Moroccan experience that had not been his but pleasantly might have been." (Stewart 1974, 21). Key here are the place of memory and the desire memory inflames. As with Proust, the memory of a previously inhabited place and time creates a desire to reinhabit those places. Writing, then, becomes an act of creative reconstruction that bridges past and present, an act that seeks to fill the space forced open by desire.

It would be difficult to place too much emphasis on the most obvious fact bearing on Bowles's writing: his expatriation, especially his contact with Morocco, fueled his artistic drive and supplied him with the ideal landscape for his fertile imagination to flourish. Writing in his autobiography, *Without Stopping*, Bowles recorded his first real vision of Morocco when he traveled there with Aaron Copland in 1931: "If I said that Tangier struck me as a dream city, I should mean it in the strict sense. Its topography was rich in prototypal dream scenes: covered streets like corridors with doors opening into rooms on each side, hidden terraces high above the sea, streets consisting only of steps, dark impasses, small squares built on sloping terrain so that they looked like ballet sets designed in false perspective, with alleys leading off in several directions; as well as the classical dream equipment of tunnels, ramparts, ruins, dungeons and cliffs."[21] Thus began his lifelong affair with Morocco, which immediately captured his imagination. The recognition that an imaginary geography actually had a correspondent reality most likely prompted the notion that another kind of dream, that of becoming a writer, might also be objectively manifest.

The bulk of Bowles's literary output can be situated in exilic space, when the writer, with what James termed a "double consciousness," is curiously attracted to his new environment while at the same time reflecting on his native home. Michael Seidel, writing about this exilic condition, notes that "the task for the exile, especially the exiled artist, is to transform the figure of rupture back into a 'figure of connection'": "So many writers, whatever their personal or political traumas, have gained imaginative sustenance from exile—Ovid, Dante, Swift, Rousseau, Madame de Staël, Hugo, Lawrence, Mann, Brecht—that experiences native to the life of the exile seem almost activated in the life of the artist: separation as desire, perspective as witness, alienation as new being."[22] Without question, Paul Bowles fits within this tradition.

At the heart of "Tea on the Mountain" is the American's encounter with Morocco and Moroccans, and the conflicts that emerge result from the projection and obstruction of crisscrossing desires. While no means one of his best, the story is noteworthy because it announces stylistic and thematic patterns that become characteristic of Bowles's fiction. The writer himself told Lawrence Stewart that while the story was "really superficial and rather trivial," it "may foreshadow things that come later in better stories" (Stewart 1974, 21). Twenty years later, for example, Bowles would write "The Time of Friendship," which more satisfactorily works out the dynamics involved in "Tea on the Mountain."

The central character in "Tea on the Mountain" is an unnamed American woman writer who, when we first meet her, has just received "a large advance from her publishers." She is in the International Zone partly because "life was cheap" (*CS*, 15). Her money and its value in Morocco, a function of the political and economic strength of her homeland, give her the freedom to come and go as she pleases. Not only does the woman come to Morocco in search of a place to live cheaply; she is also led by a vague yearning for sexual adventure. To the Moroccan male she becomes an unwitting symbol of accessible sexuality and corruption. Desire to possess the Western woman (to wrest her from her Western man) is fed by advertising and economic deprivation, and conquest is a sign of virility as well as a way of avenging a gnawing condition of political impotence. The process of corruption is symbiotic. As much as the West thrusts itself on the East, the East eagerly awaits all the freedoms and glamor it often perceives the West as offering. These psychological/historical dynamics act as a kind of palimpsest over which the individual characters in the story move.

With money in her purse, the American woman, in the story's first scene, is more receptive than usual to the friendly advances of Driss, a young Europeanized Moroccan who passes by and addresses her in French. Though previously she had maintained some distance from him, "this morning she greeted him warmly, let him pay her check, and moved off up the street with him, conscious of the comment her action had caused among the other Arabs sitting in the café" (*CS*, 15). Driss has studied and been influenced by the ways and affectations of Europeans, though he still wears a djellaba and remains thoroughly Moroccan.

Driss introduces the American woman to two young Moroccans, Mjid and Ghazi, Mjid being "more serious and soft-eyed," while Ghazi is "plump and Negroid" (*CS*, 16). Mjid, more precocious and fluent in foreign tongues than his friend, soon proposes that the three of them go on a picnic the next day. He will get a carriage and, they suggest, she will bring ham and wine, a flagrant and daring violation of fundamental Islamic tenets. Though the woman at first decides against going on the picnic, the idea of an adventure soon consumes her such that she does "not even wait until the next day to stock up with provisions at the English grocery": "She bought three bottles of ordinary red wine, two cans of Jambon Olida [the kind the boys had explicitly requested], several kinds of Huntley and Palmer's biscuits, a bottle of stuffed olives and five hundred grams of chocolates full of liqueurs" (*CS*, 18).

The picnic becomes the occasion for both the American woman and the Moroccan boys to break out of culturally imposed conventions and moral constraints. At one point Ghazi and Mjid remark on their culture's taboos and restrictions:

> "If my father could see us," said Ghazi, draining a tin cup of it. "Ham and wine!"
>
> Mjid drank a cup, making a grimace of distaste. He lay back, his arms folded behind his head. "Now that I've finished, I can tell you that I don't like wine, and everyone knows that ham is filthy. But I hate our severe conventions." (*CS*, 20)

Later on, after Ghazi has been left behind and the woman is with Mjid in a room at a villa, waiting for tea, she attributes her presence at the picnic to a dream of release and freedom. She thinks to herself: "'What am I doing here? I have no business here. I said I wouldn't come.' The idea of such a picnic had so completely coincided with some unconscious desire she had harbored for many years. To be free, out-of-doors, with some young man she did not know—*could* not know—that was probably the important part of the dream. For if she could not know him, he could not know her" (*CS*, 22). The woman's emotions described here might be taken as an expression of Bowles's own anxieties and desires. And expatriation must be seen as a search for a sense of freedom unavailable in America. The force and thrill of the exotic lie in the recognition that something will always be veiled, just beyond the understanding, and that the subject will, likewise, always be just beyond understanding. One will always be the outsider, the stranger, the interloper.

In the end neither the American nor the Moroccan young men become much more than stereotypical figures, and the story represents little more than a tourist's flirtations with a culture and the projection of her sexual fantasies on the landscape. As much as the story is about the powerful mechanisms of desire, it is about the subversion of desire by the myriad personal and cultural obstacles that stand between any two living humans. Everyone in the story seems to want something magical, yet that something never ultimately transpires. As Lawrence Stewart puts it, "Certainly it prefigures one of [Bowles's] obsessive beliefs: the need for, and the impossibility of, communication among people" (Steward 1974, 21).

The need and failure both seem to be heightened in the drama that takes place between such radically different cultures. Throughout the story both parties are, in their own ways, trying to get to know the other, attempting to break through the thick barriers that culture and gender impose on them and to establish some kind of meaningful communication. Both sides, it is clear, want something from the other, yet those wants are vague, confused yearnings. On the way to the picnic, in the carriage, Mjid gives the American woman a silver ring. When the woman asks what she can give in return, he says meaningfully, "The pleasure of a true European friend." She reminds them that she is American, not European, to which Mjid replies, "All the better" (*CS*, 19).

Gifts are exchanged and hospitality is extended, yet in the end communication fails. As Stewart puts it,

> The tea ceremony—like hospitality itself, which is to unite men in peace and understanding—here shelters perversion. The religious dietary laws are broken, and the woman is far older than the boys; she likes Morocco only for the cheapness of the land and the cheap availability of a qualified but delicious terror. We have the prelude to the sexual act, but timidity and indifference interfere. It is the hunt without the kill. Tea becomes the confederation not of those who wish to give themselves to bonds of love and friendship; it is the confederation of those who wish to get. Since terror is an essential ingredient to her pleasure, she flaunts her money and her solitude, pretending to be an easy victim. But this courting of danger is only the courting of vulgarity. As she draws money from her publisher for work that is promised but not delivered, so she extracts emotions from the boys, using Mjid as she has used Driss earlier, "putting him off without losing his friendship." (Stewart 1974, 25)

Toward the end of the story, the young Moroccan voices his dream that "Perhaps some day I shall go to America, and then you can invite me to your house for tea. Each year we'll come back to Morocco and see our friends and bring back cinema stars and presents from New York" (*CS*, 24). We know that this fantasy, shared by so many in the third world today, is but a fragile Cinderella-like scenario that comes true only in fairy tales and, perhaps, in Bowles's later story "Here to Learn," which chronicles the odyssey of a young Moroccan woman, picked up in her native village and escorted by various Western men through Spain, France, Switzerland, and, finally, Los Angeles.

The picnic in "Tea on the Mountain" is cut short by the muezzin's call to prayer, sharply reminding the American how much of an outsider she is. On the way back to the hotel, she tells her companions she will be leaving for Paris the next day. In other words, the balloon of romance has burst, dropping all parties back to the ground of reality. Read symbolically, the end of this story, much like the end of Bowles's novel *The Spider's House*, shows the mobility of the Westerner, who can come and go as he pleases, leaving the Moroccan behind in a cloud of dust.

If "Tea on the Mountain" supplies clues to the psychological forces behind Bowles's storytelling and his ties to Morocco, "The Scorpion" and "By the Water," both luminous and surreal, reveal more about the relation between reality and story in Bowles's work. In his autobiography, *Without Stopping*, Bowles tells about the circumstances of the writing of "The Scorpion," written in 1945:

> I had been reading some ethnographic books with texts from the Arapesh or from the Tarahumara given in word-for-word translation. Little by little the desire came to me to invent my own myths, adopting the point of view of the primitive mind. The only way I could devise for simulating that state was the old Surrealist method of abandoning conscious control and writing whatever words came from the pen. First, animal legends resulted from the experiments and then tales of animals disguised as "basic human" beings. One rainy Sunday I awoke late, put a thermos of coffee by my bedside, and began to write another of these myths. No one disturbed me, and I wrote until I had finished it. I read it over, called it "The Scorpion," and decided that it could be shown to others. . . . It was through this unexpected little gate that I crept back into the land of fiction writing. Long ago I had decided that the world was too complex for me ever to be able to write fiction; since I failed to understand life, I would not be able to find points of reference which the hypothetical reader might have in common with me. (*WS*, 261–62)

Several things stand out in this passage. First, "The Scorpion" is important for Bowles because it opened that "little gate" which led him "back into the land of fiction writing" he had known as a young man. The appeal of the "primitive mind," which is so clearly a theme in Bowles's work and life, can be understood here not only as a reactionary modernist rejection of scientific, rational thinking but as a means of recovering the proto-rational, unconscious origins of storytelling. This attitude explains, in part at least, the meaning of Morocco for Bowles and his interest in the traditional oral storytelling of Moroccans such as Mohamed Mrabet and Driss Ben Hamed Charhadi, whose tales Bowles has made available to English readers. In a brief introduction to his translation of Mohamed Choukri's *For Bread Alone*, he writes: "It has been my experience that the illiterate, not having learned to classify what goes into his memory, remembers everything. . . . It seems almost a stroke of good luck that Choukri's encounter with the written word should have come so late, for by then his habits of thought were already fully formed; the educative process did not modify them."[23]

The short, fablelike story tells of a woman who lives in a cave her sons have dug out for her before they leave for the town, "where many people live" (*CS*, 27). The woman gets used to living alone, away from any social or family contact: "There were many things about this life that the old woman liked. She was no longer obliged to argue and fight with her sons to make them carry wood to the charcoal oven. She was free to move about at night and look for food. She could eat everything she found without having to share it. And she owed no one any debt of thanks for the things she had in her life" (*CS*, 27). One day one of her sons returns to the cave and asks if he can come in. She answers, "No." He then decides she must then go with him. Again she protests, putting him off by insisting she needs sleep. During her sleep she dreams of a city with church bells, then of a scorpion's approach, which while at first terrifying her finally causes great happiness when "she realized he was not going to sting her." The scorpion continues its approach: "She felt his hard shell and his little clinging legs going across her lips and her tongue. He crawled slowly down and was hers" (*CS*, 30). When she wakes up, she is ready to go with her son.

The peculiar charm of "The Scorpion" no doubt owes much to the method of its composition. It can be read simply as a story, but we are also tempted to look for the figure in the carpet. Since its meanings are not readily apparent, we either accept it as surrealistic nonsense or ask ourselves, "What might this allegory of the cave stand for?" There is, to begin with, a distinct opposition between inside and outside, between the world of the cave and the social world outside: "Outside through the moving beads of water she saw the bare earth lighted by the gray sky, and sometimes large dry leaves went past, pushed by the wind that came from higher parts of the land. Inside where she was the light was pleasant and of a pink color from the clay all around" (*CS*, 27). The world of the cave is primitive, precultural, and the woman in the cave is a figure cut off from social interaction. Wayne Pounds, in his commentary on the story, has written, "The behavior of the old woman in 'The Scorpion,' who is passive in relation to the poisonous principle she *receives*, who relinquishes the civilized community for an animal existence in solitude, may indicate that a defect of will in Bowles' characters draws them to primitive experience. Transcendence, or release from a kind of consciousness felt to be stifling, is envisioned, but only invertedly, in a phylogenetically backward course" (Pounds, 72). When people pass near the cave, the old woman avoids them.

The world of the cave is, further, a world in which the imaginative faculties are loosened and dreams occur naturally and fluidly. The dream itself, like many dreams, is one of converting fear into the acceptance of demonic forces. As Pounds notes, "her dream has reassured her that in her alienated condition human contact is not a threat" (Pounds, 67). The threat posed by the scorpion, however, will always be a lurking force in Bowles's imagination and fiction.[24]

"By the Water," which, like "A Distant Episode," was written in New York in 1945, took shape in much the same way as "The Scorpion" did. Bowles once described the story as "an experiment in automatic writing. . . . I sat down with no previous idea in my head, wrote the thing without 'knowing' what I was writing, and at a certain point stopped, probably because I was physically tired, and called that the end" (Stewart 1974, 27). Yet the story has its basis in concrete facts. Bowles, for example, tells of an actual person he knew in Fez, one who resembles the Lazrug of the story: "He could only reach up to the rungs of a chair. He could reach about as far as the seat of the chair I was sitting in, with these flippers that came out of his shoulder, like a seal" (Stewart 1974, 26). The *hammam*, or public baths, in the story is the transformation of a place Bowles actually knew: "The pool is, again, from another place. The pool I'm thinking of is not really underground—it's in a sort of cave. It no longer exists, it's been destroyed by the Moroccan government" (Stewart 1974, 26). Bowles the storyteller has pulled together these details, based in reality, and woven them into the fabric of his story.

As in "The Delicate Prey," the protagonist (who is, significantly, a young man) moves from a place of safety and comfort into the region of the unknown. It is late winter when the story begins. Snow is still on the ground, and Amar, a young Moroccan, "being alone in the world, decided it was time to visit a neighboring city where his father had once told him some cousins lived" (*CS*, 31). He arrives in that city (which is never named) at night, and finds it much colder: "It was an unfriendly town; he could tell that immediately." Deciding not to try to contact his relatives that night, he at last takes "refuge" in a *hammam*. The world of the *hammam* is for Amar totally strange; he doesn't know the codes and protocols. As he enters the baths and undresses, he wonders how much he can trust these people. Through the young boy, Brahim, who takes him to the baths, he first hears of Lazrag: "It is his place here. You'll see him. He never goes out. If he did the sun would burn him in one second, like a straw in the fire. He would fall down in the street burned black the minute he stepped out of the door. He was born down here in the grotto" (*CS*, 33).

Indeed, Amar soon meets Lazrag, when a voice booms out, "Who are you?" A description of the speaker follows: "The creature's head was large; its body was small and it had no legs or arms. The lower part of the trunk ended in two flipper-like pieces of flesh. From the shoulders grew short pincers. It was a man, and it was looking up at him from the floor where it rested" (*CS*, 33). When Lazrag orders him emphatically to get out, Amar reacts defiantly—kicks him in the head, sending him rolling across the floor and into the pool—and makes a getaway. The young boy from the baths catches up with him and leads him to his home, from which, after an argument with his grandfather, they are again ejected. Their object then becomes not only to escape the wrath of Lazrag but quickly to put as much distance as possible between themselves and familial figures of authority and repression. They finally reach the sea, where "the spring wind pushed the foam from the waves along the beach" and "rippled Amar's and the boy's garments landward as they walked by the edge of the water" (*CS*, 36). The two boys, both now outcasts, create, for a short interval at least, a safe haven for each other. They share their adventure, the warmth of each other's bodies, and friendship. The last scene has Amar swimming, accosted by an enormous crab. Amar falls back, hitting his head against the rocks, and the other boy exclaims, "Lazrag!" When the crab disappears, Brahim claims victory: "'I saved you, Amar.' After a long time he answered, 'Yes'" (*CS*, 37).

Johannes Bertens, in his study of Bowles's fiction, notes the characters' outsidedness and their difficulties in trying to establish meaningful social bonds. He discusses "By the Water" within the context of his general thesis that "practically all attempts to find meaning in personal relationships, or in becoming part of a community, fail. . . . Yet such attempts are of vital importance, no matter how futile and even dangerous they often are."[25]

All three of these stories—"Tea on the Mountain," "The Scorpion," and "By the Water"—feature characters who are in some way outsiders, whether it be the American visitor to Tangier, the old woman in the cave, or the young Amar who has left his family searching for wider horizons. As such, each of the stories expresses something of the fear and exhilaration associated with living on the outside and being perceived as different. The overwhelming sense of relief and freedom is tempered by the acute recognition of vulnerability, which is heightened once the usual sustaining cultural supports are gone. Some intrinsic value, nonetheless, must be ascribed to the outsider's stance. It is, at the very least, the stuff from which Bowles spins his tales.

Tales of Gothic Horror

The dust jacket of the original edition of *The Delicate Prey* boasts that the stories "share an almost Gothic preoccupation with violence—particularly that violence arising out of the clash of the Westerner with the alien world of the East." The dedication to his mother, "who first read me the stories of Poe," acknowledges both familial and literary debts. [26] No reader of Bowles is likely to forget the gruesome twists of fate in "The Delicate Prey" and "A Distant Episode," two stories for which Bowles is perhaps best known. So controversial was the title story that it, along with "Pages from Cold Point," was excised from the first British collection of Bowles's stories, apparently because of concern for censorship.[27] After Tennessee Williams first read the story, Bowles reports that he told him, " 'You mustn't publish it. Don't publish that.' And I said, 'Why not?' And he said, 'Because everyone will think you're a monster, and it will do you irreparable harm if you publish it.' Of course I didn't listen to him. . . . I wrote it for a little magazine called *Zero*, being published in Paris at the time, and I thought, 'Well, no one would ever see it except a few hundred people who read that magazine'" (Stewart 1974, 75).

In typical Bowles fashion "The Delicate Prey" begins prosaically, almost like a fairy tale: "There were three Filala who sold leather in Tabelbala—two brothers and the young son of their sister" (*CS*, 165). They set out on a business trip to Tessalit, knowing full well, ahead of time, of the dangers posed by the Reguibat, a hostile tribe that roamed the area they would have to pass through. It had, in any case, been "a long time since the uncouth mountain men had swept down from the *hammada* upon a caravan; most people were of the opinion that since the war of the Sarrho they had lost the greater part of their arms and ammunition, and, more important still, their spirit" (*CS*, 165). In the desert they are approached by a solitary man on a camel. The stranger doesn't seem to be Reguiba, so the three travelers cautiously allow him to enter their circle. He is, they learn, Moungari, and "Moungar is a holy place in that part of the world, and its few residents are treated with respect by the pilgrims who go to visit the ruined shrine nearby" (*CS*, 167). The Filala agree to allow him to travel with them, since they are going in the same direction.

Though all is well so far, a faintly ominous tone suggests a lurking terror. At one point in the journey, the stranger goes off on foot to hunt for gazelles, saying that if they hear a shot, they should follow. Two shots are heard, and the older brother goes off. Two more shots are heard, each from a different gun, and the second brother goes off, leaving the young boy, Driss, alone. While he waits during the heat of the day, Driss sleeps, dreams, and wakes. "While he had slept," we are told, "a hostile presence had entered his consciousness" (*CS*, 168). That hostile presence grows fiercer, and the tone more ominous, as the story progresses.

Feeling a kind of terror, Driss, who has been suspicious of the Moungari from the beginning, gets on a camel and heads off into the desert, not knowing his way. Realizing the absurdity of this venture, he returns to the camp. As he approaches, he is fired on and wounded. The crazed Moungari, who evidently has been smoking hashish, leaps out at him and pins him to the ground, holding a gun to his neck. After stripping and binding him with rope, "The man moved and surveyed the young body lying on the stones. He ran his finger along the razor's blade; a pleasant excitement took possession of him. He stepped over, looked down, and saw the sex that sprouted from the base of the belly. Not entirely conscious of what he was doing, he took it in one hand and brought his other arm down with the motion of a reaper wielding a sickle. It was swiftly severed. A round, dark hole was left, flush with the skin; he stared a moment, blankly. Driss was screaming. The muscles all over his body stood out, moved" (*CS*, 170). The Moungari makes an incision in the boy's belly, where he, "using both hands, studiously stuffed the loose organ in until it disappeared." As "an ultimate indignity," he takes his pleasure with the boy.

The story might have ended there, with this most memorable and lurid passage, but it doesn't. There must be some form of justice or revenge. The Moungari takes the leather goods on to Tessalit, where suspicion is aroused and finally confirmed. The French officials turn their backs while the Filala's take their own revenge, burying the murderer alive, up to his neck, in the hot desert sand.

It is no wonder the story created a stir. Alice B. Toklas, on reading the stories in the collection, wrote to Bowles: "Your delicacy is perfect—precise and poignant—but the macabre fate—though inevitable that overtakes most of your prey is not to my taste."[28] As with all good tales of horror, this one upsets our sensibilities. It forces a confrontation with images or subject matter we might find gruesome, revolting, or repre-hensible. It displays a kind of violence we perhaps would rather deny or ignore, either as an imaginary or real possibility.

It would be a mistake, however, to dismiss lightly the import of works such as "The Delicate Prey," which are conveniently tucked into the "horror" genre with other works, either because they play off popular appetites for the sensational or because they indulge in vulgar fetishism. Rather, when engaging in the genre we should ask ourselves what it is we find unsettling and why. What repressed fears are we forced to confront? Certainly, "The Delicate Prey" gains much of its force from its vivid depiction of castration, which is apt to produce lewd fascination, violent disgust, or a mix of these and other emotions. Any castration scene (lest we consider the rare and unlikely possibility of auto-castration) involves two parties, the empowered and the powerless. Hence, at its most basic level castration invokes our fears of vulnerability, of having our most personal, productive potential violently and irrationally ripped from us. The young, relatively naive and powerless Driss, in this story, clearly becomes the victim, the "prey" to the more powerful, deceitful Moungari.

To entertain seriously the status of horror is to consider, at least imaginatively, the nature of evil and its propagation. In tales of horror there is generally a source of horror, and those which have no identifiable source, such as *The Turn of the Screw*, most upset our sensibilities. In "The Delicate Prey" the horror comes in human form, and its agency becomes a possibility only when those who are vulnerable let down their guard. Beyond the initial experience of the shock, the story urges us to think about whence this malevolence issues. What perhaps is most disturbing is not the recognition of the horror (and how much horror this century has experienced!) but that it is likely to come when we feel most safe, most complacent. "He comes from the North, not the West," the Filala say with relief when they meet the stranger.

"The Delicate Prey" displays a number of features that become hallmarks of Bowles's craft. One is the even narrative progression. The stark outlines of the story suggest its tight logic. One event follows the next, just as one sentence follows the next, surely and evenly, casting the shadow of naturalistic inevitability over the piece. This story, like so many others by Bowles, takes the form of a journey. Characters set out from a known place of safety and comfort to find themselves in an unfamiliar region fraught with possibilities of deception and terror. With Bowles, the unfamiliar setting (which can be thought of as a metaphysical condition as much as a real place) often takes the form of an exotic Morocco or a strange and tropical Latin America. A final element in the picture, one often noted by Bowles critics and seen in so many other stories, such as "By the Water" and "The Frozen Fields," is the way in which the child, here the young Driss, is victimized by the brutal force of a more powerful adult.

As improbable and fantastic as "The Delicate Prey" may seem, the tale was not purely a construct of the imagination. As with most Bowles stories, this one began with a real incident. In conversations with Lawrence Stewart, Bowles has told how the outlines of the story were suggested by a French captain Bowles met and spoke with in Timimoun, Algeria, in the winter of 1947–48, while he was working on *The Sheltering Sky*: "How the leather sellers start out over the desert and are killed en route, and how he [the murderer] did it, by getting each one separately, pretending to go shooting, and killing them one by one, and then going on and having the leather recognized when he arrives at the other side of the desert by other Filala, and the Filala go to the French and the French turn the man over to the Filala and say, 'Do what you like with him.' So they don't have any hand in it at all. Yes, that was told me. . . . But of course I hoked it up considerably" (Stewart 1974, 75). Bowles, as here, usually begins with some kind of donnée, a piece of reality, a suggestion, or a memory, which he weaves into a tale, embellishing, expanding, and cannibalizing as the needs of the emerging story demand.

Another earlier story, often linked to "The Delicate Prey," apparently owes its existence to a dental appointment. Of the genesis of "A Distant Episode" Bowles says:

> That I happened to write because of having a dental appointment. I think I was going to have an extraction. . . . I was on my way up and I took an IRT subway train from where I was, dreading the experience, but fortunately I had a little notebook with me, so I thought I would provide a counter-irritant, fight fire with fire, so I began writing a story. . . . And I had perhaps a page, or a page and a half, written by the time I got to Columbus Circle, and then I went on to the dentist's office, which was on 57th Street, and went on writing even more feverishly because the moment of truth was approaching and I do not like to have teeth extracted.[29]

The circumstances surrounding its conception may in some way explain the macabre tone of "A Distant Episode," written in 1945 when Bowles was in New York, first published in *Partisan Review* in January 1947, and selected for inclusion in *The Best American Short Stories of 1948*.

"A Distant Episode" calls to mind many of the themes at work in "The Delicate Prey." In both, unsuspecting victims walk into an unfamiliar landscape that soon darkens with horror. In both, a fragile thread of trust is broken by deception and malice. An important difference between the two stories is that while "The Delicate Prey" was populated wholly by indigenous characters, the protagonist of "A Distant Episode" is a Western linguistic anthropologist. At the story's outset, the Professor, as he is called, is on the last leg of his journey to Aïn Tadouirt (an imaginary place somewhere in the south of Morocco), carrying only his "two overnight bags full of maps, sun lotions and medicines" (*CS*, 39). Ten years earlier he had spent three days in the village, and developed a friendship with the café owner, which he hopes to revive on this trip. In the car, driving through the mountains at sunset,

> the chauffeur, whose seat the Professor shared, spoke to him without taking his eyes from the road. *"Vous êtes géologue?"*
> "A geologist? Ah, no! I'm a linguist."
> "There are no languages here. Only dialects."
> "Exactly. I'm making a survey of variations on Moghrebi."
> The chauffeur was scornful. "Keep on going south," he said. "You'll find some languages you never heard before." (*CS*, 39)

This is the first indication that the Professor may be in for more than he is expecting. His four years of studying the language of the region ill prepare him for actual experience in the field. He is, in fact, frightfully inept at reading the signals around him, a failing he suffers miserably for in the end.

After checking into the Grand Hotel Saharien and eating dinner, the Professor makes his way to the café once owned by his "friend," Hassan Ramani: "The *qaouaji* tried to make him take a seat at the other table in the front room, but the professor walked airily ahead into the back room and sat down" (*CS*, 40). The Professor, indifferent to the Moroccan's less-than-forthcoming responses to his questions, persists: "Tell me . . . can one still get those little boxes made from camel udders?" (*CS*, 40). The *qaouaji* makes an insolent reply in Arabic, yet still the Professor is undaunted. He offers the man 10 francs for every little box he can get. This leads to one of those terrifying trips, characteristic of Bowles, where the character in an unknown landscape is escorted by (that is, at the mercy of) a stranger whose intentions are unclear. As they pass together out of the village and begin their course through "a winding road between rocks, downward toward the nearest small forest of palms," the Professor thinks to himself, "He may cut my throat. But his café—he would surely be found out" (*CS*, 41). The farther away from the village they go, the more his suspicions grow. He hears dogs barking. The guide refuses to tell the naive foreigner where he is going or whether or not he plans to work the next day.

The *qaouaji* finally points ahead, indicating the Professor will now have to continue alone. The foreigner continues down the path, where he is suddenly attacked by a dog, then seized by a group of Reguibat tribesmen, one of whom presses a gun against his soft flesh. The Professor tries to use his Moghrebi to convince them to spare his life; to his dismay, it has no apparent effect. Then, his rational sensibility gaining control during a time of terror, he recalls a saying about the Reguibat— "When the Reguiba appears, the righteous man turns away"—and sees this as "an opportunity of testing the accuracy of such statements" (*CS*, 44). A moment after this thought passes, his captors begin beating him, rolling him in the dirt, and screaming in a tongue he cannot understand. He loses consciousness, and wakes the next morning to the sight of a man clutching a knife in one hand and his tongue in the other. Dizzy and speechless, the tongueless Professor is put in a bag and carried away by camel, tin cans tied to his body.

The Professor, who by now seems to have lost all memory of his past, lives with this wandering nomadic tribe for a year, acting as a kind of clown for them. Finally, he is sold to a villager and at once begins to regain consciousness. His sense of pain returns; he hears and understands phrases of Arabic. A series of events puts him in the hands of the French, and the contact with civilization triggers the return of his memory. In the final scene of the story, the Professor, thoroughly wild, breaks out of his cell and runs off into the desert, dodging the shots of a French soldier, who says to himself, "*Tiens*, . . . a holy maniac" (*CS*, 48).

The story is quintessential Bowles. Even an abridged recounting of the story line should suggest its power, beauty, and economy. Descriptive elements and action are evenly balanced. Place is all-important. The writer evokes the colors and smells of southern Morocco, often, as on the Professor's first night at the Hotel, in a single line: "The afterglow was nearly gone from the sky, and the pinkness in objects was disappearing, almost as he watched" (*CS*, 39).

The story's richness and the satisfaction it yields can be attributed not only to fine handling of narrative but to the deeper questions that meditation on the story is likely to provoke. For starters, What shapes our destiny? In the world according to Bowles, human will is not ultimately in control. Bowles's characters, in fact, exercise remarkably little willpower. Rather than shaping their own lives, larger, unpredictable external forces determine the patterns their lives take. This fatalistic conception in some ways strongly resembles the dominant philosophical perspective that so deeply governs thought in Morocco and other Arab countries. The difference, though, is that in Bowles's fictional world, events are not God-directed. There is, here, no place for a Providentially guided order. Events, rather, are the result of willy-nilly forces, almost Manichaean, more likely brutal than kind. The vision is like the one described toward the end of *The Sheltering Sky*, as Kit hears the roar of the plane that is to take her back to civilization (Kit, unlike the Professor, returns alive): "Like a great overpowering sound it destroyed everything in her mind, paralyzed her. Someone once had said to her that the sky hides the night behind it, shelters the person beneath from the horror that lies above. Unblinking, she fixed the solid emptiness, and the anguish began to move in her. At any moment the rip can occur, the edges fly back, and the giant maw will be revealed."[30]

The story also invites an examination of the impulses guiding anthropology, a rationally propelled Western science, generated out of the cultural forces of the past few centuries. In seeking to understand the dynamics of modern anthropology, Edward W. Said has suggested that our encounters with the primitive "provide us with the lively means of seeing our loss: as he was for the eighteenth-century writer of philosophical voyages, the primitive is a model for our imaginings of a lost plentitude."[31] The leap, however, as this story shows, is not easily made, and it may well be impossible to recover what we have lost. Bowles's work becomes at once an enactment and a critique of the anthropological impulse. An avowed antimodern, Bowles, like the anthropologist, has sought those ever-vanishing corners of the world uncontaminated by the touch of the technological, the modern. The world, in Bowles's view, is not becoming a better place to live in. The myths of progress and humanism are just that—myths.

Yet for the Western anthropologist in this story, the journey toward the primitive may be neither welcome nor satisfying. One thing this story does is subvert the customary end of an adventure story, or an anthropological study—the return. Significantly, in this story the Professor, like Jim in Conrad's *Lord Jim* and Kurtz in *Heart of Darkness*, does not return to tell his own story. His turn toward the "primitive" is irrevocable and fatal. There are not even any survivors capable of telling us the Professor's story, as there are in Conrad; the narrative, hence, must be omniscient (*WO*, 55–60).

Like writers such as Joseph Conrad and Paul Theroux, Bowles has inscribed from a Western point of view the dynamics governing relations between West and East, North and South, the technologically advanced and the less developed regions of the world. While it would be reductive to read this story as a simple political allegory involving the encounter between two sets of cultural assumptions, it would be just as mistaken not to consider these underlying issues. The Professor's actions easily can be thought of as symbolizing our involvement with the rest of the world and his fate, no less than a portentous omen.

Latin American Tales

Bowles's identification with Morocco has been so fixed that his Latin American stories have often been eclipsed. Yet a glance at the table of contents of *The Delicate Prey and Other Stories* shows that nearly half the stories, placed together at the beginning of the volume, are set south of the U.S. border. While these stories may not be charged with the bristling, grotesque drama of "The Delicate Prey" or "A Distant Episode," they are in their own right exceedingly fine stories, marked by distinctive Latin American landscapes and intense, often subterranean, psychological drama.

Though these stories all draw on Bowles's periodic travels in Mexico and Latin America during the 1930s and 1940s, the expressive forms they take vary considerably. Some, such as "Call at Corazón," we might presume to be semiautobiographical. Others, such as "Pastor Dowe at Tacaté" and "Señor Ong and Señor Ha," present wholly imaginary happenings set in the region. And still others, such as "The Circular Valley," unfold atavistic myths of an animistic universe. Frequently woven into the fabric of these stories are familiar Bowlesian elements: eruption of repressed sexual energies, glimpses of altered realities produced by drugs, and the Westerner's encounter with the native. What binds all these together, certainly, are the sounds, sights, and smells of the Latin American landscape: the heat, tropical vegetation, screech of monkeys, buzz of insects, and marimba melodies.

"At Paso Rojo" (1947) stood at the head of *The Delicate Prey and Other Stories* and is one of the best of the lot, inviting comparisons with Katherine Anne Porter's "María Concepción." The cultural tensions that reverberate in the attitudes and actions of individual characters throughout the story are those between male and female; master and servant; a dominant, "European" culture and an oppressed, indigenous Indian culture. At the very outset of the story, prejudices against the Indian are felt when two unmarried sisters, Lucha and Chalía, soon after their mother's death, arrive at the ranch of their brother, Don Frederico. "Indians, poor things, animals with speech," Lucha remarks (*CS*, 121). Chalía later reveals her prejudice when she scolds her brother for being too generous with the workers and servants, suggesting that his benevolence will make them soft and rebellious. "They need a strong hand and no pity," Lucha asserts (*CS*, 125). Don Frederico, meanwhile, insists on their honesty and nobility, saying none has ever stolen from him. The story's power, rather like that of *Othello*, lies in the insidious and deceitful manner by which a native, residing trust is twisted into doubt and finally broken completely.

The central drama of the story unfolds as Chalía decides to go with her brother on one of his early-morning horse rides around the estate. Lucha stays at home, judging it inappropriate to go out so soon after her mother's death. On the ride Chalía is increasingly attentive to a young Indian, Roberto, who has accompanied them. While she is viscerally attracted to him, her scorn and prejudice permit only a threatening and hostile interpretation of his actions. Mockery, she feels, lies beneath his polite words. Rather than being accepted as a deferential gesture, his addressing her as "señora" is taken as a satiric suggestion of her age, reminding her of her spinsterhood. In other words, Chalía projects her deepest anxieties and fears onto the Indian, a move often characteristic of dominant groups' scapegoating of minorities.

Chalía arranges that she be left alone with the young man as the others ride ahead, and tries to tempt the young Indian by suggestively unbuttoning her blouse, complaining of the heat and telling him she wants to dismount and rest. The Indian maintains his proper position, remaining polite and respectful, refusing to compromise his honor: "She slipped her arm around his neck and felt the muscles grow tense. She rubbed her face over his chest; he did not move or say anything. With her eyes shut and her head pressing hard against him, she felt as if she were hanging to consciousness only by the ceaseless shrill scream of the cicadas. She remained thus, leaning ever more heavily upon him as he braced himself with his hands against the earth behind him. His face had become an impenetrable mask; he seemed not to be thinking of anything, not even to be present" (*CS*, 128). When he abruptly rejects her advances, Chalía, insulted, jumps on the horse Roberto had been riding, rather than her own, and has a wild ride back to the ranch. Hers is a double outrage, since Roberto has failed not only to be ensnared by her seductive moves but also to give her the evidence that would have confirmed her view of his corruptness. Later the same day, when she is back on the ranch, Chalía spots Roberto bathing naked in the river, in a place uniquely visible from the upstairs veranda. Interpreting his behavior as willful taunting, "the idea of vengeance upon the boy filled her with a delicious excitement" (*CS*, 130).

The vengeance that follows gives this story its cutting edge. Chalía's malicious moves and devious plottings successfully undermine the integrity of both her brother and Roberto. From her brother's cigar box she steals four 10-colon notes. Later, when she sees Roberto, the smell of liquor on his breath, she whispers, "Roberto, I love you. I have a present for you," and gives him the money (*CS*, 132). Still later that night, out walking, she happens on a form that turns out to be Roberto, passed out on the ground. A light kick in the head produces only a faint moan. She pulls him to a nearby embankment and pushes him over.

Meantime Don Frederico misses the stolen money. Roberto is brought in and accused of stealing when it is found on him. When confronted, he says the money was given to him by Chalía, which she denies. Don Frederico dismisses Roberto, and Chalía is satisfied by the success of her plan. In the story's last lines, Chalía "got into the bed . . . , blew out the lamp, listened for a few minutes to the night sounds, and went peacefully to sleep, thinking of how surprisingly little time it had taken her to get used to life at Paso Rojo, and even, she had to admit now, to begin to enjoy it" (*CS*, 134–5). Even before this last exhibition of malice triumphant, the reader is likely to feel a sense of indignation at the power and success of Chalía's lies, motivated by selfishness and prejudice, and at the tremendous injustice done to Roberto, an injustice we imagine will only fuel the fires of racial distrust and hatred. The psychological dynamics of the story are taut, and as is so often the case in good stories, we are never given full explanations for why characters act the way they do. We simply see them acting. The story works on us as we follow the actions and try to ascribe motives.

Like "At Paso Rojo," "Under the Sky" pits the urban, Spanish life against the life of the Indians who live in the mountains, away from the centers. In "Under the Sky," however, Bowles admits us to the point of view of an Indian character, thus affording "us" a glimpse of "the other" seeing us. The narrative technique used in the story is one the writer employs at greater length in his novels *Let It Come Down* and *The Spider's House*.

In this story, Jacinto, a mountain dweller, has come down to a town on the hot plains to sell his goods. He goes to the railway station, where he figures he has a chance to pick up a bit of money by offering his services as a porter. Though the narration is omniscient and in the third person, we are close to Jacinto's consciousness and are invited to perceive things as he does. The technique used by Bowles is much like what Dorrit Cohn calls "narrated monologue," which renders "a character's thought in his own idiom while maintaining the third-person reference and the basic sense of narration."[32] We see this quite clearly when Jacinto spots three Americans among the arrivals of "the daily train from the north":

> From the crowd three strange-looking people suddenly emerged. They all had very white skin and yellow hair. He knew, of course, that they were from a faraway place because everyone knows that when people look as strange as that they are from the capital or even farther. . . . [H]e noticed that they were speaking a language which only they could understand. Each one carried a leather bag covered with small squares of colored paper stuck on at different angles. He stepped back, keeping his eyes on the face of the younger woman. He could not be sure whether he found her beautiful or revolting. Still he continued to look at her as she passed, holding on to the man's arm. The other woman noticed him, and smiled faintly as she went by. (*CS*, 78–79)

Jacinto turns away in anger, for he thinks the woman a whore and believes she is taunting him, knowing he would not have enough money for her.

After walking around the town, eating, and smoking a few *grifas*, Jacinto thinks again of the strangers and decides to wait near the hotel where he suspects they will be staying. Almost by sheer force of will, he seems to bring one of the women (the older one) out of the hotel. They meet and exchange a few words. Jacinto asks:

> "And you, what are you looking for?"
> "Nothing."
> "Yes. You are looking for something," he said solemnly.
> "I was not sleeping. It is very hot." (*CS*, 81)

The story then shifts to a more sinister register, rather like that in "The Delicate Prey" or "A Distant Episode." The Indian refuses to accept the woman's explanation for her solitary expedition and leads her off, threatening to kill her male companion and saying that she could, by doing what he wanted, save his life. Finally, in a cemetery, as she watches the intermittent flashes of lightning in the sky above her, he rapes her.

The rape might be thought of as Roberto's revenge. In cultural and political terms, conditions of constant abuse and economic depravity have established a psychological dynamic in which revenge is one of the only satisfying forms of justice possible. The story, short as it is, economically displays the forces at work and is made all the more effective by its backdrop: heat, lightning, fountain splash, voices carried on the wind, marimba band, and lemon trees.

Bowles certainly is not the only fiction writer who has depicted relationships involving the Western woman and the more primitive, virile Latin man. This story and others calls to mind Lawrence, especially novels such as *The Plumed Serpent* and *St. Mawr*, where the Western woman seems to abandon her Western male counterpart in favor of a more potent, natural male figure. The difference is that Bowles's Western women seem less to project their own desires than to become the unwitting, unwilling prey of male fantasies for revenge and sexual conquest. As with Mustafa Sa'eed's violent sexual exploitation of women in Tayib Salih's *Season of Migration to the North*, the conquest of the Western woman here seems to be a symbol of insubordination and prowess in the face of postcolonial forms of domination. The rape scene in "Under the Sky" can also be thought of as prefiguring the last section of *The Sheltering Sky*, written several years later, in which Kit becomes the sexual captive of an Arab camel driver, Belqassim, in a bizarre cross-desert odyssey.

With "Pastor Dowe at Tacaté," one of the lighter stories in the volume, Bowles again takes up the theme of the Westerner's contact with the exotic, this time showing that, despite the potential for tragedy, the encounter can have its comical side. The confrontation of ideologies that takes place in the story is similar to the one Melville presents in *Typee*, where the narrator, much like the anthropologist, faces a wholly new culture and measures it against what he knows. The story enacts the friction that occurs when two vastly different cultures and systems of belief rub against each other.

When Pastor Dowe delivers his first sermon at Tacaté, on the "Meaning of Jesus," he notices that his audience, while respectful, does not seem to understand his message, even though he believes himself a fairly competent speaker of their dialect. The problem, it seems, is not simply one of linguistic mastery; it is one of differing cultural beliefs. Pastor Dowe's version of Christianity does not mesh well with the beliefs those in the village have long subscribed to. To begin with, "each house in Tacaté had its own small temple: a few tree trunks holding up some thatch to shelter the offerings of fruit and cooked food" (*CS*, 138). The people of Tacaté, we learn, adhere to a rather Manichaean view of the world, incompatible with Pastor Dowe's conception of God and the universe. They have two Gods, Hachakyum and Metzabok. Hachakyum is responsible for making everything native and good. Metzabok, as the preacher's local go-between, Nicolas, explains to him, "makes all the things that do not belong here" (*CS*, 139). Hachakyum, in other words, has not created Don Jesucristo, guns, or missionaries. Not only is the pastor bothered by the natives' nakedness, but he finds it difficult to conceive of an order distinguishing primarily between things that belong and things that don't, rather than a system whose categories depend on a moral distinction between "good" and "evil."

The pastor, recognizing his alien status, begins to make some accommodations in the interest of drawing people to his faith. Bending to their demands for the incorporation of music in the service, he employs his phonograph and plays the only music he has brought along—"Crazy Rhythm" and "Sonny Boy." Nicolas advises the pastor to intersperse his talk with the music, and a new form of worship service is created.

Soon the people are asking for salt as well as music. Only reluctantly does the missionary give in, explaining that what he brought with him is just enough for his own household. "You have enough for everyone in the village," Nicolas insists. The missionary begins to justify his actions to himself: "After all, what principle am I upholding in keeping it from them? They want music. They want salt. They will learn to want God" (*CS*, 144). By and by, the preacher in his Sunday sermons substitutes local deities for biblical characters in his readings of Scripture.

In this setting the foreign pastor understandably feels increasingly isolated, begins to think about an escape, and eventually packs up his Bible, notebooks, toothbrush, and Atabrine tablets. Like so many of Bowles's fictions, this one ends with a solitary man walking away from social structures, into a completely unknown temporal and geographic territory. And like so many of Bowles's fictions, this one can be seen as a kind of parable of the dynamic between more technologically advanced nations and the third world.

"Señor Ong and Señor Ha" also has a third-world setting and, at least obliquely, points to key dynamics associated with contact between cultures of varying economic strength. We learn at the beginning of the story that a dam is being built up river from the unnamed town in which the action takes place and that this has had an economic impact. The Indians coming to town from the surrounding areas now bring money. Some in the town prosper and exchange their surplus money for radios and other modern gadgetry. One man who buys a car finds the roads too bumpy and muddy for it and so leaves it to rust.

The central action of the story revolves around a young boy, Dionisio, Nicho for short, who lives with his aunt in this small town. Rather like James in *What Maisie Knew*, Bowles constructs a narrative that closely represents the perspective of the young boy, who only imperfectly understands the operation of the adult world that victimizes him. Soon after the story begins, a strange man comes to live with Nicho's aunt, and though he notices this man is different, it is not until his friends start calling him "Chale" (Chinaman) that Nicho realizes the man's racial identity: "The name [Chale] itself would have been bearable if only it had not implied the ridicule of his home life; his powerlessness to change that condition seemed much more shameful than any state of affairs for which he himself might have been at fault" (*CS*, 175). Though Señor Ong has plenty of money and the traffic in and out of their house escalates when the Chinaman comes to live with him and his aunt, neither Nicho nor the reader knows for sure what kind of operation is being conducted. Only gradually, as the mind works through the accumulating facts, are certain meanings derived.

Against the cold and abstract world of adults, Nicho finds solace and comfort in the form of another young outcast, Luz, an albino: "Her hair was a silky white helmet on the top of her head, her whole face was white, almost as if she had covered it with paint, her brows and lashes, and even her eyes, were light to the point of not existing" (*CS*, 176). Together Nicho and Luz spin a world of shared secrets and stories, make-believe, and hiding places for pretended treasures in decaying tree trunks. One night Nicho discovers the adult equivalent of a hiding place. He finds the Chinaman chiseling out a secret hiding place in a small niche in the *sala*, behind a Chinese calendar he placed there when he first came.

The story is in part about how value is determined and the disjuncture between the child's world and adult means of determining value. The morning after discovering Señor Ong's hiding place, Nicho rushes out to see about his own valuables—sand that he and Luz have pretended is silver: "In the tree his treasure was undisturbed, but now that he suspected Señor Ong of having a treasure too, the little can of sand seemed scarcely worth his interest" (*CS*, 180). When Señor Ong goes away on one of his regular trips to visit another Chinaman in a nearby town, Nicho surreptitiously investigates the niche, finding there, behind a loose tile, a large envelope containing "a lot of little envelopes, and in some of the little envelopes there was a small quantity of odorless white powder" (*CS*, 182). Though Nicho has no idea what the stuff is, he deduces its value by the way it is stored and hidden. He takes a bit of the substance from each envelope, puts it into two envelopes, then places everything back the way it was.

Acting intuitively, Nicho begins to operate his own drug business, drawing away Señor Ong's own customers, vastly undercutting him because he doesn't know the market value of what he is selling. Señor Ong is suspicious when it becomes apparent that his customers are being supplied by someone else; however, his suspicions are directed toward Señor Ha, whom he has paid off with the provision that Ha not encroach on his territory. Nicho keeps his new activities secret from Luz, substituting the money he makes for the sand, or "silver," Luz has placed in the tree trunk, and taking pleasure in her belief in alchemical magic.

Nicho's next daring move, not so much the result of a decision as of an inevitable chain of events, is to take Luz and go by bus to Tlaltepec and warn Señor Ha that Señor Ong has threatened to kill him. Nicho has, after all, heard Señor Ong say that when he next goes to see Ha, "it will not be to ask him anything" (*CS*, 186). Soon thereafter, Señor Ong is apprehended by the police and Señor Ha, as brutal and hateful if not more so, is in line to move in with his aunt and to use Nicho as a runner in his business.

The story's ending demonstrates the usual grace, precision, and harmony with which Bowles ties his various strands and melodies together: "The town went on being prosperous, the Indians kept coming down from the heights with money, the thick jungle along the way to Mapasstenango was hacked away, the trail widened and improved. Nicho bought a packet of little envelopes. Far down the river he found another hollow tree. Here he kept his slowly increasing store of treasure; during the very first month he picked up enough money on the side to buy Luz a lipstick and a pair of dark glasses with red and green jewels all around the rims" (*CS*, 191).

"Señor Ong and Señor Ha" again reveals Bowles's preoccupation with the outlaw, the displaced, the victim, the outsider. None of the main characters is at home in the scene he inhabits; each, in his own way, is disenfranchised. Nicho, the young orphan, is a subject of whatever choices his adult guardians make for him. Luz is an albino, another outcast; perhaps it is an instinctive perception of their common plight that draws the youths together. Señor Ong and Señor Ha, as well as being ethnic Chinese living in Latin America, are operating a drug business outside the law. Nicho's aunt, female, poor, and single, is forced to rely on unsavory men in order to ensure her economic well-being.

A rather different emphasis is placed in "Call at Corazón," which, though also set in Latin America, focuses on the marital relations of an American couple. Readers of the story who know anything about the relationship between Paul and Jane Bowles will almost certainly see connections between the two writers and the American couple in the story. In March 1938 the newlywed Bowleses set out on a Caribbean cruise that took them to Colón, Panama, among other places. Elements of this trip clearly figure in Jane's novel *Two Serious Ladies* and in Paul's "Call at Corazón" and *Up Above the World*. At stake in the story is a marriage, the relationship between a man and a woman, each groping for a way to be together while at the same time preserving individual integrity. The husband in the story, like Mr. Copperfield in *Two Serious Ladies* and Dr. Slade in *Up Above the World*, is a distant, unsympathizing character who often gives the impression he would just as well live without people (including his wife) as with them. The wife, a drinker, tries to reconcile her needs for care and attention with her strong desire for independence. "I'm just trying to live with you on an extended trip in a lot of cramped little cabins on an endless series of stinking boats," she tells her husband (*CS*, 65).

The story, written in New York in 1946, opens with a dispute between the husband and wife, who are on their honeymoon. The dispute, which concerns a monkey the husband insists on taking with them on board the ship, exhibits the dynamics working in the relationship. The husband offers to do without the monkey, if taking it along is going to make his wife miserable, but the offer seems to be a ploy, almost as if he knows ahead of time that if he puts things in these terms, she will give in, perhaps fearing that later he will complain about her hemming him in, or perhaps simply being reluctant to exercise that type of power in the situation. The monkey wreaks havoc exactly as the woman predicted, eating pages of a book the man was reading. "If you want me to get rid of him, I will. It's easy enough," he again offers, to which she replies: "I don't mind him. What I mind is you. *He* can't help being a little horror, but he keeps reminding me that you could if you wanted" (*CS*, 68). The man self-righteously gives in, handing the monkey over to the steward, inwardly harboring a grudge for his sacrifice.

The tension throughout the story is between the man's ties to his wife and his impulse to strike out on his own and discover the new, foreign scene. The modern predicament women find themselves in, the man believes, makes any relationship between a man and woman as problematic as ever. While watching native women trying to clean their laundry in a river "the color of black coffee," he writes in his notebook: "Modern, that is, intellectual education, having been devised by males for males, inhibits and confuses her. She avenges . . ." (*CS*, 66). The writing is broken off.

The couple get on a second boat, swarming with insects and natives, to continue their voyage in a *Heart of Darkness*–like trip up a river in a tropical setting, the boat bumping against the banks, spasmodically lurching forward. During this wretched trip the wife goes on a drinking binge, her husband later finding her on the lower deck of the boat, half-clothed, asleep beside another man. In the early dawn the boat docks; the husband disembarks and boards an awaiting train headed for the mountain town of Cienga: "On the crowded, waiting train, with the luggage finally in the rack, his heart beat harder than ever, and he kept his eyes painfully on the long dusty street that led back to the dock. At the far end, as the whistle blew, he thought he saw a figure in white running among the dogs and children toward the station, but the train started up as he watched, and the street was lost to view. He took out his notebook, and sat with it on his lap, smiling at the shining green landscape that moved with increasing speed past the window" (*CS*, 75). And that is that.

The success of this story lies in the maintenance of a balanced view, in the reserve, in the lack of authorial comment or judgment. In the end the reader would be hard-pressed to place blame on one character or another; there is too much moral complexity in the world for us easily to make those kinds of determinations. Rather, we are inclined to sit back and say to ourselves, *Tant pis pour ils, tant pis pour nous:* too bad for them, too bad for us.

Two Tales of Repression and Perversion

"The Echo" and "Pages from Cold Point" deserve special mention. In both stories homosexuality, the problematic nature of family ties, and expatriation are intimately intertwined. The characters in these stories, like Nelson Dyar in Bowles's novel *Let It Come Down* and the American woman in "Tea on the Mountain," are fleeing the puritanical morality of America, seeking a "world elsewhere" where their romantic yearnings, as impractical or immoral as they may seem back home, have a better chance of being realized. Repressed sexual desire, often operating on an unconscious level, is the moving force behind so much of human action, as Freud all too amply demonstrated. These two stories resist depictions of overt sexual fantasizing, showing instead the effects of strong under-tows of sexual emotion, often unseen yet ever present.

The opening pages of "The Echo," written in New York in 1946, immediately draw us into the scene. A young American coed named Aileen, on a small airplane above a tropical jungle, pulls from her handbag a letter from her mother: "Perhaps I should begin by saying that Prue and I are sublimely happy here. It is absolute heaven after Washington, as you can pretty well imagine. Prue, of course, never could stand the States, and I felt, after the trouble with your father, that I couldn't face anyone for a while. You know how much importance I have always attached to relaxation. And this is the ideal spot for that" (*CS*, 51).

While we may not yet know who Prue is, what kind of trouble there has been between Aileen's mother and father, or where this "ideal" spot is, this brief extract from the mother's letter does vividly present a number of elements that coalesce and form and expatriate disposition. There is, to begin with, the deep-seated dissatisfaction with the homeland. There is, further, the family quarrel, from which one escapes. Beneath it all there is the romantic yearning for an idyllic life, somewhere one can live as one has always fantasized. Having been unable happily to build a nest in the United States, Prue and Aileen's mother have retreated to Jamonocal, somewhere in a tropical landscape near Baranquilla. Aileen too, as she begins to read the letter, is "excited to be going to a new home" (*CS*, 51).

As Richard F. Patteson points out in his book *A World Outside*, Bowles's stories frequently contain figures of home and displacement from home. Patteson perceptively suggests that man-made shelters, constructed to protect us, often prove in Bowles's fiction to be vulnerable, unable to withstand either the chaotic forces from within or the violent, unpredictable turmoil of the world outside. This can be seen very clearly in "The Echo." In her letter Aileen's mother writes that she felt "the sooner we got down here to Jamonocal the more of a home we could make out of the old place." And some house it is. With the help of an American architect, a cantilevered construction has been designed, with a portion of the home evidently hanging over a large gorge. Aileen's mother writes to her daughter: "I think there's not likely to be another house like it in the world, if I do say it myself. The terrace makes me think of an old cartoon in the *New Yorker* showing two men looking over the edge of the Grand Canyon, and one is saying to the other: 'Did you ever want to spit a mile, Bill? Now's your chance'" (*CS*, 52). The very construction of the house, its precarious perch above the abyss, becomes a symbol for the human condition as it evolves in the story. If the house is that structure meant to provide the warmth and comfort we all need and crave in life, the gorge is that lurking force outside which threatens all our ideas of order and stability.

As Aileen, still in the plane, recalls the place from her experiences as a five-year-old, "she had no memory of the gorge. Probably she had never seen it, although it was only a few paces from the house. . . . However, she had a clear memory of its presence, of the sensation of enormous void beyond and below that side of the house" (*CS*, 53). It seems as though her mother's lesbianism, like the gorge, had until the time of the story been only a vague presence, without having taken, at least in the daughter's mind, any tangible form. Aileen's arrival forces a confrontation with her mother's sexual orientation and the form it has taken in her life. Daughter and mother never talk about it directly, yet the effects of the issue are dramatically displayed. Aileen, expecting to arrive "home," finds her mother's cares and attentions directed toward this other woman. She has been displaced, left out in the cold. No longer can she expect to receive maternal warmth. And while her mother continually insists that she and Prue get along, rivalry between the mother's lover and daughter is inevitable.

Once Aileen arrives at the house, Bowles deftly uses the architectural structure to underscore the girl's emotional state. To begin with, "Aileen had asked to be put into the old part of the house, rather than into a more comfortable room in the new wing. . . . Here in her room she felt at least that the earth was somewhere beneath her" (*CS*, 56). By contrast, when she is on the terrace she feels uncomfortable: "The emptiness was too near and the balustrade seemed altogether too low for safety" (*CS*, 56). Aileen continually refuses to admit her feelings toward Prue, though obviously they are brewing inside her. As the narrator tells us, "Because Aileen could not bring herself to think what she really felt, which was that Prue was ungracious, ugly and something of an interloper, she remained emotionally unconscious of Prue's presence, which is to say that she was polite but bored, scarcely present in the mealtime conversations" (*CS*, 56).

The conflict does not long lie submerged. In a neatly arranged scene, Bowles has Aileen and Prue meet each other alone, without the presence of the mother. At one point in an awkward conversation, Aileen innocently asks whether Prue is planning to stay there long. Naturally, Prue is offended: "What the hell do you mean? . . . I live here" (*CS*, 57). Subsequently, the mother is forced to arbitrate, to maintain civility, but only makes things worse by suggesting that Aileen is a "guest," when she wants desperately to claim her rights as a full-fledged member of the family.

So much is held in balance in this story. Within the characters we feel the struggle to maintain emotional equilibrium. We feel as well the tension between internal and external landscapes, both psychic and natural. It is as though the structures of stories, lives, and houses are themselves barely sufficient for containing the charged emotional content that often goes on within them. An interlude toward the middle of the story shows Aileen taking a walk, going outside the zones of comfort associated with the house, past natives' huts, through dense foliage, into jungle and mist. At one point along her walk, she meets a young man whose "shirt and pants were tattered" and who spits a mouthful of water in her face as he leans toward her across a barbed wire fence. A rock she throws into the door of the nearby hut, in retaliation for this unexpected exhibition of hatred, evidently hits a target, judging from the screams she hears.

This violent scene glides into another. As Aileen returns to the house, she encounters Prue; their exchange is more sharp and bitter than the first. After Prue, who has Aileen's mother's ear, apparently has tattled on Aileen, her mother comes back to tell her daughter she must leave. What makes the rupture, the loss of the battle for her mother, more acute is her mother's announcement on the day of Aileen's departure that she is not feeling well enough to accompany her daughter to Baranquilla. "But it won't matter, will it?" she pleads with Aileen (*CS*, 61).

Bowles's regulation of the dramatic pace in this story is masterful. The tension escalates in a steady crescendo up until the last page, when Prue, coming across Aileen while she is eating breakfast, flaunts her sense of victory over Aileen's imminent departure. Emotions are close to the surface, and so it takes little to spark a fight. Prue grasps Aileen's arm and gives it a twist: "The reaction was instantaneous. Aileen jumped at her with vicious suddenness, kicking, ripping and pounding all at once. The glass fell to the stone floor; Prue was caught off her guard. Mechanically, with rapid, birdlike fury, the girl hammered at the woman's face and head, as she slowly impelled her away from the doorway and across the terrace" (*CS*, 62). In the end, in a scene reminding us of her arrival at the beginning, Aileen rides away on horseback from the house cantilevered over the gorge.

The story itself, as form, triumphs over the forces of disorder. We leave the story, as does Aileen, having lived through a highly charged, compressed moment. As readers, our lives, like Aileen's, have been affected, yet how and to what extent can be determined only individually. Bowles never tells us how we are supposed to feel about a story. Moral ambiguities are displayed without authorial intervention. It is up to us to think through a story's implications and meaning.

"Pages from Cold Point," which Bowles wrote aboard the MS *Ferncape* en route to Casablanca from New York, dates from the same period as "The Echo" and shares with it many similar thematic concerns. The story is one of Bowles's best known and most widely admired; Norman Mailer once hailed it as "one of the best short stories written by anyone."[33] Bold and original, the story, like "The Echo," outlines sexual configurations seldom depicted (especially in 1947) in literature, probably one reason that it, along with "The Delicate Prey," was omitted from English editions of Bowles work until 1968.

More so than "The Echo," "Pages from Cold Point" plays on escapist fantasies and displays a modernist brand of pessimism understandably appealing in our times. The story, in fact, begins with a statement of this philosophy: "Our civilization is doomed to a short life: its component parts are too heterogeneous. I personally am content to see everything in the process of decay. The bigger the bombs, the quicker it will be done. Life is visually too hideous for one to make the attempt to preserve it. Let it go. Perhaps some day another form of life will come along. Either way, it is of no consequence. At the same time, I am still a part of life, and I am bound by this to protect myself to whatever extent I am able" (*CS*, 83).

These views, inscribed by Norton, an American university professor who has found refuge on a Caribbean island, closely resemble those of the author. Bowles, like many other modernists, has often decried the state of the modern world, and nostalgically looked back toward preindustrial societies for relief and haven. His attitude, like Norton's, seems to be that we are condemned to live in a world that is, day by day, deteriorating, crumbling, succumbing to violence and irrationality. Often the writer has remarked that he dislikes going back to places he has already seen because he knows they will be worse than he had first known them to be. This response to the world and the course of human history makes sense, especially when we consider the contexts surrounding the story, at the end of World War II. Millions of innocent people, civilians and soldiers, had died in battle or in concentration camps. In August 1945 the United States dropped atom bombs on Hiroshima and Nagasaki. The landscape was bleak and devoid of hope.

Norton, one of Bowles's rare first-person narrators, is writing from an island retreat where he has lived since his wife, Hope, died and left an inheritance. He has no trouble whatsoever giving up his academic career, which had always "been an utter farce (since I believe no reason inducing a man to 'teach' can possibly be a valid one)." With delight he makes his "adieux to the English quacks, the Philosophy fakirs, and so on" and watches "the envy in their faces" when he tells them of his intention to fly to a tropical island and do "Nothing" (*CS*, 83). The scenario, which only scantily veils Bowles's attitudes toward the academy, is one that nearly every academic must, at one point or another, have dreamed of.

As in "The Echo," the opening moves of the story establish the circumstances of exile and situate the action in an exotic foreign setting. While the drama in "The Echo" revolves around three women, that in "Pages from Cold Point" revolves primarily around three men—Norton, his son Racky (Rocky in the original version), and Charles, an absent older brother of Norton's who is a successful lawyer in the United States. Charles, the narrator tells us early in the story, disapproves of nearly everything his brother does, not in the least his decision to bring his son with him to the island. No doubt Norton's retreat from America is linked to his wish to escape his brother's disapproval, which, we are led to believe, is based on some unstated moral grounds.

Critics of the story have often speculated that Charles has the goods on his brother. Lawrence Stewart goes so far as to suggest that "before they had left the States the boy had overheard a conversation between his father and his uncle and had correctly deduced that they had had, in their youth, an overt sexual relationship" (Stewart 1974, 39). Stewart's interpretation, while on track, pins down the story's subtle ambiguities too precisely. First, we are never exactly sure what Racky knows or thinks, partly because Norton is narrating. Second, there is scant textual evidence to support Stewart's claim that the brothers had had any kind of "overt sexual relationship." When the narrator recounts his brother's tauntings ("D'ye think that I've forgotten?"), we are certainly led to believe that *something* has gone on, but that "something" is never spelled out, and we can assume it is Bowles's intention to preserve a sense of ambiguity (*CS*, 84).

Once on the island, Norton decides to settle on Cold Point, away from populated areas, "quite isolated on its seaside cliff" (*CS*, 85). Early descriptions of the place portray an idyllic setting, one in which Norton can be alone with his 16-year-old son. As the narrator puts it: "I can never even think of the boy without that familiar overwhelming sensation of delight and gratitude for being vouchsafed the privilege of sharing my life with him. What he takes so completely as a matter of course, our daily life here together, is a source of never ending wonder to me; and I reflect upon it a good part of each day, just sitting here being conscious of my great good fortune in having him all to myself" (*CS*, 86).

The irony, much as in "The Echo," is that the attempt to isolate themselves from "civilization" and "external influences" ultimately backfires; it brings them in closer, undeniable proximity with the most haunting, disruptive portions of their selves. Norton thinks that, once on the Caribbean island, they will be "beyond the reach of prying eyes and malicious tongues." Not long after they arrive on the island, however, Racky evidently gains a reputation in the area for his homosexual adventures. Though the evidence is right in front of him, Norton seems the last to admit the apparent truth of the matter.

During the first half of the account, originally planned in journal form but published with dates omitted, Norton suspects nothing in Racky's wanderings; his "special" friendship with Peter, the young gardener; or his prolonged stays in the town. Norton's suspicions seem first to be aroused when he is in town—Orange Walk—one day and is confronted by "a large black woman" who says something to him, in an unfriendly tone, that he later interprets as "Keep your boy at home, mahn" (*CS*, 90). But even when Norton settles on this interpretation, he construes the words such that he averts the truth. "Suppose she did tell me to keep Racky home," he writes. "It could only mean that she, or someone else in Orange Walk, has had a childish altercation with him" (*CS*, 91).

Two incidents demand that Norton confront the truth directly. First, Norton receives a visit from the village constable, who is skeptical that Racky, whom he terms a "bad young man," is Norton's son. When Norton asks why he is bad, the constable answers, "He has no shame. He does what he pleases with all the young boys, and the men too, and gives them a shilling so they won't tell about it" (*CS*, 94). Not long after this incident, a fight breaks out between Racky and Peter, the gardener, after which Peter tells Norton what's been going on between him and Racky.

By this point in the story, the reader might well question the propriety of the narrator's response to this situation, though throughout the account the narrator himself reflects little on the wisdom of his course of action. Rather than confronting Racky with the issue, Norton chooses to let the matter pass. And though Racky lies to his father, Norton, knowing the lies, does nothing to expose them. Each, however, seems to know that the other knows. Like Marcel in Gide's *L'Immoralist*, who knowingly allows a young Arab to steal from him, Norton seems to invite the deception. As if to mollify his father, Racky flirts with him—exactly what the father may unconsciously have wanted.

One evening when Norton comes back from a walk, he finds the lights off in Racky's room and the boy in his own bedroom: "Then my mouth opened. The top sheet of my bed had been stripped back to the foot. There on the far side of the bed, dark against the whiteness of the lower sheet, lay Racky asleep on his side, and naked" (*CS*, 98).

The reader is left to imagine what, if anything, happens between Racky and his father. Norton is cagily self-deceptive on matters that could impugn his own integrity, the image of himself he vigilantly guards and believes in. He does tell us, though, that the pattern of bed sharing is regularized and that Racky taunts him about inviting Uncle Charlie down for a visit. To avoid a confrontation, Norton, an apparent victim of blackmail, takes his son to Havana, across the island, where the boy gets an apartment with a young Cuban friend.

Probably the story's most outstanding, even outrageous, feature is its twist on the incest theme. In a reworking of the traditional oedipal battle between father and son, in which the son seeks to eliminate the mother, here it is rather the mother who is considered the interloper between father and son. Once she is out of the picture, the son and father are free to play out their male-to-male dramas without interference or mediation. Longingly, the aging father most likely sees in his son a younger version of himself. His structuring of a life together, away from home, can be seen as a way of hanging onto his fleeting youth and responding to his own unadmitted, repressed homosexual desires.

In both "The Echo" and "Pages from Cold Point," children are the victims of their parents' psychological confusions. Because of the narrative technique employed in "Pages from Cold Point," however, the whole issue of deception is heightened. It would certainly be a mistake to take Norton's version of himself and his reality as indisputable, sure, or reliable. As Lawrence Stewart notes, "Norton's journal is not merely an accounting for the immediate past, nor is its writing an existential act divorced from a temporal continuum. Instead, suppressing, emphasizing, reordering, it creates a present moment with remembered materials" (Stewart 1974, 41). That reordering, his chronicle, is a masking of the truth in the guise of a fiction he can more comfortably inhabit. What is written down no doubt takes hold in the writer's mind, as it does in the reader's. The journal gives structure but affords no lasting or all-encompassing insight for its author. Norton's chronicle ends with these words: "I am perfectly happy here in reality, because I still believe that nothing very drastic is likely to befall this part of the island in the near future" (*CS*, 100).

The narrator's own conception of self is left undisturbed, and his experience takes on a static quality. The real drama occurs in the mind of the reader as he becomes absorbed in the narrative, backs off, challenges Norton's self-justifications and actions, is reabsorbed, and tries to find his own moral equilibrium.

American Tales

So lush, dense, and overpowering are the exotic landscapes in *The Delicate Prey* that it would be easy to overlook or downplay the two stories with American settings: "How Many Midnights" (Tangier, 1947) and

"You Are Not I" (New York, 1948). Though these two stories could be considered anomalies of a sort, they have a great deal in common with stories set in North Africa and Latin America. "How Many Midnights" deals with thwarted human desires to connect, and "You Are Not I" displays the workings of a deranged sensibility.

The urban setting of "How Many Midnights"; its means of narration, close to the central character's consciousness yet omniscient; and its epiphanic qualities give the story a Joycean flavor. The story centers on the romance and anticipation of an expected rendezvous. During the evening the story takes place, June, the central figure, is utterly absorbed by thoughts of Van, the man with whom she has had a relationship for some time and whom she plans to marry on Valentine's Day, 10 days hence. The night ahead of her was to have been "a special night," for Van had, the day before, meaningfully slipped her the key to his apartment. The narrator tells us: "That was surely the most exciting single thing that ever had happened between them—the passage of the keys from his hand to hers. By the gesture he gave up what she knew was most dear to him: his privacy" (*CS*, 102). Before that time, during the two years they had known each other, never "had anything ever occurred between them which was not what her parents would call 'honorable'" (*CS*, 103).

The story's narrative can be divided into two sections, the first showing June walking to Van's apartment and the second set in Van's apartment. During the first portion we are privy to the character's thoughts, given glimpses of the city, and provided with pieces of the past. The extent to which June has already invaded Van's life becomes apparent when she arrives at his apartment, carrying a rubber plant. "Practically all the adornments in his apartment were objects either of her buying or her choosing," we learn (*CS*, 104). The wood stove had also been her idea: "Many times he had said to her: 'That was one sensible idea you had,' as though the others had not been just as good!" (*CS*, 104). In fact, though she has never lived in the apartment, it all seems to have been designed and furnished to suit her tastes. The colors had been her idea, and she had also suggested the goatskin rug, the "big glass coffee table," the heavy wool curtains, and "the two enormous plaster candelabra covered with angels" that she had brought back from Mexico.

Once in the apartment, June begins to fastidiously arrange everything. We get the sense that, while her attention is focused on Van and his arrival, she is really indulging in her own fantasies, constructing her own sense of order, without much concern for his point of view. She rearranges the furniture, placing the divan in front of the fireplace, even though "it might possibly annoy Van when he first saw it" (*CS*, 106). Richard F. Patteson has noted that "just as surely as Bowles' more obvious explorers, [June] attempts to colonize new territory (in her case, Van's life) even as she charts it" (Patteson, 95).

June's neurotic efforts to put things in order ironically result in more and more disorder as the night goes on. As she moves a commode, its contents—Van's correspondence—spill out, and she nervously scrambles to arrange things, fearing Van might arrive right then. Even as midnight passes, she waits in expectation, refusing to admit the more terrifying possibility that he might not come at all. What has happened to him? On her second glass of Scotch, "she succeeded in convincing herself that the mathematical probabilities of Van's having met with his first serious accident on this particular evening were extremely slight" (*CS*, 108). She flips through a number of other possibilities before thinking "that he had deliberately avoided it, which of course was absurd." Or was it? So completely do her illusions possess her that, sitting on the divan, June imagines that he is in the room and that he jumps out the window. We are given her response: "When she got to the window there was nothing to see but the vast gray panorama of a city at dawn, spitefully clear in every tiniest detail. She stood there looking out, seeing for miles up and down the empty streets. Or were they canals? It was a foreign city" (*CS*, 110).

All this, of course, is filtered through June's consciousness. We have no way of knowing Van's intentions in giving her the keys; nor do we know anything about *his* views on the relationship. The story circumvents any desire the reader, or for that matter June, might have in reaching any sure conclusions about Van and why he didn't show up at the apartment. We might entertain various speculations: from the start, he never intended to show up; he got cold feet, the more he thought about the prisonhouse of marriage; there was an accident; he had another date; or he was an unwitting prey of the city's incalculable, indiscriminate assaults. It is this quality of indeterminacy that Jane Bowles remarks on with admiration in a letter to her husband: "It seems like an innocent enough little story when it begins and the way in which you have shaded it so that it becomes steadily more somber, almost as imperceptibly to the reader as to the girl herself, is I should say masterful."[34]

Near the story's end the mystery dissolves when June goes into Van's bedroom, looks in his closet, and finds his overnight bag gone, suggesting he had in fact planned not to return that evening. On making that discovery, in the early hours of morning, June leaves the apartment, hails a cab, takes a solitary walk in the cold morning air, and finally returns to her parents' home. Once back in her bedroom, she undresses and opens the window, and "the cold wind blew through the room" (*CS*, 111). Whatever becomes of Van and June after that we can only guess.

The story presents—granted, in stark, dramatic, fictional form—the dynamics between male and female (or, for that matter, any two people), where two wills vie for power. As with "Call at Corazón," underlying this story are deep doubts regarding the possibility, even the advisability, of giving oneself completely over to another person. How is one to maintain one's integrity with another's will pressing in so closely? As with many other Bowles stories, there is also a sharp dichotomy between inside and outside, between an almost paranoid regard for privacy and a sense of public violation. Outside it is cold, hostile, snowy; inside the apartment there is at least an illusion of refuge, a warm space where order can be constructed against the chaos of the world. For a moment June thinks, "[W]hat an ideal little vacation it would make: a night and day up there in the snow, isolated from everything, shut away from everyone but Van" (*CS*, 107). The irony is, as Richard F. Patteson points out in his discussion of the story, that this humanly constructed shelter is not sufficient. "By the end of the story," he writes, "her opening of a window to let the winter wind blow through signals an unspoken acknowledgment that her sense of security cannot withstand violation from the outside world" (Patteson, 3).

"You Are Not I," which Robert Craft, in a review of Bowles's work, calls one of the author's best stories, shares more than its American setting with "How Many Midnights."[35] Both are explorations of a neurotic human consciousness. So intense are June's fantasies that they create a reality of their own, displacing a socially shared reality. Hers, we feel, ultimately is an unstable personality. In "You Are Not I," the screw is given one more turn. Here we are in the hands of an insane, schizophrenic narrator. The intensely subjective, deranged first-person narrator in Bowles's story reminds one of Poe's narrators, say, in "The Cask of Amontillado" or "The Man of the Crowd."

In a taped conversation with Lawrence Stewart, Bowles tells of the story's genesis:

> I remember one night I woke up having—funny, I didn't see it as clearly, the story, in my dream, as I saw the words I was writing. The words were imposed on the scenes, as it could be on the screen, you

know. But I was writing the text on top of the scenes . . . just enough for me to get into it. The whole atmosphere of the beginning I had dreamed. So when I woke up I began writing, without putting the light on, in the dark—I could barely read it the next day. I just wrote, large, and turned pages and kept this up, because I was saying it from memory, almost. Down as far as putting the stones in the mouths, and then there was no more and I just went on, because I had for me what I thought was a good beginning the next day. (Stewart 1974, 156)

The first-person narrator, Ethel, tells the story of how she took advantage of a train accident briefly to escape a mental institution. "Everyone was so excited that no one noticed me," she says near the beginning of her tale. "I became completely unimportant as soon as it was a question of cut people and smashed cars down there on the tracks" (*CS*, 157). In a very detached manner, she walks along the tracks, surveying the scene, as rescue workers attend to the wounded. Apparently drawn to become involved somehow, she collects a handful of stones, which she proceeds to drop into the open mouths of victims lying along the tracks on the cinders. When a man catches her pulling off rings from the fingers of one of the victims, he cries out, "What are you doing? Are you crazy?" and the narrator, quick to construct a credible scenario, responds that the dead body is her sister's.

Eventually, Ethel is taken to her sister's house, whose address she has given the driver. Whatever insane behavior the narrator displays is explained by the shock she is presumed to be suffering. Her sister obviously doesn't want to see her and even thinks her delivery may be in error.

"Are you *sure* she's all right?" the sister asks the driver, who replies they have looked her over at the hospital. The driver, of course, is in the dark about the narrator's past. Her sister, not at all convinced she is well, calls "The Home" to give them a piece of her mind, after conversation with a neighbor, Mrs. Jelinek. The narrator presents her version: "I knew exactly what had happened even before she told Mrs. Jelinek. She had called the Home and complained to Dr. Dunn that I had been released, and he had been very much excited and told her to hold on to me by all means because I had not been discharged at all but had somehow *got out*" (*CS*, 162).

A number of the neighbors have meantime joined forces in case she needs to be restrained. When the men from the Home arrive to take her back, the narrator takes a stone from the pocket of her coat and "before either of them could stop me I reached out and stuffed the stone into [her sister's] mouth" (*CS*, 163). With this action she is able to convince herself she has traded places with her sister; they are taking her sister back to the Home and she is being left behind. At this point, the narrative shifts to the third person: "Driving in through the gate, she really broke down. They kept promising her ice cream for dinner, but she knew better than to believe them. As she walked through the main door between the two men she stopped on the threshold, took out one of the stones from her coat pocket and put it into her mouth. She tried to swallow it, but it choked her, and they rushed her down the hall into a little waiting room and made her give it up. The strange thing, now that I think about it, was that no one realized she was not I" (*CS*, 163).

"She" is the one ultimately who writes it all down, while "I am still in the living room, sitting on the divan" (*CS*, 164). As Richard Patteson writes, "The convolution at this point is almost Nabokovian in its complexity. Ethel is telling a story (the entire story) in which she tells another story (the "will power" reversal) in which her sister becomes the author of a story in which Ethel is a character" (Patteson, 120).

As with "How Many Midnights," events are served to us wholly from one point of view, an unreliable one at that, and we can only speculate how that person is viewed by the outside world. We begin to see the world through her eyes and develop sympathy for her point of view. Even though we know that what she is doing is wrong, we become willing accomplices to her devious deeds and ready companions for her deranged mind. Blurred are the lines distinguishing right and wrong, security and vulnerability, interior and exterior, sanity and insanity. At one point in the story, the narrator passes by an old woman, near the railway tracks, and remarks, "She looked crazy to me and I kept clear of her" (*CS*, 158). Comments she makes later go even further and, along the lines of Foucault in *Discipline and Punish*, call into question the very structure of authority and power that creates and enforces the distinctions in the first place: "It seemed to me that life outside was like life inside. There was always somebody to stop people from doing what they wanted to do. I smiled when I thought that this was just the opposite of what I had felt when I was still inside. Perhaps what we want to do is wrong, but why should they always be the ones to decide?" (*CS*, 158).

The Delicate Prey is a remarkably coherent volume of stories. The concern in virtually all the stories, whether they be set in Morocco, Central America, or the United States, is life on the edge. That edge might be the murky region where two cultures meet, where sanity and insanity become blurred, or where sexual desire takes forms repudiated by society. From the stories of this volume emerges an aesthetic of the Bowles short story—where narrative unrolls in a terrifyingly logical fashion and landscape seems frequently to overshadow the characters who traverse its terrain.

A *Hundred Camels in the Courtyard*

A *Hundred Camels in the Courtyard*, the first collection of Bowles's stories published in America after *The Delicate Prey and Other Stories*, owes its existence to a number of unlikely, fortuitous exchanges. When Allen Ginsberg visited Bowles on a trip to Morocco in the early 1960s, he suggested that City Lights, which under the guidance of Lawrence Ferlinghetti had published Ginsberg's *Howl*, might be interested in some of Bowles's recent stories. Bowles inquired, Ferlinghetti responded encouragingly, and Bowles wrote back, clarifying his intentions: "What I'd like to be sure of is that the word *Morocco* will be kept out of any blurb regarding the stories. The authorities here are touchy about the kif question, and since I live here and my wife is not well, I want to avoid any problems of that kind, naturally."[36]

In a subsequent letter Bowles wrote:

> The title business has kept me thinking, but not with any great degree of productivity. The difficulty with finding a word that has some reference, even oblique, to kif, is that the word will necessarily be a Moghrebi word, and thus will have no reference at all save to the few who know the region. (*Moghrebi* itself could be used, I suppose: *Four Moghrebi Tales*, for instance. But of course no kif is suggested there.) Do you like A HUNDRED CAMELS IN THE COURTYARD . . . ? On the title page we could have the whole quote: "A pipe of kif before breakfast gives a man the strength of a hundred camels in the courtyard."
>
> . . . Moghrebi Proverb
>
> That would more or less capsulize the meaning, since the theme of all the stories is specifically the power of kif, rather than the subjective effects of it.[37]

Thus was born the title for the volume of four stories that share a purely Moroccan focus and that feature, among other things, the effects of smoking kif.

Bowles has often been viewed as an enfant terrible, one of our own to be disavowed because of the threatening moral purport of his work. In

Advertisements for Myself, published just three years before *A Hundred Camels*, Normal Mailer proclaimed, "Paul Bowles opened the world of Hip. He let in the murder, the drugs, the incest, the death of the Square (Port Moresby), the call of the orgy, the end of civilization: he invited all of us to these themes a few years ago" (Mailer, 429). One man's hero is another man's demon. Admonitions such as these have made Bowles, for many, only a more intriguing, fascinating figure. While Bowles was in Morocco, seemingly distant from the American scene, his persona, work, and life-style attracted the attention of many back home, especially figures associated with the beat movement. It was no accident that Ginsberg sought out Bowles. For many, including the likes of William S. Burroughs, who tracked Bowles down in the mid-1950s and early 1960s, Morocco was seen as a place congenial to many of their radical views and irreverent practices. When these Americans made their pilgrimages to Tangier, an obligatory stop was the legendary shrine of Paul Bowles. Bowles was a man, they thought, who seemed to have been living their ideals before they had even thought of them. It is a strange irony of literary history that this expatriate American should be linked to a movement with which he had only passing contact and modestly shared sympathies. Though this young group of literary avant-garde was drawn to Bowles, his aesthetic vision is much more conservative than that of the Beats. While he may have been responsive to their radical social and political ideas, he remained skeptical about their artistic ventures, adhering to more traditional nineteenth-century notions of art associated, say, with Flaubert and Tolstoy. In a photograph of Peter Orlovsky, William Burroughs, Allen Ginsberg, Alan Ansen, Gregory Corso, Bowles, and Ian Somerville taken in Tangier in 1961, Bowles, seated on the ground in a white suit and tie, gazing toward the ground, seems to have positioned himself at a remove from the others.

The cover of *A Hundred Camels in the Courtyard*, brought out by City Lights in 1962, features a traditional Moroccan *sebsi*, or pipe, and a *mottoui*, or bag of kif, on a portion of woven straw mat. "Not much support here for Bush's drug war!" exclaimed Robert Craft, in response particularly to Bowles's "Kif Quartet," the four stories of *A Hundred Camels* (Craft, 12). Moralists and other detractors have often dismissed Bowles outright without fully exploring the aesthetic value and deeper import of his work. Anatole Broyard, for example, in "The Man Who Discovered Alienation," a 1989 article appearing in the *New York Times Book Review*, calls Bowles "the grand panandrum of paranoid expatriation" and meanly charges that " he loves awfulness, or offalness," giving the writer credit for neither his originality nor his unique place in American literary history.[38]

Far from being an advocate of the indiscriminate use of drugs, Bowles has always been much more concerned with pointing out the inconsistency and hypocrisy of America's legal and moral attitudes toward these substances. Kif, for example, is a drug Bowles has suggested may be no more pernicious than our own national drug, alcohol. In "The Story of Lahcen and Idir," one of the "Kif Quartet," we are told: "The difference between Lahcen and Idir was that Lahcen liked to drink and Idir smoked kif. Kif smokers want to stay quiet in their heads, and drinkers are not like that. They want to break things."[39]

In these stories kif functions in a manner symbolic of the operation of the imagination. In "Friend of the World," Salam, the main character, always retreats into a kif-induced world of solitude in order to plot the course of events, which nearly always involves some kind of trick or trap. Bowles neither condones nor champions the drug's use. Rather, unalarmingly and evenhandedly, he displays its operation. While kif can open the door to a world of marvelous, previously unthought-of possibilities, it can just as well muddle the mind and blur the distinction between reality and illusion. In "The Wind at Beni Midar," a soldier's troubles are complicated when, after smoking kif, he eats a lot of cactus fruit and loses his borrowed gun in the heap of peels.

In the preface to a recent edition of the stories, Bowles explains the effect of kif-smoking on the smoker's logical arrangement of the world around him:

> Moroccan kif-smokers like to speak of "two worlds," the one ruled by inexorable natural laws, and the other, the kif world, in which each person perceives "reality" according to the projections of his own essence, the state of consciousness in which the elements of the physical universe are automatically rearranged by cannabis to suit the requirements of the individual. These distorted variations in themselves generally are of scant interest to anyone but the subject at the time he is experiencing them. An intelligent smoker, nevertheless, can aid in directing the process of deformation in such a way that the results will have value to him in his daily life. If he has faith in the accuracy of his interpretations, he will accept them as decisive, and use them to determine a subsequent plan of action. Thus, for a dedicated smoker, the passage to the "other world" is often a pilgrimage undertaken for the express purpose of oracular consultation. (*HC*, xi)

Altered consciousness of the kind referred to here figures in nearly all of Bowles's fiction. His interest in drugs is much like that shown by creative talents such as Coleridge, De Quincey, Baudelaire, and Walter Benjamin. The drug experience, to them, represents wide-ranging imaginative freedom, as it gives a long leash to reality, suggests bizarre connections, and stands in opposition to the dominant, increasingly scientific, rational world that threatens to obliterate the imagination completely.[40]

If one of the distinguishing characteristics of the stories in this volume is the prominent role kif plays as an agent for liberating or twisting the imagination, another is that these stories have no Western characters at all. This in itself is a major literary achievement. While Bowles is best known for those works which have at their center the encounter between East and West, he has, as we have seen, written stories wholly from the Moroccan point of view. Though a few stories in *The Delicate Prey and Other Stories*, such as "By the Water" and "The Delicate Prey," involve only Moroccan characters, this approach becomes more distinct and significant in *A Hundred Camels in the Courtyard*. Bowles's gradual movement toward giving a fuller depiction of the Moroccan perspective is natural and logical, corresponding to his extended residence in the country over the past 40 years and the various relationships he has had during that time with Moroccan artists and writers such as Ahmed Yacoubi, Mohammed Choukri, Larbi Layachi, and, most recently, Mohamad Mrabet. John Ryle, in a review of *Unwelcome Words* and Christopher Sawyer-Lauçanno's biography of Bowles, has written that "it is the subtle infusion of an indigenous sensibility into Bowles's work that distinguishes him from other expatriate writers; it is this that rescues him from the existential wilderness."[41]

The stories in this volume present one imaginative version of Morocco, and while we must not mistake this representation as a wholly realistic one, certainly the reader acquainted with Morocco will easily recognize the real place in the fiction. Bowles's interest here is not so much in giving an accurate portrayal of Morocco as it is in telling an interesting story, though the two purposes need not be presumed as being at odds. The Morocco we enter in these stories is one in which superstitions, worship of saints, and belief in *jnun* (genies) such as Aïsha Qandisha are the operating structures determining reality. (At one point Ben Tajah, in "He of the Assembly," buys vials of penicillin to treat his case of syphilis and hangs them neatly around his neck to effect the cure.) The café and mosque are the central meeting places for the men, and the women's sphere of power is generally limited to the domestic arena. Islam, in various forms, exercises its power over processes of thought. We even get glimpses of the self-lacerating ceremonies of the Jilali and the Hamadsha, subjects of study by anthropologists such as Vincent Crapanzano and Paul Rabinow.[42] Finally, the pace of life in these stories is much slower, and events are not so much predictable, according to human logic, as they are fated by an all-knowing power governing the universe. In other words, the Morocco Bowles writes about and valorizes is the traditional Morocco, not the modern, Westernized culture dominating more and more of Casablanca and other large urban centers in the country.

Governing these stories is a kind of logic whose principles are laid out by Stenham, the American writer in *The Spider's House*, when he explains the philosophy of Moroccan life to Polly, his American companion, who understands little of what goes on around her.

> It's a culture of "and then" rather than one of "because," like ours. . . . What I mean is that in their minds one thing doesn't come from another thing. Nothing is a result of anything. Everything merely *is*, and no questions asked. Even the language they speak is constructed around that. Each fact is separate, and one never depends on the other. Everything's explained by the constant intervention of Allah. And whatever happens had to happen, and was decreed at the beginning of time, and there's no way even of imagining how anything could have been different from what it is.[43]

The surprising, unexpected logic found in these stories can be explained, in part, by the method Bowles employed in creating them. "I began to experiment with the idea of constructing stories whose subject matter would consist of disparate elements and unrelated characters taken directly from life and fitted together as in a mosaic," he writes. "The problem was to create a story line which would make each arbitrarily chosen episode compatable [*sic*] with the others, to make each one lead to the next with a semblance of naturalness. . . . I listed a group of incidents and situations I had either witnessed or heard about that year" (*HC*, ix).

The three stories resulting from this procedure—"A Friend of the World," "The Story of Lahcen and Idir," and "The Wind at Beni Midar"—have about them the kind of fairy-tale improbability we might associate with stories in *A Thousand and One Nights*. What holds the world together is God's will; the arrangement of things seems arbitrary only to the measured human mind. Within that providential order fates rise or fall at the drop of a hat, justice is administered surprisingly and cleverly outside the legal framework, spells are cast surreptitiously, and long-separated siblings are reunited magically after each presumed the other dead. The nature of these stories may seem quite different from what we are most often accustomed to in the West. While our normal expectations of a story largely conform to the Chekhovian notion of "a slice of life," the story in the Middle Eastern context often is expected to do something else. The more extraordinary or dazzling a happening is—that is, the more radically it departs from the occurences of everyday life—the better and more entertaining the story. The successful story-teller often employs twists and turns of the narrative and deftly asserts the triumph of the powerless over the powerful.

The method Bowles followed in constructing the stories results in an accentuation of the element of surprise and the breaking of traditional notions of causality. In writing "A Friend of the World," for example, Bowles chose the following three items from his "group of incidents and situations" and wove them into a story:

> A. had an old grudge against B. When B. was made a policeman, A. sent money to him, seeing to it that B.'s superior was made aware of the gift. B. was reprimanded and given a post in the Sahara.

> Finding his kitten dead with a needle in its stomach, G. decided that it had been killed because he had named it Mimi.

> K. frightened a Jewish woman by leaving the ingredients of magic on her doorstep. (*HC*, x)

These incidents, then, hooked together by the puffs of a kif pipe, Bowles weaves into a marvelously coherent, entertaining story.

As the story opens, we are told that Salam, the main character, had chosen to rent a room in a Jewish home in the city:

> He had decided to live with the Jews because he had already lived with Christians and found them all right. He trusted them a little more than he did other Moslems, who were like him and said: "No Moslem can be trusted." Moslems are the only true people, the only people you can understand. But because you do understand them, you do not trust them. Salam did not trust the Jews completely, either, but he liked living with them because they paid no attention to him. It had no

importance if they talked about him among themselves, and they never would talk about him to Moslems. (*HC*, 15)

The story is set in motion when Salam adopts a small, stray kitten he innocently names Mimi. Before long Salam notices that whenever he calls out for his kitten, a particular Jewish woman runs out of her house and meets his calls with a suspicious, disapproving look. We are told: "She would put one hand above her eyes and stare up at him, and then she would put both hands on her hips and frown. 'A crazy woman,' he thought, and paid no attention to her. One day while he was calling the kitten the woman shouted up to him in Spanish. Her voice sounded very angry. '*Oyé!*' she cried, shaking her arm in the air, 'why are you calling the name of my daughter?'" (*HC*, 18).

When several days later Salam finds his kitten dead, on eating a piece of bread with a needle hidden in it, he naturally blames the woman. He sits down, pulls out his kif pipe, and plots his revenge. "The next day he got up early and went to the market. In a little stall there he bought several things: a crow's wing, a hundred grams of *jduq jmel* seed, powdered porcupine quills, some honey, a pressed lizard, and a quarter kilo of *fasoukh*" (*HC*, 19). With the help of these items and the support of Fatma Daifa, his grandmother's sister, he convinces the Jewish woman that a spell has been cast on the young girl, Mimi. Thus, when the girl falls and skins her knee on a piece of broken glass, Salam is blamed. The Jewish woman goes to the police and complains. While the policeman intends to do nothing, he takes down the name of the accused in order to appease the woman. Soon thereafter the policeman bumps into Salam on the street and knowlingly asks him whether there was any trouble. Salem becomes worried: 'A very bad thing,' thought Salam as he hurried home with the kif. No policeman had bothered him before this. When he reached his room he wondered if he should hide the package under a tile in the floor, but he decided that if he did that, he himself would be living like a Jew, who each time there is a knock on the door ducks his head and trembles" (*HC*, 24).

Salam brings out his pipe again and devises a second ruse, this one designed to get rid of the perceived threat posed by the policeman. He enlists the support of an out-of-town friend who, on Salam's behalf, delivers an envelope containing 1,000 francs to the police station, with instructions that it was for this particular member of the force. Everything works out as Salam has planned. The chief of police intercepts the money, charges his subordinate with taking bribes, and has him transferred to a post in the Sahara where he no longer poses a threat to Salam. The story ends with Fatma Daifa coming to visit Salam and staging an argument with him that signals the removal of the spell. An unusual sort of justice is served, all the way around.

"He of the Assembly," the Bowles story most resistant to straightforward interpretation, neatly fits in this "kif quartet."[44] It dwells on the familiar themes of deception and trickery, again entirely within the dynamics of Moroccan society. Nearly always the narration in Bowles's stories is direct and chronological and employs an omniscient point of view. "He of the Assembly" is an exception and may seem more confusing for the reader until he figures out its structure and realizes also that much of the confusion is a result of the distorted, subjective views of the main characters' kif-filled consciousness.

Ben Tajah at the story's opening is sitting in the Café of the Two Bridges in Marrakech, intent on deciphering the phrase "The sky trembles and the earth is afraid, and the two eyes are not brothers." He of the Assembly (a direct translation of the proper name Boujemaa, which can also mean "Born on Friday"), hallucinating, is sitting in the same café, puzzling over the meaning of the phrase "The eye wants to sleep but the head is no mattress" (*HC*, 33–34). Stewart writes, "Bowles was determined that the surreality of Boujemaa's remarks should have a logical radiance—much the same way that Cocteau in *Orphée* made the senselessness of Apollinaire's '*L'oiseau chante avec ses doigts*' sensible" (Stewart 1974, 131). He of the Assembly's delusions are vividly rendered, such that his paranoid vision at once overpowers reality and achieves, in and through language, the status of reality. In the first scene He of the Assembly imagines he is let down into a kettle of soup, chased by police, and floating in a rowboat on the hot, liquid soup. The narrative moves, freely and with few signals, from the character's hallucinations, to omniscient comments concerning the scene at large, to narration filtered through the character's consciousness.

The second paragraph of the story focuses on Ben Tajah as he leaves the café, still thinking of the cryptic phrase—"the sky trembles . . ."—and beginning to doubt its reality when he cannot find the envelope on which he thought he had first seen the phrase written. The scene then shifts, and we see He of the Assembly, still stoned, leaving the café, trying to come up with a bit of small change. In the next section we are wholly in the consciousness of He of the Assembly as he wanders about the city of Marrakech late at night, imagining he is pursued by the she-demon Aïcha Qandicha and thinking of magic potions that might rid him of her.

Eventually, as though it were fated, the two men, pariahs, each suffering from delusions, meet and take refuge from the police in Ben Tajah's humble dwelling. This meeting too is confusing, for neither the reader nor He of the Assembly at first knows the identity of the person who has suddenly helped him escape the clutches of the law and offered shelter.

As uncharacteristic as this story at first seems, Bowles's familiar pre-occupations are only thinly veiled. As in so many of the stories in *The Delicate Prey*, and as in much of his longer fiction, the theme that emerges here concerns thwarted desire for human contact and communication. At the same time, we see the flight of the outlaw from authority. Once the two Moroccan men are together, we are told that the host, Ben Tajah, felt happy to have He of the Assembly with him, "because he was certain that Satan would not appear before him as long as the boy was with him" (*HC*, 47). The two begin to talk together, not altogether coherently, and share a pipe. While Ben Tajah is pleased to have some companionship, hoping the young man will confirm his own sense of reality, He of the Assembly, for his part, is content to receive temporary haven from his demons and the police. Connections, however, do not last; too many forces work against their extended sustenance. As in "Tea on the Mountain," "Pages from Cold Point," and *The Spider's House*, this story ends in rupture. He of the Assembly lies to Ben Tajah in order to set his mind at ease, telling him the phrases in his head are from a popular song. The night ends with the two men lying together in the same bed. Ben Tajah, to his guest's dismay, quickly falls asleep. He of the Assembly thinks to himself, "This is how he treats a friend who has made him happy. He forgets his trouble and his friend too" (*HC*, 53–54). He gets up from bed; digs in Ben Tajah's pockets for what money he can find; discovers the envelope the man has been looking for, with the cryptic words written on it; burns it; and leaves, money in his pocket. Ben Tajah, then, will wake, the victim of theft and broken trust and still plagued by his inability to settle on a sure interpretation of reality.

When Lawrence D. Stewart asked Bowles whether a sexual relation-ship between the two men was implied, Bowles responded, "In the mind of He of the Assembly there is" (Stewart 1974, 134). Stewart goes on to comment, "For the first time in a Bowles short story, the crossgen-erational relationship is one of compensatory kindness. Friendship is no longer pernicious barter and exchange, and it carries no sexual price. How far indeed is Ben Tajah's bed in Marrakech from Norton's at Cold Point" (Stewart 1974, 135).

Until it is completed by the reader, put together piece by piece, the story is apt to seem like a wildly disarrayed tapestry with no readily apparent design. Actually, "He of the Assembly" is highly symmetrical, following the same kind of ordering principles Bowles often set out in his musical compositions. Should the reader not discover the pattern, Bowles explains his design: "Here the content of each paragraph is determined by its point of view. There are seven paragraphs, arranged in a simple pattern: imagine the cross-section of a pyramidal structure of four steps, where steps 1 and 7 are at the same level, likewise 2 and 6, and 3 and 5, with 4 at the top. In paragraphs 1 and 7 He of the Assembly and Ben Tajah are seen together. 2 and 6 are seen by Ben Tajah, and 3 and 5 by He of the Assembly, and 4 consists of He of the Assembly's interior monologue" (*HC*, xi). Bowles's remarks on the genesis of the story also make its shape and meaning more comprehensible. He tells us that the two cryptic statements circulating in the minds of his two central characters were among "three hermetic statements made to me that year by a kif-smoker in Marrakech. He uttered these apocalyptic sentences, but steadfastly refused to shed any light on their meanings or possible applications. This impelled me to invent a story about him in which he would furnish the meanings" (*HC*, x–xi). Bowles subjects his readers (as well as his characters) to the same kind of insoluble puzzle he faced in Marrakech.

The other two stories in the quartet, "The Story of Lahcen and Idir" and "The Wind at Beni Midar," are similar to "A Friend of the World" in both tone and theme. "The Story of Lahcen and Idir" features two friends, one of whom, Lahcen, in order to test the fidelity and loyalty of a girlfriend, leaves her with his friend Idir: "If he brought Idir and the girl together and left them alone, Idir would tell him afterward everything that had happened. If she let Idir take her to bed, then she was a whore and could be treated like a whore" (*HC*, 64). Best let good enough alone. Needless to say, the girl prefers Idir to Lahcen, who would often beat her in his fits of drunkenness. In "The Wind at Beni Midar," a kif-smoking soldier finds a fitting revenge for his superior, who mocks him for his superstitions in front of his fellow soldiers.

Though all four of these stories also appeared in Bowles's next volume, *The Time of Friendship*, they clearly belong together as we have them in *A Hundred Camels in the Courtyard*, a small, tight, distinctive ensemble, all remarkably in tune with one another.

The Time of Friendship

The Time of Friendship, published by Holt in 1967, brings together 13 stories, many of which had already appeared in various places throughout the 1950s and 1960s.[45] The stories generally are less bristling, tamer, than those in *The Delicate Prey*. Rather than trying to outdo himself or extend the boundaries of what could be done with the short story, Bowles sticks fairly closely to themes and interests established in his first collection: the exile in an alluring yet potentially inhospitable landscape; sensibilities naturally deranged or altered by drugs; and the vulnerability of children's worlds. A maturation of style and a realization of greater complexity, however, are noticeable in many of these stories, the most powerful among them being "The Time of Friendship," "The Hours After Noon," "Doña Faustina," and "The Frozen Fields."

"The Time of Friendship"

The basic setup of the title story resembles that in "Tea on the Mountain."[46] A Western woman traveling in North Africa finds the object of her romantic yearnings in the form of a young Arab boy. This time the woman is Swiss, and she is given a name, Fräulein Windling. Fräulein Windling, a more intrepid traveler than her American forerunner in "Tea on the Mountain," spends her winters in an isolated oasis, and in the summer teaches "in the Freiluftschüle in Berne, where she entertained her pupils with tales of the life led by the people in the great desert in Africa" (*CS*, 337). "The Time of Friendship" is altogether a more satisfying story than its early prototype. A more expansive canvas is demanded to handle the greater complexities in relationships, to draw sharper distinctions, and to present a more comprehensive view of the confrontation between two cultures, one fundamentally Islamic and the other Christian.[47]

Fräulein Windling, further, is more conscious of her own motives and historical condition than the American writer in the 1939 story was. No doubt reflecting Bowles's own views, she thinks at one point in the story, "What we have lost, they still possess" (*CS*, 339). Her presence in North

Africa, like Bowles's, can be seen as an attempt to escape what she takes to be modern civilization's discontents (without clearly thinking whether they are any greater than at any other point in human history) and retrieve or recover a sense of mysticism and organic connection difficult to find in modern Western societies. Bowles purposefully accentuates Fräulein Windling's idolization of traditional man in describing her responses to the place: "Her first sight of the desert and its people had been a transfiguring experience; indeed, it seemed to her now that before coming here she had never been in touch with life at all. She believed firmly that each day she spent here increased the aggregate of her resistance. She coveted the rugged health of the natives, when her own was equally strong, but because she was white and educated, she was convinced that her body was intrinsically inferior" (*CS*, 338).

Hers is a desperate campaign to try to convince the villagers to hang on to their old ways rather than blindly embrace new technologies. When she sees the women using tin cans, rather than their old goatskins, to carry water, she explains to them the potential hazards to their health, to their way of life. They agree, and go on using the tin cans. Throughout the story we see Fräulein Windling's schemes go astray. Hers is the bind in which many people in development agencies find themselves, full of well-intentioned plans that are, to their dismay, resisted, ignored, or subverted by native communities. It is indeed a tricky business for an outsider to advise or prescribe practices.

"The Time of Friendship" is of interest not only because it further defines some of the author's thematic concerns but because it can be thought of as a matrix in which have been combined the key elements that generally go into shaping a Bowles story: actual events or experiences, literary antecedents, the writer's psychological imprint, the imagination, the story's formal demands, and the writer's craft. The story is ostensibly derived from the author's actual experience. Lawrence Stewart traces the story's origins to Bowles's wanderings in North Africa in the winter of 1947–48, nearly 15 years before the writing of the story. The setting of "The Time of Friendship" clearly resembles Taghit, which Bowles describes in his autobiography as being "probably the most intensely poetic spot I had ever seen. The tiny hotel atop the rocks was run in conjunction with the military fort nearby. There was a solitary old servant who did everything; fortunately he had only one other guest besides me, an elderly Swiss lady who taught school in Zurich and spent her winters in the Sahara. She and I got on perfectly and took long walks together in the valley to the south" (*WS*, 282). Bowles kept in touch with the Swiss woman, who, in about 1962, sent him a Christmas tree from Switzerland "and said that she hadn't been able to go back . . . and this put the idea in my head: 'the war's now keeping poor Fräulein from going to her favorite spot' (Stewart 1974, 136).

The character Slimane was also suggested by the writer's acquaintance with a young Moroccan on that same trip in 1947–48. Bowles recalls "a little boy named Suliman who used to come and see her—they were great friends—she did actually make a crèche for him, and that's about all. The rest of it's all my imagination, because I transposed it from '48 when it actually happened to, say, ten years later, after the Algerian War had been going a few years" (Stewart 1974, 140).

Echoes of literary antecedents are also heard in the story. Whether as a result of conscious design or not, "The Time of Friendship," perhaps more strikingly than any other of Bowles's works, suggests certain affinities with André Gide, whose influence Bowles has often acknowledged.[48] The outlines of the story, as well as its setting, bring to mind Gide's *L'Immoralist*. Like Gide, Bowles vividly paints the North African landscape, noting patterns of light and weather, cubistic architecture, palms, sand, and sun. Fräulein Windling, we are told early in the story, is in the habit of going on the roof of her hotel at dusk:

> It was one of the pleasures of the day, to watch the light changing in the oasis below, when dusk and the smoke from the evening fires slowly blotted out the valley. There always came a moment when all that was left was the faint outline, geometric and precise, of the mass of mud prisms that was the village, and a certain clump of high date palms that stood outside its entrance. The houses themselves were no longer there, and eventually the highest palm disappeared; and unless there was a moon all that remained to be seen was the dying sky, the sharp edges of the rocks on the hammada, and a blank expanse of mist that lay over the valley but did not reach as far up the cliffs as the hotel. (*CS*, 338)

This scene evokes many of the same images and sentiments Marcel draws on in Gide's novel.

Characters adjust their internal moral systems to the natural contours of geography and the vicissitudes of weather. Comparisons with Gide spring to mind again when we consider Fräulein Windling's wanderings through the oasis, as she searches for the objective correlative to her romantic image. Her movements resemble those of Marcel in *L'Immor-*

alist as he gets to know the boys of Biskra. The most obvious difference is that the lines of attraction in Bowles's tale are ostensibly heterosexual, while in Gide's they are homosexual. Fräulein Windling's walks around the vil-
lage and its environs take her past a group of young boys, whose individual identities she gradually comes to know. Her interest and attention become focused on a particular boy in the group: "There was one, she noted, younger than the others, who always sat a little apart from them" (*CS*, 340). This boy, Slimane, appears at the hotel one day. They meet and begin to talk, initiating the "time of friendship" around which the story takes shape.

While Bowles may have modeled Fräulein Windling after the Swiss woman he actually met in Taghit, the fictional representation also calls to mind Isabelle Eberhardt, another Swiss-born woman who, drawn to Islam and the desert, masqueraded in male garb and lived an absolutely daring life in North Africa at the turn of the nineteenth century. Bowles's preface to and translation of Eberhardt's *The Oblivion Seekers* is surely proof of his acquaintance with her life and admiration of her work.[49] The woman in early drafts of the story seems to bear more of a likeness to Eberhardt than the woman in the published version. In his first drafts Bowles writes: "[S]he had once dressed up in men's clothing, burnous and all, and ridden horseback with a group of Moungara all the way to Sidi Moungari, where she had spent the night outside the shrine, rolled in a camel's blanket."[50] For both Eberhardt and the early version of Fräulein Windling, the male disguise seems a way of breaking through the rigid attitudes and norms of a strict, patriarchal society, as well, perhaps, as playing out latent fantasies.

Bowles's revisions are prone to favor subtle portrayal of emotional and sexual dynamics over simple or graphic depiction. As with most of his work, the sexual tension in "The Time of Friendship" is implied, not overtly depicted. Plainly, there is a sexual dimension to the friendship between Fräulein Windling and the Arab boy, even if it is not fully acted out. Though one feels the presence of powerful sexual feelings, these feelings are not clearly characterized in the story as published. That Bowles was aware of the sexual dimension and that his revisions often favor the more subtle treatment of those themes can be seen when we look at an early version of the story, preserved in manuscript form. At one point in this version, the 14-year-old Slimane

> laid the palms of his two hands gently against her cheeks, and in that
> moment she saw him again as he had come along the road yesterday,

and then she understood that he had begun to visit the Ouled Naïl
girls at the bottom of the cliffs below the village.

"*Zoui-i-ina,*" he said under his breath, so low that she could scarcely
hear him, although his face was almost touching hers, "*very* nice." His
hands were still on her cheeks, but his eyes had turned aside and were
looking beyond her. (HRC)

The published version is much more subtle. The same kind of expurga-
tion of explicit sensual detail, as the writer moves from draft to final
version, can also be seen in "Pages from Cold Point."

In the creative process Bowles pulls stories away from their experien-
tial origins. Aesthetic concerns demand that rough edges be shaven
off. Once events are placed within the framework of story, they must
conform to principles of coherence, economy, and the formal expectations imposed by the genre, not merely the haphazard logic of everyday
life. These aesthetic considerations tend, for Bowles, to drive stories
away from clear subjective identifications with the author and to give
them a more objective character. Bowles is a cagey storyteller. The
reader is apt to feel the presence of a powerful authorial psychology, yet
one that has craftily erased clear traces of itself.

With his decision to have the Swiss woman visit the oasis during three
consecutive winters, Bowles emphasizes the phases of the relationship
between Fräulein Windling and Slimane. On the first visit she meets
Slimane; her second visit, during which her romance continues and
seems to blossom, was "probably her happiest season in the desert"; her
third visit begins with her landing at the North African port in a dreary
rain, observing with sadness the changes that occurred since the previous year, and ends abruptly with her unexpected departure.

The "friendship" (there is enough ambiguity in the story to support
an ironic reading of the title) that develops between the Swiss woman
and the North African boy is grounded in the curiosity each has about the
other's mysterious world. Each is, for the other, a symbol of the unknown; friendship is the means by which each tries to tame, penetrate, or
master that unknown. The sense of difference between the characters is
a powerful catalyst in the establishment of the relationship, yet it is also
a source of irritation and misunderstandings. The two must communicate in French, a language the young Arab knows imperfectly. From the
start, the older woman takes a patronizing attitude toward Slimane,
offering him candy, showing pity for his poverty, buying him various
things, thus subjecting him to the judgments and envy of his fellow

villagers. The Swiss woman's giving is foreign aid on a small scale: nothing truly valuable is given, and nothing is given without strings attached.

By the time of the third year, the relationship between the Swiss woman and Slimane is on less-than-certain ground. Her efforts to teach him the language and culture of the West have been largely unsuccessful. (She seems unable to put a dent in the Arab's admiration for Hitler, for example.) She conceives the approach of Christmas as the perfect opportunity to convey the message of Christianity, something she has been trying to demonstrate throughout the narrative, insisting on a distinction between Jesus and his Islamic equivalent, Sidna Aïssa. When she had spoken on matters concerning Islam, however, "no matter what she said (for at that point it seemed that automatically he was no longer within hearing) he would shake his head interminably and cry: "No, no, no, no! Nazarenes know nothing about Islam. Don't talk, madame, I beg you, because you don't know what you're saying. No, no, no!" (*CS*, 342). She decides, then, to dramatize her point with a symbolic reenactment of the birth of Jesus. She invites Slimane for dinner at the hotel and in the meantime constructs a crèche. The drama around the creation of the crèche and Slimane's reaction to it form the center of the story.

Fräulein Windling's ardent yet foolish efforts to impose her religious conceptions on the young Muslim, or at least display them to him, bring to mind Pastor Dowe's futile antics in "Pastor Dowe at Tacaté." The Swiss woman spends hours constructing the figures needed for the Nativity scene, using whatever materials are at hand: "She wanted only to suggest to him that the god with whom he was on such intimate terms was the god worshipped by the Nazarenes" (*CS*, 347). When Christmas Eve finally arrives, it is a dark, windy night, perhaps portentous of her project's doom. The weather is but the first indication that events will unfold in a manner wholly unlike the scenario she played out beforehand in her imagination.

Although Slimane arrives in time to dine with Fräulein Windling, the hotel porter turns him away. She eats dinner alone, unaware of what has become of the boy. Later in the evening, to the Swiss woman's relief, Slimane turns up in time for her production of the Christmas pageant. She brings out chocolates and begins to tell the Christmas story, inserting the name of Slimane's native village in the place of Bethlehem and having the shepherds and wise men come there to pay homage to the newborn child. Try as she might, however, Fräulein Windling is unable sufficiently to distinguish for Slimane the Christian savior from the

Muslim prophet. After revealing the crèche to him, she slips away to find flashbulbs for her camera, in order to take a picture of him before the crèche, in the new white turban she has given him.

On her return, she finds one of the camels decapitated and the baby Jesus missing. She is unable to avoid the realization that her scheme has been a farce built on mistaken assumptions:

> Across the seasons of their friendship she had come to think of him as being very nearly like herself, even though she knew he had not been that way when she first had met him. Now she saw the dangerous vanity at the core of that fantasy: she had assumed that somehow his association with her had automatically been for his ultimate good, that inevitably he had been undergoing a process of improvement as a result of knowing her. In her desire to see him change, she had begun to forget what Slimane was really like. "I shall never understand him," she thought helplessly, sure that just because she felt so close to him she would never be able to observe him dispassionately. (*CS*, 354)

The story's title, as John Ditsky has pointed out, suggests temporal limitations to the duration of friendship.[51] The Christmas scene is the logical outcome of dynamics established even before the beginning of the story, in the history of relations between two radically different, often opposing cultures. The very nature of the cultural differences between Fräulein Windling and Slimane determined the great odds against a long-lasting friendship. Throughout the story external events exert more and more pressure on the oasis, constricting motion and making it more and more untenable to maintain romantic illusions. The course of events drives a wedge between the Swiss woman and her young Arab friend. On Christmas Day, the morning after the reenactment of the Nativity story, she receives an order from the French commandant to leave. It but hastens the end of an already strained relationship.

As in many Bowles stories, political, cultural, and social realities brutally collide with the course of individual desires. The erosion of ground beneath this particular relationship commences at the story's outset—in fact, with the opening lines: "The trouble had been growing bigger each year, ever since the end of the war. From the beginning, although aware of its existence, Fräulein Windling had determined to pay it no attention" (*CS*, 337). The trouble referred to here is the growing indigenous resistance to French occupation and the imminent threat of large-scale violence. Yet we are also urged to entertain the notion that the circumference of that region of "trouble" could be expanded to include (a) Fräulein Windling's own personal trouble in reconciling her romantic dreams with a reality inhospitable to their enactment and (b) the whole drama involving West and East that, as contemporary world events continually remind us, refuses to go away even as we try to deny its existence. The story's capacity to speak to these large issues, as well as to individual fates, makes its resonances especially powerful.

The brilliantly executed end of "The Time of Friendship," from the point where Fräulein Windling learns she must leave to the last lines, is thickly layered with meaning. Departures and endings, especially ones thrust on us from the outside, are apt to come quickly, leaving us little time to take care of our affairs and get our houses in order. Once Fräulein Windling learns she must leave, she is beset by a host of complex responses. She is deeply sad and already nostalgic because she realizes her departure not only marks the end of her personal pursuit of a cherished romantic ideal but corresponds with the end of an historical phase.

Traditional life-styles will be disrupted, and following the struggle for freedom, people will still have to live with the ugly remnants of colonialism.[52] Like many Orientalists, Fräulein Windling's impulse is to guard and hang on to her imaginative construction of the values of the dying order.[53] At the same time, she realizes that the forces of history are against her, that the demand for change and modernization will, in fact, come from *within* the traditional culture she values. She is in the awkward position of wishing for others a way of life that they themselves are inclined to be rid of.

What, then, will she take with her of the experience she has had in the oasis? In Bowles's story the nature of this problem seems to be symbolized by a sliver the Swiss woman gets the morning of the departure. As she leaves the oasis, she takes with her, figuratively as well as literally, a sliver of experience, one that festers beneath her skin, an uncomfortable, irritating reminder of a past quickly becoming more and more inaccessible.

One of the uncomfortable ironies in the story is that while for Fräulein Windling the oasis of Timimoun is a refuge, for the natives it is a site of struggle—against French colonization, for preservation of cultural values (threatened by Windling's very presence), and for basic necessities of life. Though the war is, at the story's outset, still "far away" in the North, it has directly affected the lives of those in the oasis. Men have disappeared, apparently having been sent to French prisons. Men have gone off to fight. Slimane, even on her third and final visit, still seems not to have been affected by the forces that threaten his innocence, though his departure from his native village in the end signifies the end of innocence. It is almost as if his innocence depends on a vague, inchoate sense of time itself; the highly conceptualized and regimented version of time the Swiss woman brings with her puts extraordinary pressure on the very organic order she prizes.

As in so many of Bowles's works, the Westerner is free in the end to leave, but locals must stay and face the sometimes unpleasant facts of political and social realities. The discrepancy is seen first in an exchange between Fräulein Windling and Boufelja, the old porter/caretaker at the hotel. Once she knows she must leave, she finds herself wondering what will happen to Boufelja when the hotel shuts down, there being no more tourists like herself to patronize the place:

> "*Mon cher* Boufelja, we shall see one another very soon."
> "Ah, yes," he cried, trying to smile. "Very soon, mademoiselle."
> (*CS*, 357)

Even though both know the truth—that there can indeed be no return to the past order of things—neither openly admits it.

Windling's parting from Slimane is no less problematic. The inequality between the two characters' status is dramatized in many ways at the end of the story. Slimane arrives at the hotel with his donkey and assists Fräulein Windling with her luggage; the French have sent a jeep around for her. Wishing to postpone the final separation as long as possible, she consents to Slimane's plea to go with her as far as Colomb-Bechar, though she admits that complying with his request is "absurd" and "irresponsible." Nonetheless, she gives in, rationalizing her action by thinking to herself that "she wanted to give this ending to their story." When they are picked up by the truck leaving the village, she rides in the cab, while Slimane is in the back "with a dozen men and a sheep." She is "writing" an ending to suit *her* desires, not Slimane's best interests. She feels a twinge of guilt, realizing she is responsible for taking him away from parents, uprooting him from his culture, leaving him trapped in a space between two cultures, neither any longer wholly within reach.

No longer will he be satisfied with his life in the oasis; nor does he have the wherewithal to go all the way to Switzerland. By the end of the story, Fräulein Windling knows Slimane has used this opportunity to escape the confinement of the oasis. He has clearly decided to stay in Colomb-

Bechar. She gives him money (more foreign aid). At their final parting she sobs over him, treating him like a child, *"Oh, mon pauvre petit!!"* (*CS*, 360). As the train pulls away from the Colomb-Bechar station, she thinks to herself of Slimane's fate, absolving a gnawing sense of guilt: " 'He's too young to be a soldier,' she told herself. 'They won't take him.' But she knew they would" (*CS*, 361).

If "A Time of Friendship" can be thought of as an anatomy of friendship between Westerner and Arab, it can also be thought of as an elegy for a past world, pastoral and whole. *Sic transit, gloria mundi*: this too must pass.

"The Hours After Noon"

A number of the stories in *The Time of Friendship*, including the second and longest, "The Hours After Noon," actually date from the late 1940s and early 1950s. The corrected typescript of "The Hours After Noon" reads "Fez, May 14, 1949" (HRC), while the version in the *Collected Stories* reads "Paris-Tangier, 1950." In conversations with Lawrence Stewart, Bowles says that he actually began working on the draft *in* Tangier, where the story was set, an unusual practice for the writer, especially at this point in his career:

> I was staying in Tangier, in the Pension Callender, in that very place, and eating meals and seeing this woman, and eating every day in that dining room that I describe there, that's cold and windy and the chairs make an awful scraping noise on the tile floor. It's really journalism—in other words, it's not filtered through memory. The place I wrote about when I was actually in it, which I very seldom do. . . . It's about Tangier. I do say International Zone, and the people coming in from Gibraltar, so it's definitely Tangier, and I was thinking of it always as Tangier. (Stewart 1974, 80)

Insofar as the story focuses on Tangier, it invites comparisons to Bowles's novel *Let It Come Down*, written shortly afterward. Psychological dynamics in the story—particularly the sexual vulnerability of women—resemble those in *The Sheltering Sky*. Perhaps, though, the story has more affinities with "The Echo." Both begin with the return of a daughter to a foreign land, and both feature inept mothers whose preoccupations with their own problematic passions contribute to a failure of communication and, ultimately, to rather tragic outcomes.

"The Hours After Noon," nearly long enough to be termed a novella, is neatly divided into eight numbered sections and is preceded by an epigraph from Baudelaire that figures importantly in the conception and action of the story: "If one could awaken all the echoes of one's memory simultaneously, they would make a music, delightful or sad as the case might be, but logical and without dissonances. No matter how incoherent the existence, the human unity is not affected" (*CS*, 217). The story itself begins in medias res, in the middle of a pitched argument: "Oh, you're a *man*! What does a man know about such things?" (*CS*, 217). It takes the reader a moment or two to situate the action. We are in the dining room of the Pension Callender, which caters to Western expatriates—writers, archaeologists, businessmen, and curious travelers. Mrs. Callender is staging an argument with her husband, in front of her guests, over the advisability of allowing a certain M. Royer (read: roué) to stay in the pension, thus exposing their daughter to the dangers of his legendary moral depravity. "He's a filthy, horrible man, and he's going to be sitting opposite your own daughter at every meal," Mrs. Callender exclaims (*CS*, 218).

With this argument, the story's central theme is established. The problem—how to introduce innocence to experience without tremendous and irreparable damage—is precisely that of Prospero in *The Tempest*. Mrs. Callender's approach toward her daughter's upbringing is to limit "opportunities for learning." In recalling her own parents' lenience and her unfortunate early experiences with men, Mrs. Callender asserts, "There were many things a girl should not know until she was married, and they were the very things it seemed every man was determined to impart to her" (*CS*, 220). Mrs. Callender's staunch attitudes on the issue, stricter than those of her American husband, are determined in part by her English background. The strategy Mrs. Callender adopts is not nearly as successful as Prospero's. In the face of such an overbearing, jittery mother, Charlotte determines to find out for herself. Her mother's fears themselves drive the rebellious daughter toward M. Royer.

The story's title is derived from Mrs. Callender's habitual experience in dealing with the time between noon and evening. "It was the hours after noon," Bowles writes, "that she had to beware of, when the day had begun to go towards the night, and she no longer trusted herself to be absolutely certain of what she would do next, or of what unlikely idea would come into her head" (*CS*, 222). The "hours after noon" might just as well be thought of as a period of time on one's biological clock; Mrs. Callender, a middle-aged woman whose dawn has faded, is on some level dealing with the afternoon of her own life. She is obviously not happy. In part, her condition, a kind of paranoia, is a consequence of her life as a foreigner among Moroccans, whom she calls "brutes" at one point. (Her strategy for living among them is to have just enough to do with them as is necessary to conduct daily business.) Mrs. Callender, whose judgments are consistently misshapen, is doubtless one of the more despicable of Bowles's characters.

The second and third sections of the story feature the arrivals of M. Royer and Charlotte. M. Royer is happy to be in Morocco: "The months in Spain had been not at all relaxing; he was fed up with the coy promises of eyes seen above fans, furious with mantillas, crucifixes and titters. Here in Morocco, if love lacked finesse, at least it was frank" (*CS*, 222). He tries to give articulation to the feeling he has at being back in Morocco, finding in his memory a fragment from a book he has read (as it turns out, Gide's *Amyntas*): "*Le temps que coule ici n'a plus d'heures, mais—.*" His revery, his excitement with an idealized Morocco, is jolted by the approach of a young beggar whom Royer violently slaps and pushes away.

Like Aileen at the beginning of "The Echo," Charlotte is thinking about her mother as she lands at the small Tangier airport. Apprehensive at the prospect of once again being under her mother's constant surveillance, she tells herself "that this consistent watching was a common misapplication of maternal love, but that did not make it any easier to bear" (*CS*, 224).

On her arrival at the pension, in section 4, Charlotte has an opportunity to take in both M. Royer, whom she had already met on her ride back to the pension, and Van Siclen, a young bearded American archaeologist. To her mother's dismay, Charlotte finds the suave Frenchman much more attractive than the crude American. When Mrs. Callender calls M. Royer "an insufferable fool," Charlotte counters, "I think he's rather sweet" (*CS*, 228).

Mrs. Callender is, of course, unconsciously bringing on the fate she fears. Though she has omens of something horrible happening, she never takes steps that might avert tragedy. She fears M. Royer's perceived sexual appetites as a threat to her innocent daughter; though she has the chance to stop his visit, she doesn't, thinking instead of the money he would bring in and the silk scarf she would like to have. When the Frenchman leaves temporarily, she puts him on demipension, so as to continue the cash flow.

Ironically, it is the young bearded American archaeologist, whom Mrs. Callender has trusted and flirted with, who poses the greater threat to her daughter. The night of her arrival, Charlotte goes out for a walk. Van Siclen intercepts her and forces her into his jeep for a joyride. He gets his thrills by stepping on the gas and making his hostage in the seat beside him shriek with fear. When they get to the lighthouse, out past Bou Amar, Van Siclen, an unchecked Caliban, coerces a kiss, managing to bite Charlotte's lip in the process.

Had Mrs. Callender been truly vigilant and attentive, she might have judged Van Siclen a potential threat. In the first conversation we see between the two—after the argument about M. Royer—Van Siclen offers his view that "a girl's education has to start somewhere, some time" (*CS*, 220). In the same conversation Mrs. Callender remarks that if the man were younger, she wouldn't be so concerned. It's to be expected, she asserts, that a young man sow his wild oats. But, she goes on suggestively, "A young man is more likely to be interested in older women, don't you think?" (*CS*, 221).

The morning after the jeep ride, Charlotte goes down to the beach, where she meets M. Royer and engages him in conversation. She finds the refined, polite Frenchman a relief after her frightening encounter with Van Siclen. The meeting is observed by Mrs. Callender, who, once she has her daughter alone, launches into a wrathful diatribe. She construes the question of obedience in terms of the daughter's conforming to her mother's wishes (for which Charlotte sees no rational justification) or causing her mother's unhappiness: "Darling, please don't ruin my pleasure in your stay by being stubborn and belligerent about this" (*CS*, 234).

When Charlotte deliberately and openly defies her mother's interdiction, as much because she resents her mother's forceful grip as because of any deep infatuation with M. Royer, Mrs. Callender, who is suffering from "the aching nostalgia of her own youth," goes into a tizzy and tries to devise a way to get rid of M. Royer (*CS*, 236). She finally convinces Van Siclen to invite M. Royer to his archaeological site at El Menar, hinting that Royer will certainly accept if Van Siclen plays on Royer's known proclivities. Meantime she stews and brews a migraine, blaming her misery on the lecherous M. Royer and her daughter, who has been "intolerable since the moment she arrived. Inconsiderate and perverse" (*CS*, 238).

The story's ending is tragic. The eighth and final section of the story begins with Mrs. Callender heading off to El Menar in their station wagon, driven by Pedro, the chauffeur. Charlotte has been out late and not returned or called. At first Mrs. Callender suspects M. Royer. Pedro, however, tells her he saw Charlotte that morning with Van Siclen in his jeep. When she and Pedro reach the archaeologist's tent, far off the beaten path, she quizzes him as to her daughter's whereabouts. "It'd be more to the point to ask where Monsieur Royer is," Van Siclen responds (*CS*, 240–41). Though in their brief search in the dark that night they do not find M. Royer, in their own minds they both draw the same conclusion of his fate, the accuracy of which the narrative confirms in the story's last few paragraphs. Mrs. Callender and Van Siclen are returning to town in the jeep and station wagon:

> From the spot where he lay, he could have heard the two motors grow fainter and be drowned by the vaster sound of the sea; he could have seen the two little red tail-lights moving away across the empty countryside. Could have, if all that had not been decided for him twenty-one hours earlier. In the bright moonlight he had sat with the child on his knee (for she was really no more than a child) letting her examine his watch. For some reason—probably the sight of this innocent animal holding the thin gold toy in her tattooed hands—he was put in mind of the phrase he had not been able to recall the evening of his arrival. He began to murmur it to himself, even at the moment her expression changed to one of terror as, looking up over his shoulder, she saw what was about to happen. (*CS*, 242)

As is the case with good tragedy, it is difficult to pinpoint blame. Clearly, Mrs. Callender feels her share, for she had been the one to suggest that Van Siclen take M. Royer to El Menar. She, however, tries to displace the blame onto the archaeologist, saying he had put the idea into her head. Indeed, very early in the story, when Mrs. Callender shared with him her anxieties about M. Royer, he interjected, "Send him out to El Menar. . . . If he chases the girls around out there they'll find him in a couple of days behind a rock with a coil of wire around his neck" (*CS*, 221). Van Siclen obviously understood Moroccan values better than Royer, who had shared his views with Charlotte on the beach when she asked whether he thought it right for a man to kiss a woman against her will. Yes, that would be wrong, he says. Yet he goes on to say that it is a completely different case with the native Moroccans, who have no will. This hideously distorted position justifies his own moral depravity. He had not accurately assessed the risks involved, his position as a Christian and outsider, and the value traditional Moroccans place on a woman's purity.

As Lawrence Stewart suggests, the story is one that "forces the reader to focus upon the psychological mystery where the explanation of events is in the remembrance of rhetoric—in particular the remembrance of two sentences, sentences which are indeed the leveling upon life of judgment and punishment" (Stewart 1974, 80). At the end of the story, at the moment presumably just before his death, M. Royer comes close to completing what his memory had failed to reconstruct earlier: "*Le temps qui coule ici n'a plus d'heures, mais, tant l'inoccupation de chacun est parfaite—.*"[54] The reader should at this point recall the Baudelaire epigraph, which speculates on the effect of bringing together, at one moment in time, all of one's memories in one bundle. The effect, writes Baudelaire, "would make a music, delightful or sad as the case may be." Both Mrs. Callender and M. Royer, the characters we get the most of in the story, suffer existential torment. Each wrestles with memory in an attempt to gain consciousness and wholeness. M. Royer, at least, seems to have been on the verge of a resurrection of the unconscious. It comes too late, however. We have the feeling that, had he had more consciousness, Royer might have been able to avert his fate.

Three Fables

The Time of Friendship contains three fablelike short stories, all of which address issues involving deception, justice, and Islam. The first among them, "The Successor," which Bowles completed in Sri Lanka in 1950, is about two brothers, the younger of whom suffers the "crushing injustice" of the traditional Moroccan practice of inheritance that has made the older brother the owner of the family café (*CS*, 243). The younger brother, Ali, looks on in silent disapproval as his brother throws his money away on gifts for women he is trying to seduce and on wine for his friends. The plot of the story can be easily summarized. When during a rainstorm a Belgian tourist seeks refuge in the café, the older brother seizes the occasion as an opportunity to get a handful of sleeping pills from the foreigner in order to gain the compliance of an uncompromising young lady. Ali, who has secretly witnessed the transaction, does not seem in the least surprised when the next day his brother, highly perturbed and anxious, returns from an outing. In the story's last scene, the police come and take the older brother away, apparently charging him with murder. The reader, who has been given the story over the younger brother's shoulder, feels justice has been done when in the end Ali is left alone with the café.

"The Hyena" is a short fable that basically follows the patterns of deception laid out in the story of the gingerbread man or, for that matter, "Little Red Riding Hood." In Bowles's story, set in North Africa, an unsuspecting stork falls prey to a wise, wily hyena. Though the stork has never seen a hyena before meeting one at the edge of a pool of water, he is nonetheless wary because "he had been told that if the hyena can put a little of his urine on someone, that one will have to walk after the hyena to whatever place the hyena wants him to go" (*CS*, 291). The hyena tries to put the stork at ease, saying that he too is a creature of Allah. When the stork, who has tarried too long talking with the hyena, takes off in the dark and breaks his wing, he has little choice but to accompany the hyena back to his cave. Just when the stork seems persuaded that "there is no power beyond the power of Allah," the hyena tears open the bird's neck.

Johannes Bertens, in his study of Bowles's fiction, has emphasized this story not so much because it is a good one but because in his view it encapsules the elements of Bowles's fictional world. In Bertens's view, "the story presents a confrontation between a rather complacent but morally concerned unworldliness and its opposite, amoral worldliness. Not surprisingly, the hyena wins, not only because he is smarter, but also because of his inner strength. . . . 'The Hyena' offers a bleak picture of an amoral world . . . where innocence cannot survive. Bowles expressly withholds judgment, and aloofly records what he considers the state of affairs in the world around him. This is the environment in which Bowles' characters are forced to live" (Bertens, 201).

Though Bertens places disproportionate emphasis on this story, his observations are sound. "The Hyena" is a tale of the age-old encounter between innocence and evil, and as such the story plays out, in the form of a fable, the same kind of drama we find in much better stories, such as "The Delicate Prey," "A Distant Episode," or even, if one stretches things, "The Frozen Fields." Moreover, "The Hyena" carries in it an implicit critique of the everyday application of Islam, for all through the story the status of the faith as a moral system is in question. The hyena, who uses religious arguments to dupe the stork, says at one point that he "is not in the world to tell anyone what is right or wrong" (*CS*, 292). And at the end of the story the hyena, on his return to consume his rotting prey 10 days after the kill, thanks Allah "for a nose that could smell carrion on the wind."

While the tale wears the traditional garb of a fable, the moral is not easy to untangle. It might even be thought of as an antifable. While traditional fables tend in the end to celebrate, in epigrammatical form, the need for adherence to established moral values such as those sanctioned by religious beliefs and institutions, "The Hyena" seems to suggest that religion itself, or at least its corrupt manifestations, is a hoax and that we are naive if we do not realize the Manichaean principles by which the real world operates. Were it extended, the critical perspective on morality implied here might resemble the one developed by Nietzsche in *The Genealogy of Morals*.

Though only three pages long, "The Garden" contains a powerful message that again seems to challenge the moral legitimacy of established religion, in this case Islam. The central character in the story is a man, never named, who spends all his time cultivating a garden of pomegranates and barley at the edge of an oasis in southern Morocco. He is so happy when he returns home from the garden that his wife thinks he is hiding some kind of treasure in the garden. She proceeds to poison him gradually, hoping to wring his secret from him. She overdoes it and flees in fright. The man nearly dies, recuperates, and goes back to his garden, the rest of the townspeople now suspecting him of having done something to his wife. One day the imam visits him in the garden:

> The sun was sinking in the west, and the water on the ground began to be red. Presently the man said to the imam: "The garden is beautiful."
>
> "Beautiful or not beautiful," said the imam, "you should be giving thanks to Allah for allowing you to have it."
>
> "Allah?" said the man. "Who is that? I never heard of him. I made this garden myself. I dug every channel and planted every tree, and no one helped me. I have no debts to anyone."
>
> The imam had turned pale. He flung out his arm and struck the man very hard in the face. Then he went quickly out of the garden. (*CS*, 365)

Not long after this the townspeople come after the man with the garden, judging him to be a heretic and a threat to the community, beating him with hoes and sickles, and leaving him to die in his own garden: "Little by little the trees died, and very soon the garden was gone. Only the desert was there" (*CS*, 365).

This fable is every bit as powerful as "The Hyena." An interpretation of the story might begin with the observation that the central struggle in the tale is between individual creativity and work, on the one hand, and the stubborn, intransigent orthodoxy imposed by Islam, on the other. When push comes to shove, the heretic, no matter his productive capacities or the inherent worth of his personal values, will always be beaten by the crowd. The story points to a fundamental tension between art and religion in Islamic cultures, and the end, showing the encroachment of the desert on the garden once the heretic has been stoned, can be read as a metaphor for cultural sterility and stagnation in a world that continually seeks to defeat art.

Two Latin American Tales

The first of the two Latin American stories in *The Time of Friendship*, "Doña Faustina," dates from 1949 and was written in Tangier. Again the idea of the story was suggested by real events, transformed and extended in the writing. The story takes the form of a mystery, and as is the case with most successful mysteries, the writer withholds and releases information in measured doses he deems necessary to sustain interest and build suspense. In a manner that has become the hallmark of Patricia Highsmith, Bowles generates a modicum of sympathy for the perpetrators of heinous crimes, making a macabre comedy of the story. With a little imagination one can feel the devious chuckle of the writer, delighted by the perversity of his tale.

The nature of the unresolved mystery is stated in the beginning of the first of the six numbered sections of the story: "No one could understand why Doña Faustina had bought the inn" (*CS*, 205). A series of popular explanations are given for her purchase of the forsaken, deteriorating inn, only to be shot down, one by one. There has been no substantiation of the notion that the place is a whorehouse. The theory that a fugitive bandit has taken refuge there is given up when the man is caught. The drug ring theory is disproved. "There were darker hints to the effect that Carlota [Doña Faustina's sister] might be luring lone voyagers to the inn, where they met the fate that traditionally befalls such solitary visitors to lonely inns" (*CS*, 206), but not much credence was put in this idea. Enjoying more wide circulation was the belief that Doña Faustina was simply a bit *loca*. Still others insisted that the two sisters were sitting on a cache of riches lying hidden somewhere on the property.

All these are but theories when the police are finally prompted to investigate the inn on the disappearance of a child from a nearby village. They are given anything but a warm reception and find the place an absolute shambles. People go on thinking the women are crazy when they start making trips to far-off villages, bringing back "numerous bundles and baskets" (*CS*, 207).

Still, we suspect something fishy is going on at the old inn. It is only a matter of time before José, the sisters' docile servant, discovers a tank deep in the overgrowth surrounding the inn, and hears a heavy splash, the source of which he is never able to identify. One day he meets Doña Faustina on her way toward the tank, carrying a basket. When José asks if he could carry it, the woman reacts strongly, clutches the basket zealously, and firmly orders the servant back to the kitchen. He then shares his experience with Elena, the other old servant, withholding his knowledge of the tank.

One cold drizzly evening there is a knock at the door of the inn, and the women scurry about. Doña Faustina turns her attention to the laundry area, where she gathers "the refuse that strewed the floor and the washtubs" and takes it outside in baskets. It was not the police, as they had feared. After Doña Faustina has told her sister to lock herself in her room, she returns to her own room, where she finds herself face to face with an unsavory intruder. When he doesn't find what he wants in the room, he settles for sex, a little to the woman's surprise, given her age. When he asks her to hand over money, she insists she has none, and offers "something more precious." She proffers him "a small parcel done up in newspaper" (*CS*, 210).

When he looks inside at its contents, he asks, "What is this?" "*Ya sabes, hombre*," she says calmly. "*Cómelo*" (*CS*, 211). The man accuses her of witchcraft but finally gives in to her exhortations and eats the contents, as she tells him it will give him the power of two: he "lifted the thing to his mouth and bit into it as if it had been a plum" (*CS*, 211).

Before long, Doña Faustina announces to her sister that she is pregnant. Far from being dismayed, Doña Faustina rejoices because the child will "have the power of thirty seven" (*CS*, 213). Very economically, in a tone almost comic, Bowles describes the birth of the child, a boy, whose name, Jesus Maria, perversely fuses the Virgin and the Christ Child. When no one reveals the identity of the father, José suggests that the boy is a child of the Devil. José meantime identifies the source of the splash he has heard in the tank when he sees the large crocodile for himself, and rushes off to tell Doña Faustina, for whom we suspect the news is no surprise.

The two women escape just in time. The police find not one but two crocodiles, which, along with the discovery of heaps of blood-stained clothing from the missing infants, allows them to piece together the nature of the mysterious goings-on at the inn, more hideous than any had ever suspected: Doña Faustina had cut up her tiny prey in the laundry area, extracted and eaten their hearts, and fed the remains to the crocodiles. Though we have almost no access to Doña Faustina's thoughts, we might assume her mental logic would turn with that uncanny, seductive regularity we associate with Poe's deranged narrators.

The story ends with an account of what becomes of Jesus Maria. Fifteen years after the two women have fled the inn, the young man is taken on as a servant in the home of the chief of police in the country's capital. Subsequently, he joins the Mexican army and quickly moves up the ranks to become a colonel by the age of 25. In that capacity the greatest power he exercises (the power of 37, remember) is releasing a notorious bandit and 36 of his men, who are put under his authority. Though Jesus Maria's deed cannot be proved, he loses his rank.

As John Ditsky has pointed out, the story beautifully and irreverently interweaves Christian, Aztec, and literary mythology (Ditsky, 383). The mother, ritualistically devouring the hearts of her victims like Aztec warriors ate their enemy's hearts, makes a pact with the Devil. From this union is unimmaculately conceived Jesus Maria, the savior of criminals and outcasts.

In the fall of 1957, Jane Bowles's health worsened, and so she and Paul left Tangier for London, where she could receive better medical diagnosis and care. In London Paul fell ill himself. In his autobiography he describes his feverish condition and the accompanying birth of another Latin American story:

> That autumn, in the course of a London epidemic, I caught Asian flu. During the nine days I spent in bed, I ran a high fever which prompted me to write a story about the effects of an imaginary South American drink, the *cumbiamba*. It was called "Tapiama" and was something of an experiment for me, being the only fever-directed piece I had written. On the tenth day, when the story was finished and typed in duplicate, my thermometer showed ninety-eight and six-tenths. I got up, dressed, and went to Harrod's. A few hours later I was delirious. (*WS*, 338)

The resulting story, which returns to the familiar Bowlesian themes of drugs and the vulnerable foreigner traveling in a strange and exotic locale, bears the traces of the delirium that was its midwife. The interest in "Tapiama" lies less in its central conceit, which is by now well worn, than in the psychological insight the story provides into the questing instinct that seems to have motivated Bowles for much of his life.

The story's protagonist is a nameless photographer who remains a distinctly flat, hazily developed character. Rather like the traveling writer, the photographer apparently hopes to capture alluring images of the places he visits in order to show and sell them back home. We first see the man in a hotel room of some unnamed third-world country. Plagued by heat, insects, bad food, and a delirious half-sleep, he decides to get out of the hotel. This move out of the hotel might be taken as yet another figure for expatriation. The hotel room, like the homeland, offers shelter, yet the price one pays for staying inside those boundaries is constant irritation and discomfort. Though he seems to have almost no idea where he will go or what the consequences will be when he first sets out, the photographer has reached the conclusion that life where he is is intolerable and that he simply must get out.

The narrator describes the sense of freedom the protagonist experiences on his midnight walk: "There was a difference between this walk and innumerable other midnight jaunts he had made, and he was inclined to wonder what made it so pleasant. Perhaps he was enjoying it simply because the fabric here was of pure freedom. He was not looking for anything; all the cameras were back in the hotel room" (*CS*, 279). Just beyond this point the photographer continues thinking about freedom: "The question of freedom was governed by the law of diminishing returns, he said to himself, walking faster. If you went beyond a certain point of intensity in your consciousness of desiring it, you furnished yourself with a guarantee of not achieving it. In any case, he thought, what is freedom in the last analysis, other than the state of being totally, instead of only partially, subject to the tyranny of chance?" (*CS*, 279).

These remarks on the logic of freedom are ones we would expect to hear from the author. What is proposed here is a life on the edge, far from the banal conventions of society yet just short of that dangerous point of annihilation—in other words, the kind of life Bowles has enjoyed for so long in Morocco. Just prior to this scene, the photographer stops short of taking off his clothes and walking naked, telling himself he would then have the bother of carrying his clothes along with him. (Of course, he might have just left them there!) In any case, being "subject to the tyranny of chance" is quite different from willfully hurling oneself into the elements. The notion of freedom expressed here is one requiring a minimal exertion of will; the object goes with the flow, watches for the signs, and follows them.

Twelve minutes into his walk, the photographer comes to a critical juncture. He had arbitrarily imposed on himself a 15-minute limit. But why? He questions the very basis of his own self-imposed boundaries and decides to go on. Since we are in a Bowles story, we cannot expect that the photographer's walk will be uneventful. We might even wonder, with stories such as "A Distant Episode" behind us, whether he will even live through the story.

From one point to the next, the photographer moves on. His first destination is a bonfire burning close by, aboard "a gently swaying craft." A naked man, apparently in command of the boat, asks the photographer, "*Tapiama? Vas a Tapiama?*" The photographer, never having heard of Tapiama, stutters a bit and finally says, "*Sí*" (*CS*, 280). When he gets aboard the craft and finds two other passengers there, the photographer notes the absurdity of the whole situation: "He told himself, 'Things don't happen this way,' but since beyond a doubt they were doing so, any questioning of the process could lead only in the direction of paranoia" (*CS*, 280). The photographer, then, rather than asserting his own will, gives himself over to the journey.

Before long, after the boatman has indicated that the people in this area are none too fond of Americans ("I'm Danish," the photographer quickly asserts), they find themselves at a rustic cantina, a setting evocative of Conrad, Graham Greene, or Paul Theroux: "In another minute they were there: all in the dimness an open space, a dozen or so palm-leaf huts at one end of it, at the other a platform which must be a loading dock, the empty night and openness of water behind it; and half-way between the dock and the cluster of dwellings, the *cantina*, itself only a very large hut without a front wall" (*CS*, 281).

Once inside the cantina, the only company the photographer finds are two men drinking at the bar. As the outsider, he wonders how to handle the scene. "When in doubt, speak," he determines, only to admit that the opposite strategy—"When in doubt, keep quiet"—would be just as reasonable. Before long, the photographer orders his first of several *cumbiamba*, "the coastal region's favorite drink, a herbal concoction famous for its treacherous effects" (*CS*, 282). The photographer's grip on reality subsequently slips away. The bar begins to fill up with scantily clad black natives; a mulatto woman approaches him and tries to undo his fly; he is besieged by a swarm of tiny ants.

The photographer is all at once exhilarated and apprehensive. The excitement stems in part from the transfiguring effects of the drug, which opens him to wholly new sensations: "It was not that he felt drunk as that he had become someone who was not he, someone for whom the act of living was a thing so different from what he imagined it could be, that he was left stranded in a region of sensation far from any he had hereto known" (*CS*, 284). After an unsettling conversation with a soldier who wonders what attracts the stranger to this godforsaken place, and after his fourth *cumbiamba*, the American's apprehension of imminent danger grows. He thinks to himself at one point, "This is not going to work out right, at all. It's just not going to work out" (*CS*, 285). Another white man at the bar, evidently more acquainted with the surroundings, warns him of the danger in no uncertain terms. The charged atmosphere intensifies. The mulatto vomits outside, dogs bark, a fight is in the air, and knives are pulled out. All the photographer has to do is hang on: "The important thing was to remember that he was alone here and that this was a real place with real people in it. He could feel how dangerously easy it would be to go along with the messages given him by his senses, and dismiss the whole thing as a nightmare in the secret belief that when the breaking-point came he could somehow manage to escape by waking himself up" (*CS*, 286). The scene in the cantina becomes more and more surreal, bizarre, riotous, and violent, distorted in the consciousness of the hallucinating photographer.

Seemingly without thinking of his actions, the photographer makes his way out of the cantina's bacchanal and back to the punt. This traveler is more fortunate than many of Bowles's other Western pilgrims who are left, feverish and demented, to die in hostile climes. Though we are not certain of the photographer's fate at the end of the story, there is some chance that he will find his way back to civilization after his nightmarish ordeal. He pushes the punt into the water, climbs aboard, and floats *à la deriva*, watching the tropical dawn, his revery interrupted about midday when "five young men, all of whom looked remarkably alike, surrounded him" (*CS*, 289). He asks them to take him to Rio Martillo. By the end of the story, they are within earshot of the whistle of the Compañia Azucarera Riomartillense, the photographer's fate still uncertain.

American Tales

In an interview with Lawrence Stewart in 1963, Bowles said he had thought of doing a whole series "of stories based on memories of childhood": "I had several incidents that I thought would make nice stories, and then I thought No, one must not write about—it's a self-indulgence to write about—one's own life and one's own childhood. I thought it was bad, and so I stopped it. One should reach out beyond. It's the sort of thing that nine out of ten American writers do, you know. So I didn't want to get into that."[55] These comments reveal much about Bowles's attitudes toward homeland and art and even suggest how the yen for traveling and aesthetic principles have been united in his life. Felt here is the need to do something fresh and different from the mainstream American tradition. One way to effect that is to move away from that native experience and expose oneself to a wholly new cultural scene.

The few stories with American settings in *The Time of Friendship* are striking and interesting anomalies, just as they were in *The Delicate Prey*. Bowles's literary output suggests not only an absorption with the foreign but an attempt to bury, transcend, or elide his Long Island origins. Thus, those occasions when he has gone back to his early past for fictional material, as rare as they may be, are especially significant. These stories give us an idea of what kind of writer Bowles might have been had he been limited solely to American material. The most important American story in *The Time of Friendship* is "The Frozen Fields." A second story, "If I Should Open My Mouth," set in New York City, has no apparent autobiographical echo. Nor does "Sylvie Ann, the Boogie Man," another American story from this period that was not included in the volume.

"The Frozen Fields" supplies some explanations for Bowles's subsequent expatriation, explanations that lie in deeply rooted psychological responses to his father and to the cultural restraints on the expression of passion and the practice of art. In its sublime use of weather and its depiction of a debilitating New England morality, as well as in its aesthetic balance, "The Frozen Fields" calls to mind *Ethan Frome*, that masterpiece by an earlier American expatriate for whom Bowles has expressed admiration.[56] The beauty of the story lies partly in the way elements are held in balance. There seems little room for warmth or comfort between the biting cold outside and the strict puritan atmosphere inside.

Comparisons with Joyce's *Dubliners* or even his portrayal of Stephen Dedalus in *A Portrait of the Artist as a Young Man* also come to mind, for the two writers, at least in this instance, have very similar aesthetic and thematic concerns. The way in which the adults in "The Frozen Fields" try to shield Donald, the story's six-year-old protagonist, from the more embarrassing aspects of their own world has a Joycean air, as does the story's tight epiphanic quality. The argument at Christmas dinner between Aunt Emilie and Donald's father, over the father's treatment of the boy, calls to mind Dante's pitched quarrel with Simon Dedalus and

Mr. Casey over the right of Catholic priests to meddle in politics in *A Portrait of the Artist*.

Bowles has always preferred to write in an environment that "is not a continuation of anything" (Stewart 1982, 67). "The Frozen Fields," like many of Bowles's works, began to take shape in the author's imagination while he was traveling on board ship. "Being in motion always excites me apparently," Bowles has said, "and I begin scribbling. . . . A train or a ship gets me started. . . . Usually I'm in the bed, lying out flat, with pillows behind me" (Stewart 1982, 67). Late in 1956 Bowles and his companion, Ahmed Yacoubi, a young Moroccan painter, were once again en route to Ceylon, this time to see about selling Bowles's island, Taprobane, off Weligama, which Bowles bought in 1952. Bowles had been going frequently to Ceylon since 1949 and had written parts of *Let It Come Down*, completed *The Spider's House*, and produced numerous stories and journalistic pieces there. On the 1956–57 trip Bowles had no literary project in mind. He was going to visit the wildlife preserve at Yala, in southeastern Ceylon, to photograph the animals. After that he would go to Kenya to compare the animal preserves there with those he had just seen. And so it was that in December 1956 he "took a ship from London and had to go all the way around Africa—Cape Town and up." (The Suez Crisis had closed off the more direct route.) There, in the Indian Ocean, "between Durban and Colombo . . . [in] the spring of '57," he wrote what was to be "The Frozen Fields":

> The detonating scene [a childhood memory of his grandparents' Happy Hollow Farm, in Massachusetts] was something which I didn't even put in: I was lying awake at night in this cold room "at the Happy Hollow Farm"—very early in the morning before dawn and hearing a fox howling, barking outside. . . . This was in Massachusetts. . . . On shipboard I remembered it: I was just there, on the ship, and I suddenly thought of the fox howling—I'll never know why. How does one know what makes one think of things? And then I went to the captain of the ship and asked if I could have a room to work in, and he gave me an empty cabin. I would leave my own cabin and go down to this place where nobody ever bothered me at all. And I had my typewriter and paper in there. And I went every afternoon after lunch and wrote and had it all done, and when I got to Colombo I sent it right off the first day, to New York, and it was immediately published in *Harper's Bazaar*. And then it was put in an anthology that year: the *Best Short Stories of '58*." (Stewart 1982, 67)

It was the last of his fictional works written before Jane Bowles had her stroke in April 1957. "I did not know it," he writes of this period in his autobiography, "but the good years were over" (*WS*, 336).

The opening scene of the story reconstructs the originary scene of the creative act and dramatizes the oppressive force of the father over the young artist. When we first meet Donald and his father in the second paragraph of the story, they are on the train headed toward the grandparents' farm for Christmas: "Donald had started to scratch pictures with his fingernail in the ice that covered the lower part of the windowpane by his seat. His father had said: 'Stop that.' He knew better than to ask 'Why?'" (*CS*, 261).

What is at stake in this first evidence of a struggle of wills is the very impulse to create, which is abruptly checked by the father's firm command to "Stop that." Donald scores what he considers to be a minor triumph, perhaps in retaliation for his father's injunctions, when on their arrival at the station his Uncle Greg and Uncle Willis, in greeting him, lift him in their arms and plant kisses firmly on his mouth. "Men shake hands," his father had once told him. "They don't kiss" (*CS*, 261). When he arrives at the farm, Donald's initial sense of freedom dissolves when he realizes "his father's presence here would constitute a grave danger, because it was next to impossible to conceal anything from him, and once aware of the existence of the other world he would spare no pains to destroy it" (*CS*, 362). With these carefully selected details, presented early in the story, Bowles announces his central theme–the nature of authority and the threat the father poses to the child's imaginative world.

The story, much like "The Echo" and "Pages from Cold Point," exerts critical pressure on the institution of family. The family we see here is completely dysfunctional; it is no wonder Donald looks for a means of escape. No doubt expectations for familial bliss are heightened by the Christmas atmosphere, for during this season, above all others, families are supposed to be happily united. The scene in Donald's family, however, is noticeably tense. Soon after arriving at the farm, Donald (significantly the only child present) listens to his adult relatives talking about his Aunt Louisa and Uncle Ivor's plans; they will be coming the next morning:

> "Mr. Gordon, too, I suppose," said his mother.
> "Oh, probably," Uncle Greg said. "He won't want to stay alone Christmas Day."

His mother looked annoyed. "It seems sort of unnecessary," she said. "Christmas is a *family* day, after all."

"Well, he's part of the family now," said Uncle Willis with a crooked smile.

His mother replied with great feeling: "I think it's terrible."

"He's pretty bad these days," put in Grampa, shaking his head.

"Still on the old fire-water?" asked his father.

Uncle Greg raised his eyebrows. "That and worse. You know. . . . And Ivor too." (*CS*, 264)

Donald overhears this conversation, trying to piece together its meaning. We are never sure just how much Donald grasps the references to drinking and drug use, which are purposefully disguised by the adults. It is rather unlikely that he understands much about the relationship implied here between his uncle and the mysterious Mr. Gordon. The disturbing truth the adults cryptically and jokingly allude to is that Mr. Gordon, who has come as a guest of Uncle Ivor, is a particular sort of friend. We are given all sorts of clues but never told outright. Right after the portion of conversation just cited, Donald's mother exclaims, "Oh, honestly . . . I don't see how Louisa *stands* it" (*CS*, 264). When Mr. Gordon finally appears, he regally, even queenly, displays "two big diamond rings on one hand and an even bigger sapphire on the other" (*CS*, 267).

The selection and arrangement of material in the story clearly are designed to emphasize affinities between the young Donald and Mr. Gordon. Both are cast as outsiders, set apart from the family. Even before Mr. Gordon's arrival, Donald is curious about him and favorably disposed: "Everyone had talked so mysteriously about Mr. Gordon that he was very eager to see him" (*CS*, 266). Once there, Mr. Gordon immediately establishes a friendship with the young boy, by showing him his "fat watch with a little button, and tiny chimes struck, inside the watch." At one point during the Christmas visit, Mr. Gordon praises Donald's behavior before his father. "Discipline begins in the cradle," asserts the father. "It's sinister," Mr. Gordon mutters in reply (*CS*, 270). And later, after a charged family quarrel, Mr. Gordon, in remarks seemingly directed to Donald, says, "Family quarrels. . . . Same old thing. Reminds me of my boyhood. When I look back on it, it seems to be we never got through a meal without a fight, but I suppose we must have once in a while. . . . Well, they're all dead now, thank God" (*CS*, 272).

The atmosphere becomes even more tense when it comes time for opening gifts. Once again Mr. Gordon becomes the focus of family scorn because his gift giving is, by their standards, inappropriately lavish. The first gift Donald opens, from Mr. Gordon, is a three-foot-long fire engine equipped with all the gadgets guaranteed to delight a six-year-old: "'Oh . . . isn't . . . that . . . lovely!' said his mother, her annoyance giving a sharp edge to every word." After this are even more gifts: "There were, of course, the handkerchiefs and books and mufflers from the family, but there was also a Swiss music box with little metal records that could be changed; there were roller skates, a large set of lead soldiers, a real accordion, and a toy village with a streetcar system that ran on a battery" (*CS*, 268). All these toys far overshadow the tan cashmere sweater given to him by his mother and father.

As fascinated as Donald is with Mr. Gordon, his family clearly tries to keep him away from his uncle's special friend. The extravagance of Mr. Gordon's giving is just one concrete manifestation of Mr. Gordon's unsettling effect. It is as though the family fears that if the young Donald touches or talks with him, he too might become homosexual. Both parents are obviously upset by Mr. Gordon's presence, and handle their son's natural curiosity with something less than frankness. When Donald asks his mother why Mr. Gordon lives at his Uncle Ivor's, she replies limply, "Dear, don't you know that Uncle Ivor's what they call a male nurse?" (*CS*, 270). Particularly disturbing to the family are comments Mr. Gordon offers as he, Uncle Ivor, and Aunt Louisa are readying to leave the family gathering. He says Donald "reminds me a little of myself, you now, when I was his age. I was a sort of shy and quiet lad, too" (*CS*, 275). With this remark, Donald's mother strengthens her grip on her son.

Their implicit fear of Mr. Gordon and the threat his homosexuality poses to the family, might, on some level, be valid. Yet it is the cold, inept way Donald's parents handle their son, especially the tyrannical means by which Donald's father tries to exert his power, that more than anything else accounts for the young boy's positive response to Mr. Gordon. Lawrence Stewart notes the logic of the affinities: "Donald is unconscious of Mr. Gordon's presumed sexual interest in Uncle Ivor. But when Mr. Gordon had said that he was glad that all of his own family are dead, Donald recognized in him an ally, the speaker of his own concealed thought about his father" (Stewart 1982, 65). His father's cold, authoritarian manner and his mother's lack of candor drive Donald away from his family, toward a decision, not reached in the story, to get as far away from them, and have as little to do with them, as possible.

The tension between father and son comes to a head later in the story when Uncle Ivor takes Donald out to the henhouse, using his egg-collecting mission to mask another intent—to separate Donald from the others and talk with him. Ivor delicately asks the boy questions aimed at determining the extent of domestic violence in the family, and finally gives up: "Well, it's a great pity your father ever got married. It would have been better for everybody if he'd stayed single" (*CS*, 273). Into this scene rushes his father, screaming "Donald!" They walk off in the snow together, his father, sergeantlike, giving him sharp orders about his posture. After throwing a snowball at a distant tree and hitting it, his father challenges Donald to do the same. Donald's defiant refusal provokes a rather violent response, quite sharply described: "Suddenly he was rubbing the snow violently over Donald's face, and at the same time that Donald gasped and squirmed, he pushed what was left of it down his neck. As he felt the wet, icy mass sliding down his back, he doubled over. His eyes were squeezed shut; he was certain his father was trying to kill him" (*CS*, 274).

Following this incident, on the way back to the farmhouse Donald, feeling a sense of detachment from the whole scene, is surprised by his lack of resentment. This description sheds light on Bowles's own modus operandi. One is very often struck by how much the man has been able to detach himself from painful or intimate experiences. Those mechanisms for coping might have their origins in childhood experience, as might the impulse to give experience some kind of objective, literary form. Like Stephen Dedalus, Bowles has chosen, in the interest of art, to distance himself from family, country, and religion.

Recurring throughout the story is Donald's fantasy of the wolf, symbolic of those unsettling aspects of the unknown. At one point Donald fantasizes that the wolf breaks through a windowpane and seizes his father by the throat. "The Frozen Fields" ends with a scene in which Donald imaginatively allies himself with the primitive forces outside, opposed to his father's brutal civilizing schemes. Upstairs in his bedroom Christmas night, after Ivor, Louisa, and Mr. Gordon have left, he again enters the magical world of his own imagination. Donald, as "he lay in the dark listening to the sound of the fine snow as the wind drove it against the panes," first creates a vivid picture of the wolf outside in the wilds, then imagines he himself is outside. The wolf then approaches, lies down beside him, "putting his heavy head in Donald's lap" (*CS*, 276). In the story's last line, the two are running together across the frozen fields.

Most readers see the final scene as Donald's provisional triumph over his father's tyranny. Stewart suggests that the wolf "has released, momentarily, the freezing grasp that attempted to hold Donald through cruelty and denial" (Stewart 1982, 65). John Ditsky says the flight is "one in which fantasy and the darkest promptings of nature are accepted without subjecting them to question and judgment on the basis of some abstract system of values or other" (Ditsky, 386). Richard F. Patteson writes that "Donald has successfully, at least for the time being, domesticated the outside, bringing it into a new interior of his own creation. And a denizen of that formerly outside world, the wolf, becomes the agent of destruction of the father, who is the real source of Donald's discomfort" (Patteson, 13). That Patteson ends his study of Bowles's fiction with references to the story is an indication of his judgment of its importance. When Donald is taken as a fictionalized version of the young Bowles, the boy's move toward personal autonomy can be seen as a critical step in the writer's subsequent development.

It has already been noted how "The Frozen Fields" makes use of autobiographical material. The author's memories of visits to the country to visit his grandparents, August and Henrietta Winnewisser, supplied him with the setting. Lawrence Stewart, addressing the issue of the autobiographical sources of this work, writes:

> Knowing what we do of Bowles's upbringing, we inevitably look for correspondence between the facts of his life and the events in his fiction. But Bowles himself resists the correlation. "I don't ever want to be in them [the fictional works] at all. I am *not* in them. That's why I object when people say 'That's you!' or also, 'What was your idea in writing this; what was your method?' Well, I didn't have any idea or method—not that I'm aware of—so I can't answer these questions." Nevertheless, if we look at some of the chronicled events, as well as his announced intentions, we can see where small bridges have been built between his personal activities and the dramatic action in his stories. (Stewart 1982, 66)

The Paul Bowles collection of the Humanities Research Center of the University of Texas at Austin, has the 37 handwritten, bound-notebook sheets of the first draft of the story, as well as two typescripts, each 24 pages. They tend to confirm the author's assertion that "nobody is invented. They're all real—they're all my relatives. . . . The uncle who was a trained nurse and had this elderly man that he brought for

Christmas, and so on. . . . Several members of the family didn't particularly like the man that my aunt had married. Eventually he got her
taking morphine, I don't wonder. She died from too much morphine—
she went on taking it for years. . . . In the story even that is alluded to
too: They say 'Is he still on the old firewater?' and he says, 'That and
worse' " (Stewart 1982, 67).

Although the farm in the published story has no name, in the holograph manuscript it is always the "H.H.F." (Happy Hollow Farm). The
published story makes no mention of the father's occupation, but the
holograph draft observes that "Donald's father was a doctor, and
he talked a great deal about germs and diseases." (Bowles's father was a
dentist.) While in both holograph and printed versions Donald is six, in
the former he would turn seven "five days after Christmas"—that is, 30
December, which is Bowles's own birthday. The typescript deliberately
blurs these biographical facts; as in the published account, Donald
becomes seven "the day after New Year's" (Stewart 1982, 67).

The struggle between Donald and his father is clearly a thinly veiled
fictional portrayal of the writer's relationship with his own father. In his
autobiography Bowles frequently displays his feelings toward his father.
Especially dramatic is the story Bowles tells (with seeming pleasure) of
how his grandmother believed his father had tried to kill him when he
was a baby:

> When you were only six weeks old, he did it. He came home one
> terrible night when the wind was roaring and the snow was coming
> down—a real blizzard—and marched straight into your room, opened
> the window up wide, walked over to your crib and yanked you out
> from under your warm blankets, stripped you naked, and carried you
> over to the window where the snow was sailing in. And that devil just
> left you there in a wicker basket on the windowsill for the snow to fall
> on. And if I hadn't heard you crying a little later, you'd have been dead
> inside the hour. "I know what you want," I told him. "You shan't do
> it. You'll harm this baby over my dead body." (*WS*, 38–39)

Though the reliability of the story might be questionable, one gets the
sense Bowles wants to believe it. A little earlier in the autobiography, he
recalls with some resentment another memory from when he was a boy
of five. His father would shout at him to "Fletcherize," while monitoring
his chewing, making sure every bite was chewed 40 times before swallowing (*WS*, 24). Without question, Donald's father is modeled on

Bowles's own, and the story itself might be thought of as the son's revenge.

Uncle Ivor too has a real-life counterpart, in Bowles's Uncle Guy. In his autobiography he writes, "Uncle Guy was a novelty: he wore Japanese kimonos and spent a good deal of time keeping incense burning in a variety of bronze dragons and Buddhas" (*WS*, 40). It was through his Uncle Guy that Bowles innocently witnessed his first homosexual scene, rather like Donald's brush with Mr. Gordon in the story. One time when the young Bowles was visiting his uncle in Northampton, Massachusetts, his uncle put on a party in Aunt Emma's apartment next door. Paul, attracted by the music and loud noise, went and looked in. Glimpsing at the studio, he found "it was crowded with pretty young men dancing together" (*WS*, 41). The appearance of his angry uncle put an end to his observance. In "The Frozen Fields," it seems, something of the content of this memory is preserved. Yet despite the evidence, Bowles will insist that "I wasn't trying to recreate myself at all. I was making a story. I was making fiction out of it, of course" (Stewart 1982, 67).

The New York setting of "If I Should Open My Mouth" is not nearly so fully depicted as the farm in "The Frozen Fields," yet in its own way it is every bit as much a determining factor in the story's action. Written in Tangier in 1952, the story dwells on the bizarre psychological workings of a deranged mind. Its Poe-like tone and Dostoyevskian thematic concerns place the story alongside "You Are Not I," "He of the Assembly," and perhaps Bowles's fourth novel, a thriller titled *Up Above the World*.

As in "Pages from Cold Point," the narrator speaks through diary entries, which in this story are dated. In the first entries a 55-year-old madman describes the progress of his criminal plan, giving us a view rather like the one we get of Raskolnikov in the opening book of *Crime and Punishment*. While we might not know at once just what the diarist's intentions are, we surmise that the plan has something to do with gum and subways. Our interest in the narrator (indeed, perhaps the author's own interest) may lie in his being a writer as well as a madman. The diary, in fact, contains the writer's reflections on not only his plotting in the world but his activity qua writer:

> I don't know why it is that ideas never occur to me except when I lack
> the time to put them down or when it is literally impossible to do so,
> as for instance when I am seated in a dentist's chair or surrounded by
> talking people at a dinner party, or even sound asleep, when often the

best things come to light and are recognized as such by a critical part of my mind which is there watching, quite capable of judging but utterly unable to command an awakening and a recording. . . . I am not a literary person and I never expect to be one, nor have I any intention of showing my notebooks to my friends. . . . I am using up pages of my notebook, minutes when I might be strolling on the beach smelling the sea, in scribbling these absurd excuses, inventing alibis for not living, trying to find one more reason why I should feel justified in keeping these nonsensical journals year after year. (*CS*, 252)

The trouble the narrator is having writing the diary is related to the difficulty he is having telling his story "truthfully." The narrator's own reluctance to tell, of course, contributes to the suspense of the story. Only in little bits, as the writer musters the courage to put it down, do we form a full picture of his operations. "I delivered the first twenty boxes today," he writes at one point. Yet we don't know what the boxes are, how he delivered them, or what he expects to happen. The narrator, however, soon does tell the story of how he rode the Eighth Avenue subway, planting his own specially prepared boxes of Chiclets in the machines at various subway stations along the route. With glee he notes that he has seen a woman take the bait, exclaiming to her friends, "Gee, I'm gettin' good. . . . I got two." Far from having any moral qualms about his "silly project," he feels "hugely righteous about it all" (*CS*, 251), and on the day he carries out his plan he "kept marveling at the peculiar pleasure afforded by the knowledge that one has planned a thing so perfectly there can be no room for the possibility of failure" (*CS*, 253–54).

Again like Dostoyevski's Raskolnikov, the narrator eagerly scans the papers looking for accounts of his deed and its victims. When he finds none, he first suspects that the police are putting a gag on the story, then wonders whether he actually had done what in his diary he has said he did. His subsequent discovery of both the untampered and the tampered boxes challenges the ontological status of the act. In this way, Bowles plays with the relation between madness and sanity, between belief and fiction.

The story can also be seen as a fable of what can happen to the mind in a modern urban context. The writer of these diary entries is a profoundly alienated figure. Though there are references to a past relationship with a woman named Anna and to his present housekeeper,

Mrs. Crawford, he seems to be living an existence thoroughly cut off from any human contact. The narrator lives in a post-Rousseauvian world where he feels his intellect has become his worst enemy. The narrator belongs to the ranks of a whole host of real and fictional disaffected characters of the modern era—Friedrich Nieztsche, Auguste Strindberg, Raskolnikov, Hamsun's hero of *Hunger*, Gregor Samsa, Kurtz, Sartre's Roquentin, and Camus's Meursault.

Acknowledging the breakdown of his own mental condition, the narrator writes: "I am left only with vague impressions of being solitary in the park of some vast city. Solitary in the sense that although life is going on all around me, the cords that could connect me in any way with the life have been severed, so that I am as alone as if I were a spirit returned from the dead." He concludes that "in order to *be*, one must not only be to one's self: it is absolutely imperative that one be for others" (*CS*, 258). His imaginary scheme of planting poisoned Chiclets in machines must be seen as a kind of frantic attempt to have an impact on the world, to overcome a feeling of boredom and impotence. In the last paragraph of the story, the narrator submits one more potentially devious scheme. It occurs to him to "take all forty boxes to the woods behind the school and throw them on to the rubbish heap there. It's too childish a game to go on playing at my age. Let the kids have them" (*CS*, 259). Who is to say whether he will carry through with this plan or not, or whether this too will be yet another imaginary plot?

While "Sylvie Ann, the Boogie Man" was not published in *The Time of Friendship*, the story dates from this period.[57] As an explanation of why the story was omitted from both this early collection and his *Collected Stories*, Bowles has expressed his concern that the story, which portrays the relationship between the black protagonist, Sylvie Ann, and one of her wealthy white employers, Mrs. Lauder, might be misinterpreted, especially at a time America was engaged in civil rights struggles.[58] While certainly not one of Bowles's strongest stories, "Sylvie Ann, the Boogie Man" quite vividly depicts, with its sharp ironic contrasts, the unpleasant form racist attitudes can take and the pain they can cause. Compounding the racial differences are the underlying differences determined by class and economic standing.

On her fiftieth birthday Sylvie Ann goes off to do laundry for Mrs. Lauder, the favorite of her three wealthy white employers. Somewhat ironically, the same day Mrs. Lauder is hosting a luncheon ("If Mrs Lauder used the word *luncheon*, it meant automatically that there were going to be guests; otherwise she said *lunch* like everybody else" [*CC*,

164]) to celebrate the birthdays of several of her friends. When later in the day Mrs. Lauder learns that it is Sylvie Ann's birthday, she has "a glass of iced grape-juice and four thin cookies" sent down to the laundry room, a gesture that only stirs Sylvie Ann's ire (*CC*, 168).

Sylvie Ann's sense of embitterment and hurt peaks when, just as she is about to leave work that day, she overhears a conversation between Dr. and Mrs. Lauder:

> "I'd have given her some little thing, but she only told me at lunch."
>
> Dr. Lauder snickered. "Like a compact full of stove polish?" he suggested. Sylvie Ann stood absolutely still, not breathing.
>
> "Charles, for heaven's *sake*!" cried Mrs. Lauder in an agitated voice. "She's still here. I *told* you she hadn't gone yet."
>
> Neither one of them said anything for a moment. Sylvie Ann went on standing like a statue, listening. The closet smelled of naphthalene. Then Mrs. Lauder continued in a very low but perfectly audible voice: "She said she was fifty. How *could* she be, Charles? She must be older than that."
>
> "I hope you don't think she really knows her age," replied Dr. Lauder. "They never do, that type, I mean. I bet she's got no idea how old she is." (*CC*, 170)

The Lauders' racist, patronizing attitudes become even more visible and reprehensible when, sensing something is wrong, they follow Sylvie Ann in their car and try to smooth things out. Dr. Lauder finally hands the maid her wages from the car window.

The period during which most of these stories were written was a productive one for Bowles. He kept on the move. In addition to the stories and a number of musical compositions, Bowles completed two novels, *Let It Come Down* (1952) and *The Spider's House* (1955). In these works we notice a maturation of style and a deepening of thematic content, seen for example in "Pages from Cold Point" and "The Time of Friendship." The transgressions and crossings here, while not as prickly as in Bowles's earlier Gothic tales, are no less poignant.

Things Gone and Things Still Here

The decade between the publication of *The Time of Friendship* (1967) and *Things Gone and Things Here* (1977) was not a particularly fruitful period for Bowles, no doubt in large measure because of the stress associated with his wife Jane's long illness that led, eventually, to her death in 1973. In 1966 Bowles's fourth novel, *Up Above the World*, was published. In 1972 Putnam brought out his autobiography, the writing of which the author has often referred to as a painful ordeal. It was a task he would not likely have undertaken had there not been the prospect of financial remuneration. Most of his literary output during this time took the form of translations. He began working with Mohammed Mrabet, translating taped stories from the Moghrebi into English.[59] His translation of a collection of Isabelle Eberhardt's stories, *The Oblivion Seekers*, was published by City Lights in 1972, and Mohamad Choukri's *For Bread Alone* came out in England in 1974. Bowles quite likely directed his energies toward translation projects not only because of his belief and interest in the works and lives of the storytellers he translated but also because of an apparent flagging in his own creativity during this period.

Of the nine stories constituting *Things Gone and Things Still Here*, none has the arresting power and originality that so many of his earlier works have. Though the volume is, as a whole, weaker than its predecessors, it is of interest because of stylistic developments—affected no doubt by his translation work—and because it raises questions concerning the shifting relations between author and material.[60] Travel for Bowles had always been a source of material, providing inspiration and settings for his writing. What, then, happens when the writer becomes older and his life becomes more settled?

The stories in *Things Gone and Things Still Here* and subsequent volumes rely more heavily on memory. Bowles occasionally dips far back into his past experiences and retrieves a story, or reshapes and tells various tales he has gleaned from his life in Tangier, or invents or refashions local legends. Rather than go off in search of stories, more and more he has had to be content to sit back and let stories come to him. This practice, however, might be thought of not so much as a departure from as an extension of writing methods Bowles has always employed, for he has, as we have seen, usually preferred to gain some spatial and temporal distance from the originary scene of a story before writing it.

In 1966 Bowles signed a contract with Little, Brown to write a book on Bangkok, to be a part of a series of books the publisher was doing on cities. At first the publisher suggested Cairo, but Bowles recalls that "the prospect of going to live in Cairo for a year was not seductive" (*WS*, 356). Finally, he decided to propose Bangkok—"where I had never been and about which I knew nothing"—and Little, Brown accepted. Bowles got as far as visiting Thailand but never wrote the book. Several years later, however, in 1971, he wrote a story, "You Have Left Your Lotus Pods on the Bus," that owes its existence to that trip.

Bowles was not altogether pleased with his trip to Bangkok. In his autobiography he records his reactions to the place:

> Bangkok was not the verdant and hushed city of canals and temples I had expected. The place had lost so much of its original Thai flavor that what little was left seemed perverse and absurd in the midst of so much determined Westernizing. . . . By the time I reached it in the autumn of 1966 it was hopelessly overpopulated and its thoroughfares were choked with motorized traffic. Everywhere the waterways were being filled in; those that were left had become putrid and noisome, so that the process was having to be carried ahead with increasing rapidity. My initial reaction to the city was one of severe disappointment. (*WS*, 359)

The narrator at the opening of "You Have Left Your Lotus Pods" echoes this disappointment: "I soon learned not to go near the windows or to draw aside the double curtains in order to look at the river below. The view was wide and lively, with factories and warehouses on the far side of the Chao Phraya, the strings of barges being towed up and down the dirty water," (*CS*, 393). So dirty is the landscape, with its "factories and warehouses," rather than views of more exotic, "indigenous" architecture, that the traveler chooses to keep the curtain closed.

This trip to Thailand was to be one of the last of Bowles's great adventures. Following a brief stint of teaching at San Fernando Valley State College in 1968, instigated by his friend Oliver Evans, whom he visited in Thailand, Bowles has remained in Tangier, a stack of old, dust-laden suitcases standing by the door of his apartment in the Inmeuble Itesa. Something of this condition is implied in the title *Things Gone and Things Still Here*. Bowles now seems content to remain in Tangier, knowing full well that the world is becoming neither younger nor more beautiful. Travel in the 1960s was nothing like travel in the 1930s, when, as Evelyn Waugh put it, "the going was good." The airplane, which Bowles detests, has replaced the ship as the primary mover of people across oceans. It has become harder and harder, further, to escape the physical reminders of "Westernization," as Bowles found on his trip to Thailand. No less, the intrepid traveler's advancing age makes travel less appealing. What is left, perhaps, are the suitcases by the door and whatever memories one is able to reconstruct of earlier and better times.

"You Have Left Your Lotus Pods on the Bus," the only story in *Things Gone and Things Still Here* with a setting other than North Africa, is sometimes selected for anthologies seeking to demonstrate the kinds of misunderstandings that frequently occur in cross-cultural encounters.[61] The story, which chronicles the initial responses of the traveler to the new setting, displays a sense of discomfort and confusion rather than the deeper understanding of foreign manners and customs that characterizes the North African stories.

In the first scene the narrator, clearly a Bowles persona, sits in his posh hotel room with his American friend, Brooks (modeled after Oliver Evans, who was on a Fulbright in Thailand at the time of Bowles's visit), and three gold-clad Thai monks. It becomes apparent that the room is more luxurious than anything the three Thai monks had seen before, and that the narrator himself feels somewhat awkward, cut off from the world around him by the insulating walls of his Western, five-star hotel, a type of outpost of civilization so common and so prominent in the third world today. The Americans and the Thai seem hardly to know how to begin to understand each other. The oldest of the three monks, Yam-yong, says, "We appreciate the opportunity to use English. For this reason we are liking to have foreign friends. English, American; it doesn't matter" (*CS*, 394).

Though the Thai guests are equipped with enough knowledge of English to conduct an elementary conversation with the Americans, their understanding of customs and cultural codes is far more feeble. The most memorable portion of this scene occurs when one of the Thai visitors asks the narrator about the significance of the necktie:

> "You mean, why do men wear neckties?"
> "No. I know that. The purpose is to look like a gentleman."
> I laughed. Yamyong was not put off. "I have noticed that some men

wear the two ends equal, and some wear the wide end longer than the narrow, or the narrow longer than the wide. And the neckties themselves, they are not all the same length, are they? Some even with both ends equal reach below the waist. What are the different meanings?"

"There is no meaning," I said. "Absolutely none."

. . . "I believe you, of course," he said graciously. "But we all thought each way had a different significance attached." (*CS*, 394–95)

Ascribing meaning to cultural differences is indeed a tricky business, for the casual traveler and the anthropologist alike. First one must know what merits attention; then one must construct a valid interpretation.

Sometime after this first scene, Brooks and the narrator join their Thai friends for a trip to Ayudhaya. The hosts are amused by Brooks's excitement with water buffalo and his reactions to lotus pods, mangosteens, local instruments, and food. This time it is the Americans who are baffled by the meaning of certain peculiar behavior. On the bus ride home from their visit to the ruined temples, the two Americans are bothered by the rantings of a man at the back of the bus. To their amazement, nobody else on the bus seems to notice. When they politely make inquiries, Yamyong merely says the man is very busy. The Americans fail to understand. Yamyong, sensing this, goes on to explain that this man is calling out, helping the driver navigate the vehicle around various obstacles and warning of possible dangers along the way:

"All the buses must have a driver's assistant. He watches the road and tells the driver how to drive. It is hard work because he must shout loud enough for the driver to hear him."

"But why doesn't he sit up in front with the driver?"

"No, no. There must be one in front and one in the back. That way two men are responsible for the bus." (*CS*, 399)

The Americans still fail to see the logic of it all.

The course of the narrative in "You Have Left Your Lotus Pods on the Bus" follows quite closely what we might imagine to be the sequence of incidents that engendered the story. In other words, perhaps because of its slight plot and undramatic quality, the story seems to lean toward journalism. One has only to compare this story with earlier works such as "The Frozen Fields," "Pages from Cold Point," or "Doña Faustina" to get a clear impression of what is lacking.

For "Reminders of Bouselham," written in 1976 and one of the strongest stories in the volume, Bowles draws on what he had known and heard about expatriate lives in Tangier. The narrator of "Reminders of Bouselham," a young Moroccan-born English expatriate, tells about the relationship between his mother and a young Moroccan gardener, Bouselham. The focus in the story is not the affair itself but the mystery of his mother's abrupt break with the gardener and her subsequent departure for Italy.

It takes the storyteller some time to get to the core of his story, which, as it turns out, is another nested story, supplied to the narrator by Bouselham himself, the primary agent and subject of both his own story and the narrator's. We discover that the break comes when the narrator's mother learns that Bouselham has sold his sister off to a wealthy Moroccan merchant. The act seems so repugnant to her that, with no explanation, she completely severs her connection not only to Bouselham but to Morocco and, to a great extent, to her son who remains there.

In a manner reminiscent of Conrad's *Lord Jim*, though on a much smaller scale, this story represents an understanding of events that, over time, the narrator has developed by piecing together material from various sources and organizing it into a coherent form. The narrator's formation of this story is a way of giving coherence to a set of troublesome, complex events. Indeed, the story prompts speculation on the generation of stories and the social and personal purposes to which they are put. Under what conditions can stories be told? To whom and why are they told?

One necessary condition for their telling seems to be an initial perception of shared sympathy. There is, further, at work in the exchange a dynamic that functions rather like the one anthropologist Marcel Mauss has described in *The Gift*.[62] Both teller and audience have to feel they are getting something from the activity, whether it is simply pleasure or something more tangible, such as some piece of desired information; that is the implicit nature of the bargain. When Bouselham tells his story, for example, he satisfies the narrator's curiosity by offering key clues that assist in the narrator's quest to understand more about puzzling events intimately tied to his life. For his part, Bouselham makes no attempt to hide his expectation of a payoff. He begins to tell his story to the narrator, and won't go on until he has assurances from his interlocutor that he will help with legal expenses. Bouselham also gains some social credit as he boasts to his friends and acquaintances around Tangier about outwitting the rich Nazarene merchant. "To him," the narrator explains, "it was a business matter in whose success he took a healthy pride" (*CS*, 391). The rich merchant, in turn, tells Bouselham stories of his own "troubled romance," wholly unaware that his listener is none other than his girl-friend's brother/pimp.

A good story, particularly one involving scandal or sexual intrigue, circulates within a community, whether that community be a town such as Tangier, a community of expatriates, or a community of readers. Stories are one means by which the fabric of society is held together. "Reminders of Bouselham" enacts these social dynamics: it enacts the patterns of circulation stories take, and it demonstrates how stories take hold. Things get started, for example, when the narrator hears something of the story from a woman "who had just arrived here, and so had no way of knowing that the subject of her story was my mother" (*CS*, 388): "As usual the gossip got the basic facts fairly straight, but the motivations wrong. Everyone was certain that Father had left home because of Bouselham, when actually it was because he could no longer bear to be in the same house with Amy." (*CS*, 386).

The power of a story to move its listeners depends largely on its credibility. The role of belief, as Coleridge has noted, is pivotal. So long as the narrator's mother refuses to give credence to the story of Bousel-ham's use of his sister, she is not compelled to act. Once she finally *believes* the story, however, she pronounces "the whole thing" as "vile" (*CS*, 391). The story, or so the narrator would have us *believe*, is what provokes her sudden flight to Italy.

Bouselham had not anticipated the drastic consequences stories about him would have. "The way he saw it," the narrator tells us near the end of the story, "he had been turned out of the house for no reason at all" (*CS*, 392). His bewilderment and surprise, we might guess, can be explained by his unfamiliarity with the values of a Western audience. Stories that would be thoroughly understandable in one context might seem obtuse in another. Stories that would shock in one context might seem perfectly normal in another. The narrator admits, at one point, that the story of Bouselham has not affected him in the way it had affected his mother: "Mother has lived in this country for many years, and should not have been so deeply disturbed by Bouselham's behavior, particularly since it had nothing whatever to do with her. To me what he did seems natural enough, but then, I was born here," (*CS*, 388).

As we have seen, "Reminders of Bouselham" inscribes a variety of contexts involving storytelling in which the roles of teller and listener are often reversed and intertwined. Stories are told inside the story, by Bouselham and others. The narrator himself is telling the story to an unspecified audience. And, of course, outside it all is Bowles, who writes the story down, publishes it, and claims authorship. Bowles's motivations for telling might not be so different from those found inside the story. The act of telling connects him with a distant, English-speaking audience, meeting some deep psychological need, and if commercially successful his efforts provide him with the financial means to keep on living there. He has come to depend on his talents as a storyteller for his livelihood.

Richard F. Patteson, who notes thematic similarities between "Reminders of Bouselham" and Flannery O'Connor's "The Comforts of Home" and "The Lame Shall Enter First," uses the story as evidence to support his thesis that "many of Bowles' plots move toward epiphanies in which characters recognize their outsidedness" (Patteson, 7). This statement also characterizes the thematic lines of "Allal," one of several of Bowles's tales of transformation, and the final story in his *Collected Stories*.

Allal, the offspring of an illegitimate union, is abandoned as an infant by his 14-year-old mother at the hotel where she has worked. From the beginning, then, Allal is cast as an outsider, and the supernatural occurrences in the story, like those effecting the transformation of Gregor Samsa in Kafka's "Metamorphosis," seem to be a logical, figurative extension of that fundamental sociopsychological state. The townspeople continually call him "son of sin" as he is growing up, cruelly reminding him of his illegitimate status.

It is no wonder the boy feels a natural affinity for an old, white-turbaned snake merchant when he sees the villagers tormenting him because of his bag of snakes. Time and time again in Bowles, narrative patterns join the lives of two previously separate male outsiders—for example, Donald and Mr. Gordon in "The Frozen Fields," Amar and Stenham in *The Spider's House*, Amar and the young boy in "By the Water," and the two men in "He of the Assembly." Allal invites the snake merchant home, gets acquainted with him, learns about the snakes, and determines to steal a snake he develops an unusually powerful passion for: "One reddish-gold serpent, which coiled itself lazily in the middle of the floor, he found particularly beautiful. As he stared at it, he felt a great desire to own it and have it always with him" (*CS*, 411).

Allal's stratagem, which involves getting the snake stoned on a kif-and-milk paste, works. He hides the snake and the merchant leaves, upset that he has "lost" one of his most prized serpents.

With the aid of the kif paste, Allah makes friends with the snake. One day he decides to push the friendship to new heights. He undresses, invites the snake to crawl along his naked body, and lies "in a state of pure delight, feeling the snake's head against his own, without a thought save that he and the snake were together" (*CS*, 414). After this tantalizing, sensual interlude, the story becomes more and more surreal. Allal, evidently hallucinating, slips from his own body into the snake's. He then sees things, including his own abandoned human form, from the snake's point of view: "It did not strike him as being at all strange; he merely said to himself that now he was seeing through the eyes of the snake, rather than through his own" (*CS*, 415). The wonder and novelty of his experience, however, soon take a frightful turn when he is cornered and attacked by a number of villagers. The naked boy, who once was Allah, comes to his aid, but the boy's perceived madness is a ticket to the local asylum. When the villagers come after Allal-transformed-into-snake, he finally gets his revenge, though it carries a heavy price: "The men nearest him were on their hands and knees, and Allal had the joy of pushing his fangs into two of them before a third severed his head with an axe" (*CS*, 417).

Wayne Pounds, in his book on Bowles's fiction, *Paul Bowles: The Inner Geography*, devotes considerable space to "Allal," pruning the story's meaning to fit his concern with myth and the "divided self," suggested by the work of Jung and R. D. Laing. The snake that swallows Allal can be thought of, Pounds argues, as "an archetype of the Terrible Mother," and "the slit eye of the snake as a secondary displacement of the *vagina dentata* [tooth-studded womb] of the Teeth Mother." Invoking Laing, Pounds suggests that "at the same time that we read [the story] as the perilous adventure of the inner self released from the body to a fantasied omnipotence, we read it as a hallucinated reality representing the contents of the unconscious" (Pounds, 121).

While such psychoanalytic readings tend to be terribly reductive, Pounds is right to dwell on the story's importance and to identify the conflict within the self that is at its heart. "Allal's transformation into the serpent," he writes, "is the rending of the veil of the false self, permitting the venting of his hatred. . . . [T]he felt omnipotence of the inner self exists only in fantasy, and the havoc which it wreaks causes its own final dissolution" (Pounds, 124).

"Allal," rife with all the connotations that serpents, from the time of Adam and Eve, have been unable to shirk, is a wild tale of seduction and of avenging an intolerant community. The story is yet another manifestation of Bowles's preoccupation with "otherness." Here the difference, most often portrayed in East-West terms, has taken the form of human versus serpent. While the underlying psychological currents in the story are strong, it is not easy to articulate their meaning. On some level the story seems to act out a kind of wish fulfillment in which the subject consummates his fantasy of actually transforming himself into his object of fascination and desire, a transformation realized first through physical intimacy and ultimately through a radical exchange of consciousness.

For other stories in *Things Gone and Things Still Here*, Bowles turns to local legends and mythologies. In the background of "Afternoon With Antaeus" is the Greek myth in which Hercules (Erakli, the Arabic version in the story) comes to the northwestern tip of Africa (presumably about where Tangier now stands) and fights with the giant Antaeus (Ntiuz, in the story), son of Poseidon and Gaea. As legend has it, the giant could not be beaten so long as he remained in contact with the earth. Hercules lifts him up and strangles him to death. Bowles's tale stands the Greek myth on its head. In fact, the speaker of this dramatic monologue is none other than Ntiuz, who has evidently survived Erakli's attack. The implied listener, in a position much like the listener in Browning's "My Last Duchess," is an unnamed visitor from Argos: "Killed me! Is that what he told them back there? And when you got here you heard I was still around, and so you wanted to meet me? I understand" (*CS*, 367).

While the story ostensibly has a historical setting, Hercules might be recognized merely as a predecessor to the modern-day Western traveler. Any recent visitor to Tangier—or, for that matter, to any other so-called third-world country—will readily recognize the rhetorical ploys and strategies used by Ntiuz as being virtually identical with those used by his modern-day counterpart, the hustler. The speaker, who boasts a kind of Rifian toughness, first tries to allay the visitor's apprehensions, offering nuts to his guest, saying that "only savages attack a stranger walking alone" and that "we let people go through without a word" (*CS*, 367). The naive guest apparently buys the line, perhaps hoping for some adventure he can go home and talk about, and accompanies his guide into the forest, where Ntiuz apparently steals his purse. Charged with theft, the guide responds, "A pouch? I don't think you were carrying anything. There's no need to make a face like that. You don't think I took it, do you? I thought we were friends. I treated you like a friend. And now you pay me back" (*CS*, 370).

And so on. The Westerner is left to find his own way out of the forest with a warning that he should be quick about it. Allegorical interpretations are tempting. The conflict between Ntiuz and Erakli symbolically represents the age-old conflict between East and West. As such, the story belongs to the same fabric from which Bowles's *Points in Time* was cut.

Things Gone and Things Still Here also contains a handful of colorful Moroccan tales, akin to "The Garden" and the four stories of *A Hundred Camels in the Courtyard*. The best of these is "Mejdoub," which, like many of the stories of Nasrudin or Hadidan Aharam, features a clever, witty protagonist and the veiling or unveiling of deception or injustice.[63] As the story begins, we see an ordinary man watching a *mejdoub*, a possessed holy man, making threats and collecting money. He soon gets the idea that he too could wield that sort of power and make a profession of it. After carefully watching the gestures and actions of the "real" *mejdoub*, the man leaves for another town, where he gets a dirty djellaba and has an iron scepter made, then begins to practice his art with amazing success. He reasons "that Allah did not mind if he pretended to be one of His holy maniacs" (*CS*, 373).

At one point, the man decides to test his powers by asking a taxi driver to take him (without charge, of course) to Sidi Larbi's tomb: "He told the driver to wait, and jumped out of the taxi. Then he began the long climb up the hill to the tomb. The driver lost patience and drove off. On the way back to the town he missed a curve and hit a tree. When he was let out of the hospital he spread the word that Sidi Rahal had caused the car to go off the road. Men talked at length about it, recalling other holy maniacs who had put spells on motors and brakes. The name of Sidi Rahal was on everyone's lips, and people listened respectfully to his rantings" (*CS*, 373). The incident resembles an anecdote Bowles has told of an encounter in Tangier with a local holy man who once accosted him and his driver, urgently demanding that he be taken at once to the nearby tomb of a certain saint. The driver consented, fearing the consequences of noncompliance.

With money he has earned in his newfound occupation, the fake *mejdoub* goes back to his home and buys a house. Over time he develops two lives—his ordinary life in the winter in his hometown and his new life in the summer as *mejdoub*. Each is distinct and separate from the other, one secret, the other public. His two-personaed life has a certain appeal. As in the story of "The Prince and the Pauper," it enables the character to escape from the confines and boundaries of self and allows for a dramatic shift of perspective.

All goes well for the man until a law is passed prohibiting begging in the streets. (Such things have been known to happen in Morocco.) For a while, fretting about the injunction, he stays home in summer, but soon his yearning to return at least temporarily to his life as a *mejdoub* overcomes him: "Now he began to understand that the life here at home had been a pleasure only because he had known that at a certain moment he was going to leave it for the other life" (*CS*, 373).

The man's fate is sealed, however, when he is rounded up with the other usual suspects (beggars) and arrested for having no papers. He becomes trapped in his role as beggar/*mejdoub* and is placed in the madhouse, unable to convince authorities of his "true" identity. In the end, we might think, a perverse form of justice prevails. The fake *mejdoub* is caught in his own phony fabrication. As such, the tale could be read as a moral concerning the dangers accompanying pretense and duplicity. Yet we might also, to a degree, sympathize with the *mejdoub*'s attempt to break loose of the rigid confines of unitary personality, and feel his apprehension as just another example of how social structures limit and contain the radical imagination.

"The Waters of Izli," like "The Garden" and a number of stories in Bowles's next collection, *Midnight Mass*, challenges the authenticity of divine revelation. The tale is of two towns, Tamlat and Izli, the former more prosperous—literally on higher ground—than the latter. A fine spring is all Izli has in its favor, though no one from outside the village recognizes its value until, as a result of a stratagem, the spring becomes the burial place of a famous local saint, Sidi Bouhajja. Sidi Bouhajja's black stallion was to determine where the saint was buried. The saint's body would be attached to the horse, and the horse would be allowed to go where it pleased. And so, on the saint's death, Ramadi, owner of the property on which the spring was located, used his own mare (and the assistance of a snake charmer) to lure the saint's stallion to the spring. With this, "the men from Tamlat hid their chagrin and accepted the will of Allah" (*CS*, 383). Izli subsequently becomes the site of pilgrimages, and its prosperity soon surpasses that of Tamlat.

The weakest stories in the volume are "Things Gone and Things Still Here," "The Fqih," and "Istikhara, Anaya, Medagan, and the Medaganat." The title story, if indeed it can be called a story, is little more than a meditation on the status of superstitions and beliefs in contemporary Morocco. Like "The Garden," "The Fqih" (religious leader) gives a rather unflattering view of orthodox Islam. A young man goes to the *fqih* when his older brother is bitten by a dog and asks him what to do. The *fqih* advises that he lock his brother up. That he does, hitting his brother on the head with a hammer to gain his compliance. After a lengthy ordeal that takes the mother off to a neighboring village in search of the *fqih*, the boy is released. Fearing his brother's reprisals, he leaves for Casablanca.

"Istikhara, Anaya, Medagan and the Medaganat," set in the Sahara in the mid-twentieth century at a time when France was trying to establish hegemony over the various tribes of the region, is more anthropological in nature. It begins with a description of the concepts of *istikhara* and *anaya*, the first a sincere, formal prayer for dreams to guide the suppli-cant's actions, and the second a means of receiving amnesty from one's enemy. The upshot of the story is that the social order breaks down when traditional protocols are not followed: "To a Moslem, the failure of Medagan's attempt at *istikhara* is implicit in the facts. One may pray, but if one is not in a state of grace the prayer fails to get through. Once Medagan had betrayed his protectors, he was not in a condition which permitted contact with the Deity. And having construed his dreamless night as an instruction to seek *anaya*, by going out and requesting it immediately, without making even a gesture of self-defense, he doubt-less helped to bring about his own defeat," (*CS*, 403–4). The trouble with this piece is that no story is told. Though the setting here is that of "The Delicate Prey," the action remains flat and undramatic.

The tone and pattern of these last stories is similar. All, in one way or another, present scenarios that challenge claims based on divine revela-tion. In "Mejdoub" no one even suspects the difference between the real *mejdoub* and his impostor. We are left to believe that anyone claiming access to divine inspiration would go unchallenged. In "Fqih" we are left questioning the judgment of the Islamic judge. In "The Waters of Izli," what is attributed to divine causation is actually the result of self-interested human intervention, discreetly concealed. And in "Is-tikhara, Anaya, Medagan and the Medaganat," we see the results of corrupt and insincere applications of traditional moral codes.

Things Gone and Things Still Here, as the title suggests, dwells on the meaning of modern life in a period of tremendous social change. The nostalgia for the waning past order, felt in "The Time of Friendship," becomes even more apparent in later Bowles stories in which one senses an effort to hang onto those things which are vanishing or have already vanished. The storytelling impulse itself can be viewed as a conservative force, a feeble effort to keep, if nothing else, at least the memory of a past order alive.

As an outsider, a participant-observer, Bowles, like the anthropologist, is placed in an inherently awkward relation to his subject.[64] His is a longing for a past that is not his own, and his representations of Morocco, fictional though they may be, have always seemed to validate the traditional, at the same time containing faint mockery of superstitious habits. This attitude has, at various times, made Bowles a controversial figure within Morocco. Charges have been made that Bowles's fictionalizations of the country merely reinforce traditional stereotypes of Morocco as being a place of superstition, magic, and wonder—images the modernizers would like to downplay. Some of the stories in *Things Gone and Things Still Here* certainly present many of those images and suggest how popular beliefs are shifting with modernization and urbanization. In the title story, for example, Bowles writes:

> For people living in the country today the djinn is an accepted, if dreaded, concomitant of daily life. The world of djenoun is too close for comfort.[65] Among the Moroccans it is not a question of summoning them to aid you, but simply of avoiding them. Their habitat is only a few feet below ours, and is an exact duplication of the landscape above-ground. . . . City people often say there are no djenoun, not any more, or in any case not in the city. In the country, where life is the same as before and where there are not many automobiles and other things containing iron, they admit that djenoun probably still exist. But they add that the automobiles will eventually drive them all away, for they can't stand the proximity of iron and steel. Then it will be only in the distant mountains and the desert where you will need to worry about them. (*CS*, 407–8).

Clearly, the bias is in favor of the *djenoun*-based worldview, as opposed to the rational, secular world of the city, even though Bowles would say that it is next to impossible for the Westerner to wholly enter into those "primitive" forms of belief.

Bowles has faced a number of the same criticisms leveled against other colonial and postcolonial Western writers.[66] His detractors sometimes go on to point out that his Morocco is not only an imaginary place but a place that bears little resemblance to the modern country beset by problems of unemployment, overpopulation, hunger, and illiteracy. His representations, the argument goes, do the country an injustice by ignoring real social problems and by perpetuating and playing off of Western perceptions, fantasies, and images of a primitive, superstition-ridden Morocco.[67] Without wishing to overlook or underestimate the nature of these charges, I would suggest that Bowles's life and work should, rather than being dismissed or disparaged for these reasons, be put in the context of colonial and postcolonial dynamics and recognized not only for its artistic merits but for the way it uniquely inscribes a chapter in the continuing history of relations between East and West.

Midnight Mass

The stories brought together in *Midnight Mass* (1981) and *Unwelcome Words* (1988) have not yet enjoyed the popularity that those in Bowles's *Collected Stories* have, despite the inclusion of many of them in *A Distant Episode: The Selected Stories* (1988). These recent volumes, however, contain many splendid stories, demonstrating the author's versatility and mastery of the genre. Bowles does not simply serve up tried and popular dishes, though familiar flavors are recognizable. He rather offers novel treats, lending both expected and surprising pleasures.

These later stories, consistently sharper than those of *Things Gone and Things Still Here*, depict a more settled mode of life and experience. There are, to be sure, expatriates in many of these stories, yet they tend now, like Bowles himself during this period, to be rather sedentary, and the conflicts that arise generally pertain to managing local help or dealing with property, rather than those arising from more daring wanderings into hostile, foreign terrain. They describe a Tangier beset by the pains of growth and often inscribe the conflicts of values that accompany modernization. Though no more optimistic about the plight of the world, Bowles seems to have adopted more of the wry, ironic wit that sometimes accompanies the resignation to one's fate in old age.

Midnight Mass signals stylistic as well as thematic shifts. Bowles's characteristic sense of sureness and economy is as sharp as ever. Each sentence drives the story a step closer to its logical outcome. The storyteller gives his listeners what they need when they need it. We get not a word more than necessary. These stories, especially those in *Unwelcome Words*, have that pellucid, bonelike quality we associate with Beckett's later work. This the writer achieves in part by abandoning the use of quotation marks to indicate dialogue, so that speech, description, and the subtle intrusion of the narrator's ironic wit merge fluidly, creating the semblance of a seamless, integrated whole.

Many of these stories, like those in the preceding volume, have a discernible "oral" quality about them; they often give the reader the sense that the storyteller is right there, telling us the story. More frequently than before, Bowles chooses a first-person narrator. Again the writer's involvement with translation projects during this period, particularly in collaboration with Mohamad Mrabet, is probably responsible in part for these stylistic developments.

If there be a central motif in this collection of stories, a figure in the carpet, so to speak, it might be the preoccupation with houses, the structures we inhabit. The pattern and theme of many of these stories supply yet further examples of what Richard F. Patteson identifies as one of Bowles's central concerns: "That which lies outside is presented as potentially hostile and threatening, yet the barriers, the shelters, erected to keep the danger out are insufficient" (Patteson, 3). The titles of two of the stories, "In the Red Room" and "The Little House," point to this emphasis, as does the content of many other stories.

In some instances stories begin with the presentation of a house, which becomes a fragile haven for human life or a contested site of opposing values. In "Madame and Ahmed" Mrs. Pritchard's house, surrounded by impressive gardens, "was at the top of a cliff overlooking the sea; the winds sweeping through the Strait of Gibraltar struck the spot first, and blew harder there."[68] Two worldviews compete with each other under one roof, literally, in "The Little House," which opens, "The little house had been built sixty or seventy years ago on the main street of what had been a village which seemed several miles outside of town; now the town had crept up on all sides" (*MM*, 21). In either case, the ensuing dramas reveal a strain the structure ultimately withstands only after a reconfiguration of those patterns of life which they contain.

In the title story, "Midnight Mass," a Westerner actually loses possession of his childhood home in Tangier. Eight years after his mother's death, he comes back to Tangier to reclaim the house and finds it "in even worse condition than he had expected it to be. He had naively assumed that because he paid their wages promptly each month, the servants would make an attempt to keep it in order" (*MM*, 10). He should have known better.

At a Christmas Eve party, the man agrees to let a Moroccan painter use a room in the house. This foothold is all the Moroccan needs. The Westerner is squeezed out: "He did not go to Tangier at Eastertime, nor yet during the summer. In September he got word that the painter's very rich and influential family had taken possession of the entire house" (*MM*, 19). His lawyer is unable to evict them. The story symbolically shows the end of a certain kind of European postcolonial presence and the growing determination of Moroccans to conduct their own affairs.

Part 1

The Morocco of the 1980s was far different from that Bowles had first come to, in its colonial period, 50 years earlier.

Both "The Dismissal" and "Madame and Ahmed" are stories involving relationships between Western expatriate home owners in Tangier and their help. Built into the structure of these relationships are not only a difference in culture but a difference in class. Given the value of foreign currency and the very low wage levels in Morocco, most expatriates have easily been able to afford help. In some cases—such as that of the late Malcolm Forbes, one of Tangier's most notorious expatriates, best known for his collection of toy soldiers and the pair of Harleys he kept by the door of his Marshan mansion—the difference was vast indeed.

Naturally, stories about maids, drivers, and gardeners—their level of competence, their mishaps, their cleverness, problems in communication and trust—circulate in the expatriate community. "Madame and Ahmed" tells of one episode in the relationship between a wealthy Western woman and her Moroccan gardener, Ahmed: "She felt that they knew and understood one another in a basic and important fashion, even though Ahmed never had learned to pronounce her name. For him she was Madame" (*MM*, 100).

When the garden is doing poorly, her friends urge her to get rid of Ahmed, her gardener of 11 years. Ahmed, in order to keep his position, employs his wit when occasion presents itself. One day a man comes and persuades Madame to buy some plants Ahmed recognizes as being from the municipal garden. The man makes no attempt to hide his intention to take Ahmed's position. That night, after the plants have been put in, Ahmed sneaks out and snips the roots off them. The next day Madame notices the plants wilting in the sun, discovers the cause, and blames the thieves, just as Ahmed had hoped she would. To get rid of the thieves when they returned, Ahmed lies, saying Madame knew where they got the plants from and would report them to the police if they ever showed their faces again. "Ahmed, what would I do without you?" Madame exclaims in gratitude. When she asks what Ahmed said to get rid of the men, he lies again: "I told him no true Moslem would play tricks on a woman with no husband" (*MM*, 105).

The story is rife with deceit. Everyone is guilty of something— Madame for thinking of dismissing her longtime gardener, the peddlers for stealing the plants, and Ahmed for tricking and lying to his employer. Not much harm comes to anyone, however, and we feel that in the end each got what he deserved.

The expatriate in "The Eye," which appeared in the collection of *Best American Stories of 1979*, meets a worse fate than Madame at the hands of his help. We might imagine this story of an eccentric expatriate, Duncan Marsh, to be a popular one with those in the community.[69] Bowles's telling, in the first person, seems to be but one more telling of a well-known tale, heard second- or thirdhand, transformed and embellished in so many retellings. Calling the story "laconic, chilly, passionless," Joyce Carol Oates has noted that it "reads as if it had no narrator at all, and aspires to a condition of sheer narrative bereft of character—a tale told by no one in particular (its 'hero,' never directly glimpsed, is dead before the story opens), which nevertheless possesses an uncanny suspenseful power."[70]

"Ten or twelve years ago," the story begins, "there came to live in Tangier a man who would have done better to stay away" (*MM*, 151). Members of the English-speaking community, we are told, said he got what he deserved. With a very sharp understanding of how expatriate communities function, Bowles writes, "These people often have reactions similar to those of certain primitive groups: when misfortune overtakes one of their number, the others by mutual consent refrain from offering him aid, and merely sit back to watch, certain that he has called his suffering down upon himself. He has become taboo, and is incapable of receiving help" (*MM*, 151). This sacrificial abandonment no doubt occurs partly because expatriates, especially in places such as Morocco, where manners and customs are so different from their own, live shipwrecked existences and feel they can ill afford to cast a rope to a drowning compatriate without the risk of being pulled along with him into the hostile sea.

Marsh, whom the narrator says he never himself knew, evidently came to Tangier, rented a home in the Djamaa el Mokra area, became ill, and eventually went back on a stretcher to his home in Vancouver, Canada, where he soon died. The scuttlebutt was that Marsh was but "one more victim of a slow poisoning by native employees" (*MM*, 152). Two interesting facts turn the case into a mystery for the narrator. First, Marsh left the nightwatchman with a certificate guaranteeing his livelihood should his employer leave Morocco. Second, the doctor examining Marsh reported curious patterns of incisions on the bottoms of the patient's feet.

The narrator himself becomes a kind of sleuth when he meets, seven or so years after the affair, the nightwatchman, Larbi, now a waiter in a Tangier restaurant. When Larbi lets the narrator see the written document Marsh left with him, he finds it is worded in such a way that the waiter could not collect a cent. Driven by his desire to solve the mystery, the narrator makes it well worth Larbi's while to accompany him to Marsh's vacant villa, where, on the porch, the Moroccan unfolds the story.

All would have been fine, apparently, if Marsh had not decided to replace his cook, Yasmina, who came with the place. Larbi is called in to find a replacement. The replacement brings her baby, whose crying drives Marsh to distraction. One day, in order to try to stop the baby from crying, Marsh gets down on all fours and makes a fierce face at the baby, causing it to burst into hysterics. When the baby becomes ill, of course, everyone concludes it is because this Westerner has put the evil eye on the girl. The incisions cut on Marsh's feet, Larbi says, were part of what was necessary to undo the spell.

Even with a number of the questions answered, the narrator admits "a vague sense of disappointment" because he had "not only expected, but actually hoped, to find someone on whom the guilt might be fixed. What constitutes a crime? There was no criminal intent—only a mother moving in the darkness of ancient ignorance" (*MM*, 162).

Both the narrative technique and the thematic content of "The Eye" call to mind "Reminders of Bouselham" in *Things Gone and Things Still Here*. The story, which turns on the belief in the evil eye, reveals sharp differences in worldviews. Beyond this, the story presents the language issue in a way no other story in this volume does. English is the native tongue for the narrator, as well as for Bowles himself, yet in order to draw the story from Larbi, he uses Spanish, establishing a kind of neutral ground, much in the same way Bowles uses Spanish on a daily basis with his own driver, Abdelouahaïd, and with Mohamed Mrabet, who comes in every day to cook Bowles his dinner. When the narrator wants to gain even more trust, he speaks Arabic with Larbi. Bowles, like the narrator, understands and speaks the local Maghrebi dialect, though he does not read or write Arabic.

The 85-year-old French diplomat in "Rumor and a Ladder," unlike Marsh, engineers a smooth and fitting departure from Morocco. M. Ducros must in some way dispose of El Hafa, his home in Tangier, which houses a collection of mementos from his diplomatic career, and get as much as possible out of the country. Again we notice the postcolonial setting. The ruse by which M. Ducros gets his money out develops, as do most schemes, as a wedding of chance and design. Things begin with the old man falling from a ladder and breaking his leg. This brings to his home an Italian doctor, who, seeing some of Ducros's artwork, tells the diplomat, "[F]or the five Soutines alone I can get you two million French francs tomorrow" (*MM*, 142). The skeptical, law-abiding Ducros rejects the idea, saying it would be impossible to get the money out of the country because of laws restricting currency outflow.

In the meantime, M. Ducros tries to leave the country but is stopped by officials at the airport who, knowing he has been trying to sell his property, suspect the cast on his leg and rip it open. When Ducros lands back in Dr. Rinaldi's hands, they concoct a scheme. Ducros decides to sell his paintings and take out the money in the cast, fairly confident that this time the authorities will dare not check. As he puts it, "I've already been punished. Now I want to *deserve* that punishment!" (*MM*, 147).

The story succeeds not merely because of this central ironic twist but because of its wit and fine structure. A portion of the story near the beginning is told through a letter M. Ducros has written to his daughter, explaining the accident. It then moves back to an omniscient narrator, returning in the end to the letter, creating a kind of symmetry Bowles often achieves in his short musical compositions.

In a response to her reactions to the story, Bowles wrote to Millicent Dillon:

> It's interesting that you imagined that Monsieur Ducros had been "manipulating" from the beginning. I don't know from which part of the tale you got that impression; I thought I had arranged it logically. The reason I say it's interesting is that in reality "Monsieur Ducros" denounced himself anonymously after breaking his leg, thus making certain he'd be detained and examined. Then when nothing was discovered in the cast, he made a great geshcrei and got the French Ambassador in to complain, again making certain that when he took the money out he wouldn't be bothered. He got the money out safely. The only difference is that in my story there are paintings, and Monsieur Ducros is not premeditating anything; it's his mistreatment that causes him to make his decision.[71]

Bowles, as it turns out, had evidently told Dillon of the original incidents he transformed into a story.

These later stories, it should be added, are generally lighter in tone than earlier ones. One memorable comic moment in "Rumor and a Ladder" occurs when the diplomat and the doctor are confirming the price of the paintings:

You said two million as I recall.

Dr. Rinaldi laughed. If you want to throw in the Vlaminck, the Roualt and the Kokoschka, two and a quarter.

Monsieur Ducros threw up his hands. Kokoschka, indeed! I don't know one from the other. They're all equally inept. (*MM*, 147)

Another is in the closing portion of the letter to his daughter in Kuala Lumpur, where M. Ducros invokes Cocteau's playful *jeu de mots* on Kuala Lumpur—"*kuala l'impur*"—to which he adds, "But there are places far more impure!" (*MM*, 149). Tangier, for one.

The central characters in many of these later stories, such as this one, "Unwelcome Words," and "In Absentia," are older than in earlier works. One feels in the tone, and through the preoccupations of M. Ducros, the passing of an era, the attempt to cling—in memory if nowhere else—to a time gone by. When M. Ducros finds that the stationery in his Paris hotel, from which he writes the letter to his daughter, is printed—not embossed, as it had been on his last visit—he sees it as "a symbol of the times . . . The slow encroachment of poverty on all sides" (*MM*, 139). We might assume here that the character's response to his own times echoes that of the writer, who himself is keenly aware that his generation is passing and, with it, many cherished ways and values of a past era.

It would be a mistake to assume that Moroccans practice their peculiar forms of "justice" solely in regard to foreigners. While the wife in "The Husband" works as a maid for the Nazarenes and the boy gardens for an Englishman, the story centers on their own domestic lives, not on the interaction between expatriates and help. This story too begins with a house: "Abdallah lived with his wife in a two-room house on a hillside several miles from the center of town" (*MM*, 113). Abdallah commences an affair with a woman named Zohra. To help support himself and his new lover, he takes and sells a handful of silver spoons his wife had evidently already stolen from her employers. With the money he buys 10 goats, 2 of which, while Abdallah is napping, wander onto the road and are killed by a passing vehicle. Because farmers are held legally responsible for such incidents, Abdallah hires a boy to get rid of the carcasses. Finally, however, the law catches up with him and he is forced to give up 4 of his remaining goats to pay the fine. Word gets back to his wife, who makes a complaint and, with the help of the law, collects her husband's remaining goats. Again we feel as though justice, oddly enough, has been rendered.

A number of the stories without Western characters embody in some way the tensions within Moroccan society between traditional and modern values. In "The Little House" the clash between the old and the new is seen in the relationship between Lalla Aïcha and her daughter-in-law, Fatoma: "Ever since the older woman had moved in with them, Fatoma had been trying to persuade her to discard her haik and wear a djellaba like other women of the town, but Lalla Aïcha disapproved strongly of djellabas on women, saying that Moulay Youssef would surely have forbidden such a shameless custom. For Fatoma the haik was an emblem of rusticity; above all she did not want to be taken for a girl from the country. It filled her with shame to walk in the street beside a tottering old woman in a haik" (*MM*, 22–23).

When it comes time for the older woman to have a tumor removed, she "made it very clear that she had no faith in Nazarene medicines" (*MM*, 23). Lalla Aïcha places her faith in traditional saints and works her ways with poisons. Abdelkrim, in "The Dismissal," on the other hand, admits to himself, during a Jilali ceremony, that "if he himself were to invoke Sidi Maimoun or Sidi Rahal, he was certain they would pay him no attention; it was too late for young men to expect to get in touch with the saints" (*MM*, 40). For the younger generation of Moroccans, complete faith in traditional belief structures is doubtless more difficult in part, at least, because of intensified contact with a secular, capitalistic West that has seduced them with more profitable, glamorous expectations.

"The Empty Amulet" perhaps best demonstrates this conflict between old and new values. Upholding traditional "Islamic" values is Habiba's "unusually strict" father, who bars his daughter from getting an education and insists she stay at home. She has no say whatsoever in the family's plans for her marriage. The man to whom Habiba's father consents to give his daughter is a medical intern named Moumen, "a young man with modern ideas" who, we are told, "did not lock his bride into the house when he went out to work. On the contrary, he urged her to get to know the married women of the quarter" (*MM*, 129). These married women, Habiba discovers, are always complaining of various aches, pains, and maladies, and to remedy them, they make pilgrimages to the tombs and shrines of Sidi Hussein or Sidi Larbi, a practice Moumen, who works in a modern hospital, finds primitive and embarrassing.

Finally, in order to stop what he judges to be her foolishness, he has an amulet made for her. Instead of holding a real *baraka*, or inscription from the Koran with the blessings of a sheikh, however, it merely contains a crumpled cigarette paper. After the birth of their first child, Habiba discovers the bogus *baraka*, becomes furious with her husband's sacrilegious trick, and asks for a divorce.

The shape this debate between fundamental religious values and secular ideas takes in this story resembles the clash between modern, "Western" medicine and traditional spiritual values in the fine novella by the Egyptian writer Yahyia Haqqi, *The Saint's Lamp.*[72] We are told, for instance, in Bowles's story, of Habiba's fear of "the nauseating medicinal odors, the bins of bloody bandages, the shining syringes" (*MM*, 130). Moumen, on the other hand, "considered the pills and injections used by the Nazarenes superior to the baraka of the saints" (*MM*, 131). In Haqqi's story the English-educated Isma'il returns to Egypt to find his cousin/fiancée stricken with an eye disease. Alarmed and disgusted, he rejects the cure of the oil from the lamp of the Sayyida Zainab Mosque in favor of Western, scientific methods. Finally, though, when the condition worsens under his own treatment, he returns to the mosque for the lamp's oil. While Haqqi's story seeks an integration of West and East, old and new, Bowles's tale merely presents the dynamic, the way in which the two worldviews clash, without offering any judgment on the value of one or the other, or concluding with a symbolic reconciliation. The divorce at the end of the story might even suggest that the two views cannot very well coincide.

This conflict between East and West takes a somewhat different form in "Here to Learn," the longest, most ambitious, and most innovative story in the volume. As with so many of Bowles's stories, the narrative structure of this novella is determined by the cause of a journey. This time, however, the conventional routes are reversed. Rather than following the journey of a Westerner traveling to the East, the story chronicles the journey of a young Moroccan woman, Malika, as she moves from the familiar East to the strange and somewhat exotic West. The story's title is taken from a comment Malika's father had often made: "Allah has sent us here to learn."

Along the course of her journey, Malika learns many things. Elevators, light switches, hot and cold water faucets, skiing, birth control, and the English language are just a few of things she encounters for the first time. For the Western reader of the story, the familiar is defamiliarized; customs, habits, and structures we take for granted are cast in the uncanny strangeness of the first encounter. We look at ourselves through the eyes of the other, very much as we would look through the eyes of an anthropologist from the Trobriand Islands trying to comprehend Los Angeles.[73]

In the opening scenes we see Malika in her native Moroccan village. The first thing we learn about her is that she is pretty, which only makes her an attractive prey for men in the village. She must always remain on guard, hiding her beauty the best she can with veils or dabs of mud. It would seem that with the sexual oppression, the strict family control, the debilitating effects of poverty, and the lack of hope, Malika would have been more than ready to leave home. We are told, however, that "it had never occurred to her to hate the town, for she assumed that anywhere else would be more or less the same" (*MM*, 45). There were not many options for a woman in Malika's position.

Fate, not exercise of will or the development of a plan, is responsible for Malika's escape. One day on her way to market, Malika happens on a scene with a group of villagers surrounding a long, yellow car driven by a "Nazarene." They are upset that the man is trying to take pictures of the women, a violation of Muslim principles. Because she had learned Spanish from Catholic nuns, Malika is asked to communicate their objection to the foreigner. Before she knows it, she is in the car with the foreigner, driving away from the village, expecting that at some point he will buy her eggs, then send her on her way. When the man asks whether she would like to be taken back to the village or go on with him to Tetuan, she chooses to go with him. After all, it would be an adventure. In her own view of things, *Mektoub* (it was written): "It seemed to her that she had always known something strange like this would happen to her one day" (*MM*, 49). That rather fatalistic worldview which governs her consciousness accounts for Malika's yielding almost passively to every new turn of her bizarre, fairy-tale-like journey. All that happens is meant to happen, and her role is not to try to alter the course of destiny (for that would be absurd) but to take things as they happen and do the best she can.

This incident with the Nazarene and the car is merely the beginning of a chain of events that unfolds with a surprising, inevitable logic, as she moves from the company of one man to the next, her journey's trajectory introducing her, step by step, to the West. The first man, whose name she learns is Tim, puts Malika up in his apartment in Tangier, teaches her the ways of lovemaking, and obtains a passport for her. When Tim must go to London on business, he leaves her safely in the hands of two men who, he assures her, "don't make love with girls" (*MM*, 56). Then along comes Tony, a tall, well-to-do Irishman whose Maserati and promises to buy her more clothes impress her enough to accept his proposal to accompany him to Spain. Madrid, where Malika's wardrobe is upgraded and expanded, seems but a prelude to Paris, where Malika meets Tony's "sister," Dinah, who in turn takes her to Cortina d' Ampezzo while Tony is off in London.

Malika's fundamental curriculum throughout her journey consists of magazines, especially fashion magazines, from which she gets her ideas, models her poses, and shapes her desires. Even the idea of skiing had been placed in her mind from pictures in magazines Malika continually studied and amused herself with: "Malika saw that the ground was white and the people, whose clothing was not at all elegant, wore long boards on their feet" (*MM*, 64). This, we assume, would certainly be exotic from the perspective of someone who had lived in North Africa all her life.

In Cortina Malika meets Tex, the last in a string of Western men, who takes her first to Switzerland, marries her, and flies with her back to his home in Los Angeles. By this time she begins to realize how far she has come from home. On the flight "[s]he shut her eyes and sat quietly, feeling that she had gone much too far away—so far that now she was no where. Outside the world, she whispered to herself in Arabic, and shivered" (*MM*, 76).

Los Angeles is about as far as Malika could get, geographically and in every other imaginable way, from the Moroccan countryside. It is, in short, exotic from her point of view. Malika takes in the freeways, the social habits, the rights of married women, the architecture, and the arrangement of space all with a sense of awe and incomprehension. In the narrative presentation of these first impressions, we can see ourselves through strangers' eyes: "During these weeks, when she watched the life in the streets, she could find no pattern to it. The people were always on their way somewhere else, and they were in a hurry. . . . In Morocco, in Europe, there had been people who were busy doing things, and there had been others watching. Always, no matter where one was or what one was doing, there were the watchers. She had the impression that in America everyone was going somewhere and no one sat watching" (*MM*, 79).

Tex's sudden death shocks Malika primarily, it seems, because she is uncertain what will happen to her now. Tex had, in a chauvinistic way, kept her from certain knowledge, particularly concerning financial matters. At the time of Tex's death, Malika does not know the value of money, how much Tex has, where it comes from, or how to handle it. This is just one of the things she learns about on her journey. In a comic moment after F.T., Tex's financial consultant, has assured Malika that she need not worry about money, that she will have an income of $50,000 a month, Malika innocently asks, "Is that enough?"

After Tex's death, Malika remains independent and continues her education under the tutelage of a Miss Galper until, at Miss Galper's suggestion, they set off by ship, from San Pedro, on a European tour. At Cadiz Malika thinks of home again and plans a return to her village. As she encounters the stares and crude habits of Arab men in Algeciras she is forcefully reminded of her native country, just across the straits. Going home, going back to her mother, was, Malika concludes, "included in the pattern" (*MM*, 93). Her hopes for a happy, triumphant return are crushed when she finds the village transformed almost beyond recognition, her mother dead, and herself also radically different:

> She made her way up along the empty moonlit street until she came to a small open square from which, in the daytime at least, her mother's house was visible ahead, at the edge of the barranca. Now as she looked, the moon's light did not seem to strike it at all; she could see no sign of it. She hurried on, already assailed by a nightmarish premonition, and then she stopped, her mouth open in disbelief. The house was not there. Even the land where it had stood was gone. Mina Glagga's and all the houses bordering on the gully had disappeared. Bulldozers had made a new landscape of emptiness, a great embankment of earth, ashes and refuse that stretched downward to the bottom of the ravine. The little house with its garden had been just below where she now stood. She felt her throat tighten painfully as she told herself that it no longer existed. (*MM*, 95–96)

The action in "Here to Learn" is consistently presented, much like in, say, James's *The Ambassadors*, from the perspective of the main character, Malika. The effect of this technique in this story is that we, as readers, experience the novelties of Malika's encounter with the West much as Malika herself experiences them. Bowles is able, thus, to generate sympathy for his central character and at the same time maintain a control over the narrative that allows for comic, ironic play. An example of this is Bowles's handling of Malika's first exposure to homosexuality. When Tim tells her that she will be looked after by his friends Bobby and Peter, she thinks "how clever Tim was to have been able to find two such presentable eunuchs with so little apparent effort." And she soon realizes "that there were a good many more eunuchs in Tangier than she had suspected" (*MM*, 56).

Another impressive feature of this story is the amount of ground covered. Both time and space are collapsed in the novella. We move from Morocco to Spain to Switzerland to Paris to Los Angeles with astonishing rapidity, creating a pace and sense of movement not unlike that in Voltaire's *Candide*. With the succession of these short and episodic sections we are given not merely a slice of life but something more like the extended development of the character's life, though without the depth of character we generally associate with a novel.

In shaping Malika's narrative, Bowles simply inscribes, this time reversing the direction, a process of cultural encounter he himself had experienced when, as a young man, he moved from America to Europe to Morocco. We might also speculate that Bowles's extended exile in Morocco helped him sympathetically to construct Malika's journey to the West, looking at it with the strangeness of an outsider. The writer had also had experience watching Moroccans encounter the West for the first time—Ahmed Yacoubi, Larbi Layachi, then finally Mohamed Mrabet, who went with him to Los Angeles in 1968.

Malika's travel takes place under conditions far different from those normally governing the Westerner's travel to Morocco. To begin with, she does not leave independently. She must rely on men, whose motives are far from altruistic, for her escape. Her beauty is, time after time, her passport to fresh men and new destinations. Until Tex dies, she is totally dependent on men, a position that, given her upbringing, she understandably does not try to alter. Her freedom, then, in the form of Tex's inheritance, is not the outcome of a hard-fought struggle. Malika is at no point an ardent feminist. She merely takes things as they come, and her story is as fanciful and delightful as that of Cinderella.

Midnight Mass, like a number of previous volumes, contains stories set in places other than North Africa. Particularly noteworthy are "Kitty," another tale of transformation, and two set in Asia. As a story of transformation, "Kitty" belongs to the same category as "Allal," "The Scorpion," and, perhaps, "The Circular Valley." The story of Kitty, however, is considerably more benign and reads almost like a children's story. Bowles, in fact, has said that it was written as a child's story, for a Simon and Schuster collection titled *Wonders* (personal interview).

The story is different from "Allal" in that the young girl in the story actually wants to become something else. She asks her mother why her name is "Kitty" and, receiving no satisfactory response, decides "her name was Kitty because some day she was going to grow up into a cat" (*MM*, 107). Her interpretation begins to shape her destiny. Gradually, she begins to grow whiskers, ears, and fur. Her limbs are transformed, and she develops padded paws and claws, enabling her to catch birds. "When one of the birds came very close to her," Bowles writes, "she sprang forward and caught it. And at that moment she knew that she was no longer a girl at all, and that she would never have to be one again" (*MM*, 108).

Despite all of this, her mother refuses to believe in the transformation. The reader too is likely to think of the transformation as being wholly psychological until Kitty's neighbors recognize her as a cat when she goes to them to get some milk, meowing. They exclaim "Well, if that isn't the cutest kitten!" (*MM*, 109). External perceptions now validate and reinforce the changes Kitty, internally, had begun to effect. So smooth is her transformation that one would be hard-pressed to determine where Kitty's identity as a young girl gave way to her identity as a cat.

As is so often the case with stories of transformation—notably, the most famous of all, Kafka's "Metamorphosis"—this one displays deep psychological yearnings and unfulfilled desires. Barely masked beneath this narrative surface, just as in Kafka's "Metamorphosis," are the familiar features of the child-parent struggle. It is, in part, we might speculate, the mother's rejection of Kitty's fantastic constructions that energizes and stimulates the actual transformation. This same frustration with adult reluctance to engage in the make-believe world of children is, as we have seen, a theme in many other Bowles stories, such as "Pages from Cold Point," "By the Water," and "The Frozen Fields."

In the end, Kitty is recognized and affirmed by her mother for what she wants to be. When Kitty goes home, fully transformed into a cat, she finds her mother crying over her lost daughter, before a policeman: "Well, the pretty pussycat. . . . Where did *you* come from?" Kitty then jumps into her mother's lap and receives the affection she has craved. "At last," we are told, "she was living exactly the life she always had wished for" (*MM*, 111).

Though "At the Krungthep Plaza" is the weaker of the two Asian stories in the volume, issues raised in it are pertinent. The conflict between the American abroad and the native is raised to the level of governmental policy and local reactions to that policy. The central character in the story is a Thai hotel manager who capitulates to an American security request to search hotel rooms along the route to be taken by the visiting American president's motorcade. The manager must then deal with his guests' complaints, primarily those of an

Englishman who submits that "It's an affront to your guests to allow the Americans into the rooms" (*MM*, 127). The hotel manager won't be cowed, and slips into his role as an able henchman of American interests in Thailand.

Far superior is "In the Red Room," set in Sri Lanka. Included in Shannon Ravenal's collection of *The Best American Short Stories of the Eighties*,[74] the story came out first in an exclusive, fine edition published by Sylvester and Orphanos of Los Angeles. Three hundred and thirty copies of the story were printed (at a price of $50), all signed by the author. Three hundred were numbered, 26 were lettered, and 4 bore the printed names of their recipients.[75] Because of publishing agreements Bowles had made for this exclusive publishing venture, the story did not appear in the first Black Sparrow edition of *Midnight Mass*, though it has appeared as the last story in subsequent editions.

"In the Red Room," like "The Eye," is told by a first-person narrator who, in the course of telling the story, presents and solves a sort of mystery. As is generally the case with mysteries, a veil lies between the teller and/or detective and comprehensive knowledge of the scene. Behavior is seen, but it is not understood until, through deduction or details supplied by outside sources, an understanding of the past is gained.

Part of the complication in this story can be attributed to the American narrator's position as outsider. The narrator begins the story by saying that his parents were visiting him when the events he is about to describe took place: "Originally I had felt some qualms about encouraging their visit. . . . But I had underestimated their resilience; they made a greater show of adaptability than I had thought possible, and seemed entirely content with everything" (*MM*, 163). Events central to the story begin to unfold when they visit the Botanical Gardens and are accosted by a young Singhalese whom they have never seen before: "He wore white flannels and a crimson blazer, and his sleek black hair gave off a metallic blue glint in the sunlight" (*MM*, 165). Somehow, despite the narrator's usual inclination not to get involved with strangers, they get wrapped up in conversation with the young man, who later introduces himself as Justu Gonzag, and finally accept his invitation to join him for a cold ginger beer.

After they have drinks together in the pavilion, Gonzag lures them to see a house he thinks would be just right for them. Ensnared in the web of his hospitality, they follow. Once they are in the house, he escorts them into the red room: "It was a small room, made to seem still smaller by having been given glistening crimson walls and ceiling. Almost all the space was filled by a big bed with a satin coverlet of a slightly darker red" (*MM*, 169). He behaves a little strangely, and they leave, remarking how the young man seemed to treat the room in the unoccupied house as a kind of shrine and wondering why he has taken them to the red room in the first place.

The mystery remains unsolved until, quite by accident, the narrator one day becomes involved in a conversation with Weston, an employee of the Chartered Bank, who fills him in on the story of Gonzag: "[It] began on the day after Gonzag's wedding, when he stepped into a servant's room and found his bride in bed with the friend who had been best man. How he happened to have a pistol with him was not explained, but he shot them both in the face, and later chopped their bodies into pieces" (*MM*, 172). The room the narrator and his parents had been shown was, we learn, the scene of the crime, a place Gonzag liked to bring visitors to.

The question left with the narrator is whether or not to relay this solution of the mystery to his parents, who are about to leave the country. When the subject comes up just as they are about to leave, the narrator is faced with the choice of either revealing or withholding what he knows, and chooses to spare them. His mother, after all "had got to the core without needing the details" when she guesses that the "room had a particular meaning for him. It was a kind of shrine." The narrator replies, "Of course, there's no way of knowing":

> She smiled. Well, what you know won't hurt you.
> I had heard her use the expression a hundred times without ever being able to understand what she meant by it, because it seemed so patently untrue. But for once it was apt. I nodded my head and said: That's right. (*MM*, 174)

From a letter Bowles wrote to Millicent Dillon in 1982, we learn that the story, written in 1980, "came in a letter from Leonardo de Arrizabalaga, who had had the experience in Baguio, Filipinas, when he was traveling with his parents." Bowles goes on to say that he changed the setting and substituted his own parents: "The only important difference between the actuality and the fiction is the son's decision not to tell his parents the story behind the red room. In reality the parents as well as the son heard it, after they got back to Manila."[76]

In his introduction to *The Best American Short Stories, 1984*, John Updike justifies his selection of "In the Red Room." "Paul Bowles," he

117

writes, "describes, with an eerie indirection and softness of tone, a blood-soaked private shrine." Updike places the story in the context of others that admit us to a kind of personal sanctuary: "The inner spaces that a good short story lets us enter are the old apartments of religion. People in fiction are not only, as E. M. Forster pointed out in his *Aspects of the Novel*, more sensitive than people one meets; they are more religious. Religion and fiction both aver, with Kierkegaard, that "subjectivity is truth"; each claims importance for the ephemeral sensations of consciousness that material science must regard as accidents, as epiphenomena. Fictional technique and the craft of suspense are affected: without a transcendental ethics, of what significance are our decisions?"[77] Indeed, that is the question we are left asking on reading Bowles.

Unwelcome Words and Other Stories

Bowles has often, for one reason or another, turned to small presses for the publication of his stories. That works are published one place or another—or not at all—is often a result of configuration of various factors, including personal friendships, the writer's knowledge of and felt affinities with particular journals and publishers, editors' tastes, expectation of financial gain, desired audience, luck of the draw, and so forth. On one of our walks through the streets and alleys of Tangier, I remember Bowles complaining to me about how little he got from his publishers—a common complaint among authors, evidently justified in this case. When I ventured that his stories might easily be taken on by a major U.S. publishing house, he looked at me with something like disbelief and said, "You really think so?" I went on to ask why he often chose to publish with relatively small firms, such as Black Sparrow and Peter Owen. He replied that he had never liked being rejected and would rather send his work somewhere he thought it had a good chance of being accepted and published than risk it being turned down.

That Bowles has often chosen small presses might be linked to his expatriate status and his personal wishes, as much as to necessity. Expatriation has marginalized the writer to some extent and, to his relief, saved him from much of the hype and hoopla that surrounds the American publishing industry. The specter of sitting in a bookstore signing hundreds of copies of books an hour would be anathema to Bowles. Yet he seems also to have had an uncanny sense of the market value of his image as outsider, connoisseur of the exotic.

One can imagine the name of the publisher of one of Bowles's most recent collections of stories, Tombouctou, as being particularly appealing to the writer. Michael Wolfe, publisher of Tombouctou, offers this anecdote of how he came to publish *Unwelcome Words*:

> It came about naturally, as I recall. I had published two translations of Mrabet's work; transcribed a long book by Larbi Layachi, *The Jealous Lover*, which Tombouctou also published; and written *Invisible Weapons*, set in Tangier. We were sitting in Paul's *sala* talking about an

essay of his about parrots. I wondered if he'd written anything since on the subject. He went into his study and brought back two of the monologues in typescript. I read them while he sat there. They contained nothing about parrots, but we agreed to publish them anyway, along with a third monologue he showed me the next day. When I returned to the U.S. I balked at producing such a tiny volume; he sent me everything else he had finished by that time. I arranged the pieces into a sequence that seemed agreeable to me, and he approved. Then, I set about getting the money to publish the book. That part took, nearly, forever.[78]

Until the publication of *A Distant Episode: The Selected Stories of Paul Bowles*, none of the stories in this volume had been widely known, because of their limited circulation. Some of them bear likenesses to those in *Midnight Mass*: they display with knifelike precision the eccentricities and perversions of local characters, stories gleaned from Bowles's long-term residence in Tangier and transformed through the art of telling. There is also something new in a number of these stories. First is a refreshing stylistic variation, introduced in a trio of dramatic monologues. Then, in the title story—and in "In Absentia," a story published after the volume was produced—the usually reticent Bowles (or a character like him) coyly inserts himself as the letter writer in the story.

"Julian Vreden's story is a classic and uniquely American tale of revenge."[79] Thus ends the volume's first story, "Julian Vreden." This "classic and uniquely American tale of revenge," as it turns out, is a tale of patricide and matricide. Once again Bowles has made the son's battle for autonomy the subject of his fiction. Its particular characterization here, however, is further removed from the author's personal experience than is the case with, say, "The Frozen Fields."

The storyteller begins by situating himself in the present (the 1980s, we presume) and calling up the memory of a past incident, seemingly true, given the reference to its journalistic source: "Roughly four decades ago New York newspapers carried the report of a domestic tragedy, poignant but unexceptional. A middle-aged husband and wife celebrated New Year's Eve by remaining quietly at home and joining in a suicide pact" (*UW*, 11). What initially appears a double suicide turns out otherwise. The narrator unravels the mystery in a few swift strokes, and accounts for motives. Not long after the "suicides," the couple's 20-year-old son, Julian, and "his friend Mark" cash in on insurance policies and move from Florida back to New York—into his parents' apartment. Suspicions grow, and the police apprehend Julian, who admits to doctoring his parents' cocktails with poison on New Year's Eve. "Indeed," we are told, "he made it clear that he considered himself amply justified in his behavior" (*UW*, 12).

His justification, we learn, stems from mounting resentment of his parents' restriction of his personal liberties. The parents, thus, in Julian's mind, stand in relation to him as does a tyrant to an oppressed constituency. His mother would chastise him for reading poetry. His father would exclaim, "What a fairy we've got for a son!" (The son may, in fact, be homosexual.) In short, the murder was the logical culmination of years of "uninterrupted long-term parental persecution" (*UW*, 12).

For his misdeed, Julian and Mark "are condemned to life imprisonment in a New Jersey hospital for the criminally insane." Though he stops short of condoning the acts, the storyteller's sympathies seem to lie with the young murderer, who has—granted, in an extreme fashion—acted against elements that repress the creative spirit and the free development of sexual identity. In the end, the narrator reflects on the act and on the nature of punishment: "Criminal? Yes. Insane? Not likely. The desire to avenge acts of injustice committed against one's person can scarcely be considered a sign of dementia" (*UW*, 14).

"Hugh Harper" and "Dinner at Sir Nigel's" depict other forms of perversion. These stories confirm a claim Bowles made as early as 1958, about living in Tangier: "Living in Tangier means being witness to an array of unlikely episodes in a whole series of strange characters. Nowhere have I seen a larger collection of eccentrics."[80] In her book *The Dream at the End of the World: Paul Bowles and the Literary Renegades in Tangier*, Michelle Green offers a veritable feast of the most bizarre, perverse, and outrageous behavior imaginable. As for Hugh Harper, his "purely gastronomical" habit, we are told, "consisted in a taste for human blood." When Harper's unconventional appetite comes to light in any community he happens to be residing in, it is viewed with grave suspicion, even outrage, though apparently "it had no sexual facet." His family, fearful of scandal, ushers him out of England, a country known to have little tolerance for publicly demonstrated deviance. When, finally, he is booted out of Naples, "it was to be expected that the next place for Hugh Harper to settle in would be Morocco" (*UW*, 29). Tangier seems just the place for his queer habit to thrive, until his glib talk about his proclivities prompts local intervention. The imam proclaims that "the Christian must be prevented from drinking any more Moslem blood," and Harper is given eight days to leave the country: "Where he went after being declared *persona non grata* in Morocco is not known" (*UW*, 31).

Sir Nigel Renfrew is another notorious member of Tangier's expatriate community. As with many of the later stories, the storyteller dips into the past ("In those days," the story begins) for his subject. Sir Nigel is enigmatic in a way reminiscent of Duncan Marsh in "The Eye." Before he is invited along with a group of Western journalists to dine at Sir Nigel's, the narrator knows only what everyone else knows—that Sir Nigel had just two servants.

The surprise comes after dinner, when Sir Nigel announces, "You're going to see something you'll not forget, by God. And remember, they come of their own accord" (*UW*, 46). The evening's entertainment, the floor show, so to speak, begins when "a tall, muscular black woman strode in." Five more girls follow her, each taking a seated position beside a drum. Once the rhythm is established, Sir Nigel appears, wearing jodhpurs and black leather boots, "brandishing a long circus whip." He cracks the whip above the girls' heads and they begin to go wild, fiercely attacking one another until the show is called off, and they are, according to Sir Nigel, once again locked up until, we assume, the next performance. The climax of the evening, though, comes when Sir Nigel invites any of his male guests to spend time with any young lady of his liking. All decline and go home.

We are told that subsequently Sir Nigel, like Hugh Harper, is forced to leave Tangier. Even Tangier, it seems, has its threshold for deviance, boundaries that, however broad, can be transgressed: "He did return, however, to die of a heart attack sitting at a table on the terrace of the Café de Paris, in the center of Tangier, at noon" (*UW*, 50).

Interspersed between these tales of perversion are three dramatic monologues. Considered in toto, the three stories—"Massachusetts 1932," "New York 1965," and "Tangier 1975"—deal with three critical temporal-spatial matrices in the author's life. We are reminded of the importance of Massachusetts and New England for the young Bowles when we read "The Frozen Fields." New York was in many ways a hub in Bowles's middle years, serving as an originary location for contracts, friendships, and voyages. Tangier, of course, has become the center of Bowles's later life.

The sense of fluidity and dreamlike quality produced in these monologues can be accounted for, in large measure, by the complete absence of punctuation. Central in each monologue is the speaker's voice, which, like Molly Bloom's in the final chapter of James Joyce's *Ulysses*, reveals so much of the character's concerns and psychic condition simply in its vocal tone and cadence. Bowles, in fact, has said that these stories began with a clear impression of the speaker's voice. When asked how he came on this mode of telling, he has said, "Well, it's hard to say. I don't know. I heard the voice of the woman telling about the peacocks, and heard it very strongly in my ear and so I started writing what she would say, and what she did say, in her kind of speech. Once I had written one, I found it fun to become someone else and write what words I heard in my head—rather like writing music (personal interview).

The story Bowles refers to here is "Tangier 1975," in which the unnamed female speaker is obsessed with a portion of her past during which she and her husband, Anton, stayed, on invitation, in a guest cottage of another unnamed expatriate woman. The big villa, we are told, is now owned by Saudis; "they've got most of the good properties" (*UW*, 51).

Before coming to the main incident in the story, the speaker shows her contempt for the owner of the villa. At first the speaker had assumed that the woman invited them to stay because of her interest in her husband. She then complains that the woman gossiped about them and treated them as squatters. Her moral indignation and jealousy, as is so often the case, seem more a product of imagined than actual behavior: "she had lovers always native of course . . . it wasn't that she had lovers or even that her lovers were natives but that she appeared with them in public that was a slap in the face for the European colony and they didn't forgive it but she couldn't be bothered to care what anybody felt" (*UW*, 53–54). When the wealthy socialite asks them to serve as bouncers for a party she is throwing, they can hardly refuse, given their indebtedness. The morning after the party, the woman comes down to tell them that "the Duchesse de Saint Somethingorother was missing her evening bag where she'd put her emerald earrings" and blames it on their faulty gatekeeping.[81] The speaker is unable to hold back her swelling resentment: "my dear lady I said do you realize we were in that booth for five hours you told us it wouldn't take more than two I hope you're aware of that well it's most unfortunate she said I've had to call in the police" (*UW*, 58–59).

Although told in a novel way, this monologue betrays the same kinds of postcolonial anxieties seen in many of the stories in *Midnight Mass*. Less than a month after that party, "some teenage hoodlums" broke into the villa while her lover was away and "tortured her all night long trying to make her tell" where her large cache of money was hidden. The next day the woman died from the severe wounds.

By the end of the story, we learn the reason for the speaker's compulsion to tell the story—her own guilty conscience. The police track down the hoodlums, who have in their possession the duchess's evening bag: "the criminals had arrived late the night of the party and slipped in along with a group of Spaniards after Anton and I had left the gate and of course that gave him the opportunity of examining the house and grounds for the break-in later so I felt terribly guilty of course I knew it wasn't my fault but I couldn't keep myself from thinking that if we'd only stayed on a little longer she'd still have been alive" (*UW*, 59–60). Like so many of Poe's narrators, or like the Ancient Mariner, the speaker seems doomed to repeat forever those highly charged incidents of her life.

Jealousy seems to be the primary motivation behind the words in "New York 1965." The speaker begins with a tirade against a certain Kathleen Andrews, who has evidently become a highly acclaimed poet. Andrews's success, the speaker submits, can be attributed to her mother's wealth and influence, not the intrinsic merits of her verse.

As in the preceding monologue, the speaker's moralistic tendencies quickly surface, as she judges Andrews, her one-time roommate at Sarah Lawrence, for becoming an unwed mother a year or so after graduating from college. Late in her monologue the speaker openly admits her lack of tolerance: "I suppose I'm getting less tolerant but I have no patience with people who refuse to abide by the rules of the game" (*UW*, 25). Kathleen ignores the speaker's generous counsel, refusing to accept and abide by such strict boundaries for social behavior.

Kathleen finds refuge in Tangier, as did many others of her generation (hippies, beats, and outcasts) who sought to escape the strictures of puritanical and philistine values.[82] The speaker learns in a letter that Kathleen "was in the native quarter of course and Alaric [her son] was learning about life with his peers playing with the Moroccan boys in the neighborhood" (*UW*, 21). It comes as no surprise to the reader that when the speaker finally tracks down her former roommate in Morocco, after winding endlessly through dark alleyways, she is absolutely repulsed by what she finds: "well she was there dressed in some sort of flashy native costume the place had no furniture in it just mats and cushions and a big table in the middle of the room and here's the payoff on the table was an enormous pile a mountain of marijuana I saw it from the street before I went in without knowing what it was Kathleen I said that stuff is forbidden" (*UW*, 22). She goes on raving about the marijuana and expressing disbelief and outrage over the conditions in which Kathleen and her son lived, among the natives. "I was thinking how can she possibly live like this it smelled exactly like a stable," she says (*UW*, 23). The pièce de résistance is when Kathleen's six-foot-three black boyfriend walks in. The speaker quickly retreats, leaving in disgust, never to hear from her "friend" again, at least up to the time the story is told.

The enjambments and the sense of dramatic irony produce a unique kind of wit. For example, the speaker tells us that "anyway I was sitting there trying to make conversation with the two of them and suddenly there was this terrible gurgling animal sound in the next room it echoed my God what's that I asked her she was perfectly matter-of-fact about it it's just our sheep we've had it now for a month fattening it up for the festival next month" (*UW*, 23). The American visitor's squeamishness and the ambiguous origin (sheep or speaker) of the outcry "My God!" provide amusement.

Christopher Sawyer-Lauçanno suggests that, in writing "Massachusetts 1932," Bowles may have dipped back in his memory and pulled up a scene from a visit he made to New England in 1933: "He arranged . . . to go up to Massachusetts to stay for a time with his Aunt Emma. A few years before, she had divorced Guy Ross and was now living in Westhampton, Massachusetts, married to a farmer named Orville Flint. Flint's former wife had killed herself with a shotgun one evening in the parlor of the farmhouse; Aunt Emma refused to go into the room where it had happened. The story so intrigued Bowles that he never forgot it. Nearly half a century later he wrote his own account of it, which was published in 1984 as 'Massachusetts 1932'" (Sawyer-Lauçanno, 148–49). While traces of that experience can be sensed in the story, the mode of presentation and the act of telling radically transform whatever original experience might have triggered the story.

Unlike the other two monologues, "Massachusetts 1932" uses the visit of an outsider to provide the occasion and an audience for the speaker, rather like the situation in Robert Browning's "My Last Duchess." This lonely New England farmer (who seems to come from the pages of E. A. Robinson or Robert Frost) takes advantage of the visit of a prospective buyer of his house, whose voice we never hear. "Don't see so many people these days somebody comes I open up I guess," the speaker says. In a seemingly ceaseless flow of language, intensified by the threat of an approaching thunderstorm and liberally lubricated by rounds of applejack, we (and the visitor) learn of the tragic history of the owner's residence in that particular house, the house in which he had been born and lived with wives of two separate marriages, both of whom kill themselves with a shotgun.

The first wife, Susan, before she pulls the trigger, seems to have been going a bit stir-crazy living all alone in rural New England with this half-crazed husband of hers. As he tells the story, "I begin to notice that Susan isn't in such good shape she's sort of going to pieces I don't know nervous as a witch and can't sleep and I have to put up with her nagging nag nag day and night night most of all wouldn't let me sleep so finally I slept on a sofa we used to have in here" (*UW*, 36).

His second wife, Laura, he meets just after the funeral of his first wife, on a trip to New York. She hears gossip about the death of his first wife, and soon becomes obsessed with it. The relationship begins to look more and more like its predecessor: "We were getting on each other's nerves something terrible and she was spending more and more time at the piano what kind of music God I don't know but it was always loud." They argue about the piano. She stops playing completely, has a mental breakdown, cuts off her nose, then pulls the trigger: "anyway one morning I was out in the field hoeing and I heard a funny noise in the house by God I said she's playing with that shotgun and I started to run well I found her in the parlor she'd done it the same way as Susan both of them I couldn't believe it couldn't believe it" (*UW*, 40).

Like the speaker in "Tangier 1975," the man cannot help feeling guilty. If he had just told his second wife what happened to Susan before she found out on her own, he tells himself, after the fact, it might not have happened. It is no wonder he is condemned to play out that story, over and over, until death.

"Unwelcome Words" and "In Absentia," both longer epistolary stories, speak more directly from and about the author's life than the usual Bowles story. In both the writer is an older expatriate living in Tangier, complaining about the deterioration of modern life. In "Unwelcome Words" there is a certain perceived sympathy between the letter writer and his correspondent on this question of cultural decay: "I think the most important characteristic you and I have in common . . . is a conviction that the human world has entered into a terminal period of disintegration and destruction, and that this will end in a state of affairs so violent and chaotic as to make any attempts at maintaining government or order wholly ineffective" (*UW*, 74). The voice of the letter writer, singular and direct as those in the monologues, closely resembles Bowles's own, as we hear it in his published journals, in his letters, or in his *sala*. In "Unwelcome Words," in fact, the writer refers to himself as

"Paul Bowles." We recognize as Bowles's own many of the views expressed on a variety of subjects, such as the habits of Moroccan dogs, the declining quality of the postal service, the horridness of nineteenth-century romantic music, and the poor quality of Moroccan hashish.

"Unwelcome Words" is a series of six undated letters written by the fictionalized "Paul Bowles" to another older man he has known in the past who is now confined to a wheelchair, having suffered a stroke. "You ask for news about me: my daily life, what I think about, my opinions on external events," Bowles writes to his correspondent, and goes on to depict a postcolonial condition where resentment and greed thrive, and foreigners are often preyed upon. He tells of one instance in which a Jewish woman is murdered because the assailant mistakenly thinks she is rich. In another, "two old Americans (I don't think you ever knew them) who lived in a small house high up on the Old Mountain" are both badly beaten as thieves try to get them to tell where their money is. The couple was penniless, it turns out. The attitude implied here is much like that Bowles voices in a *Rolling Stone* interview, where he recounts that Moroccans once were pirates pillaging vulnerable ships from Christendom and have merely adapted that art to fit the modern world (Rogers).

These letters, meant evidently to give the reader a sense of the rhythm of the writer's everyday life, are laced with depictions of the occasional amusing incident that breaks the routine pattern and, for a time, amuses us. One such story woven into the fabric of the letters of "Unwelcome Words" is that of "the incredible Valeska." When I first read the story in print, I recognized it as one Bowles told to a group of friends one afternoon in his *sala*; then, however, the story was told as undisguised truth, the name of the "real person" freely invoked.[83] The story (in its original and fictionalized forms) involves Paul and his driver Abdelouahaïd (real person/real name), who, having taken a certain dislike to one of Paul's frequent visitors, "Valeska," one day "found his chance and sprang."

Seeing Abdelouahaïd arrive at her hotel one day in the Mustang, without Paul, Valeska jumps up excitedly, crying, "Where's Paul? Where's Paul?"

Soberly and sadly, Abdelouahaïd says, "Paul's dead." As they race off for the Itesa (Paul's apartment), Valeska exclaims, "Oh Christ! My camera's at the hotel. Never mind. Go on" (*UW*, 68–69) Of course, when she realizes she has been the brunt of a mean joke, she fumes.

Incidents such as this one, in which Bowles is erroneously presumed dead, may be part of what prompts the pronouncement in one of these letters, "*Ma vie est posthume.*"

Both correspondents seem immobilized in time and space. The unnamed recipient of the letters not only is physically constrained but reads no literature written before the nineteenth century and experiences failure of memory. In one letter "Bowles" nostalgically recalls songs from his childhood in the 1920s—"Barney Google," "Yes, We Have No Bananas," and "Second Hand Rose." The letter writer in "In Absentia" similarly admits he has no idea who the current movie stars are, knows fashions only from secondhand reports, and talks about friends he hasn't seen in 15 years; he also notes that friends in Tangier have died or moved away.

Rather like the late Henry James, the writer of these letters returns in memory to pictures of an American past, robust, healthy, and rural, and to recollections of hotels in Paris as they existed in his younger days. The present is anathema. At one point, Bowles imagines one aspect of contemporary American life with horror: "Although I haven't been in an American kitchen in years, I know that they're inclined to look more and more like laboratories" (*UW*, 81).

Life in Tangier is little better. It is as though all that Bowles has spent his life detesting and trying to avoid has finally caught up with him, and he can no longer escape it. In one letter "Bowles" complains about the changes going on in his neighborhood, around his apartment in the Itesa Inmeuble: "They're building fancy villas all around me. They're well-built but hideous, and look like old-fashioned juke boxes, their facades plastered with wrought iron and tile work. Each one is required by law to have a chimney, but in no case is the chimney connected with anything inside the house, being purely decorative. The builders are waiting for buyers who don't arrive. Will they ever? The prices seem very high: between $125,000 and $200,000, and there's no heat, of course—no furnace, no fireplaces—and often no space outside for a garden" (*UW*, 69–70). If one has recently been to visit Bowles, one would easily recognize the scene. The qualitative difference between life in Tangier and life in America, we are led to believe, may not be so great. The writer's preference for Morocco, however, is related to the fact that it has been for so long, and still is, home. The deterioration is perhaps tolerable only because the onlooker has taken in those changes gradually, thereby mitigating their shock value.

The letter writer in "In Absentia" has similar complaints about modern life in Tangier. Money from abroad is held up in Casablanca, with the government collecting the interest; imported goods are hard to come by ("You may, or you may never, get your saucepan or your powdered milk or your trowel or your broom or your Gruyére or your spatula");[84] roads are congested with traffic and lungs with air pollution.

"In Absentia" tells more of a story than "Unwelcome Words" does. The work consists of a series of letters written to two correspondents: Pamela Loeffler, who evidently has, at the beginning of this portion of the exchange, just got a handsome divorce settlement and moved to Hawaii; and a 17-year-old Mount Holyoke coed, Susan Choate, the writer's father's sister's great-granddaughter. We are dropped into the correspondence knowing next to nothing of the past relationships between the correspondents. What becomes interesting as the story progresses are the blind, frantic gropings of the narrator, trying to see what is going on, to plot action, and to control people from a distance. In his letters he orchestrates a meeting of the two correspondents. To Pamela Loeffler he casually inserts the news that his young niece— "(I think I told you I was financing her education)"—would be visiting Honolulu and "might enjoy a visit with you" ("Absentia," 15). To his young ward in Massachusetts he suggests that it might be more advisable for her to travel to Hawaii than to Morocco for the summer, noting that he knows someone there who might put her up: "Besides solving the vacation problem, your sojourn there could prove advantageous in other ways" ("Absentia," 17). In a follow-up letter he spells out his motives less cryptically: "Staying with Pamela out there you would be in a position, if you were clever enough, to receive financial assistance for the coming year. That wouldn't have occurred to you in your youthful innocence. But it occurred to me, and I see it as a distinct possibility" ("Absentia," 17–18).

The scheme, then, is to introduce his ward, who is in need of money, to the older woman, who evidently is amply bankrolled. If all went well, he might be relieved of some of the financial burden. Or, so we presume, his scheme goes.

Once Susan and Pamela have met, however, the writer finds himself no longer able to influence the course of events. He doesn't hear from Susan for a long time and shares his anxieties in letters to Pamela. From Pamela he hears that Sue has been in the hospital because of a relapse, he assumes, of hepatitis contracted on a previous visit to Haiti. His removal, his distance from the scene, while relieving him of responsibility, precludes the possibility for action and produces anxieties associated with uncertainty. In short, it leaves him helpless, save the power of his words.

After receiving a postcard from Fiji from Pamela, indicating that the two women had gone there together, the writer expresses his astonishment and exasperation. To Loeffler he writes, "It strikes me as an irresponsible act to gather the girl under your wing and fly off with her to God knows where and for God knows how long" ("Absentia," 24). He conveniently seems to forget his own role in engineering the meeting in the first place. It gradually becomes apparent that the two women have talked together about him, proving his earlier remarks: "How can I advise you from here, or dictate a course of behavior? Or foresee the complex choreography of subterfuges and dissimulations which make up your conversation? Women know how to handle each other, and need no man's advice ("Absentia," 19). When it becomes clear that Suky (Susan) is choosing not to return to school in the United States, the writer informs Pamela of his intent to sever his support for the young girl. In the last letter to Pamela Loeffler, he writes: "She expects me to mind that things didn't work out in the way I thought they would. But that's only because she doesn't know me. What she must consider to be my archaic epistolary style has helped her to think of me as an opinionated and uncompromising old bastard. Nevertheless, please believe me when I tell you that she can fall in love with a Japanese garage mechanic, sleep with you, and marry an orangutan, and it will all be the same to me. There's not enough time in life for recriminations" ("Absentia," 26).

Some doubt remains in the end whether the writer is sincere or whether he is displaying mock ire, smugly pleased that somehow his plot has worked. We can assume this is the way Bowles would have it, purposefully ambiguous.

The voice in the letters in both stories seems remote, speaking faintly across a great distance, the speaker perhaps wondering just what effect, if any, his words are having on his audience. Yet the letters, as fragile as they are, are lifelines, giving the writer the opportunity to tell of his life, to feel some slight connection to others. The epistolary form itself harks back to earlier times, as, in a letter to Pamela Loeffler, the writer states: "I see you understand the pleasure that can be got from writing letters. In other centuries this was taken for granted. Not any longer. Only a few people carry on true correspondences. No time, the rest tell you. Quicker to telephone. Like saying a photograph is more satisfying than a painting. There wasn't all that much time for writing letters in the past, either, but time was found, as it generally can be for whatever gives pleasure ("Absentia," 9).

But words have effects sometimes unanticipated by their users. They are, indeed, sometimes unwelcome. Toward the end of the series of letters in "Unwelcome Words," "Bowles" notes that his correspondent has not been appreciating his letters. In the face of what he takes to be hostility, the writer exclaims, in desperation, "There's obviously nothing I can do from here to help you" (*UW*, 85). He does not close, however, before offering a final plea that the correspondent at least recognize the noble intent his words represented: "I hope you'll remember (you won't) that I made this small and futile attempt to help you remain human" (*UW*, 85–86).

This final admission of the dubious power of the word, and plea to be taken seriously, might be thought of as Bowles's own modest apologia for a body of work that has at times provoked disgust yet always remained, at its core, profoundly human.

Epilogue

Implied throughout the preceding pages has been an argument for the aesthetic merits and cultural value of Paul Bowles's literary output. Few other American writers have had such a sustained involvement with the short story form and enjoyed so much success with it. Certainly, no other American writer of any note has lived so long in an Arab country and given us, through the lens of fiction, such an alluring aperture onto that intriguing culture.

While some have found Bowles's preoccupation with the exotic and his extended residence in Morocco unsavory if not unpatriotic, it is precisely his adamant insistence on maintaining the outsider's stance that has yielded his unique vision. In our own cultural moment, as we begin to recognize the importance of exploring and granting respect to the "other"—both within ourselves and as manifest in cultural differences—it would seem that Bowles's work takes on even greater significance.

Those who have in the past sought to save Bowles's fiction from neglect may be encouraged by recent interest shown in the writer/composer. Bertolucci's movie *The Sheltering Sky*, regardless of its merits, brought the author to the attention of many who had not heard of him before. Two recent trade books, Christopher Sawyer-Lauçanno's biography, *An Invisible Spectator*, and Michelle Green's gossipy treatment of the modern expatriate experience in Tangier, *The Dream at the End of the World: Paul Bowles and the Literary Renegades in Tangier*, provide further evidence of continued interest in the Bowles legend.

Bowles's reputation as a master of the short story has, it seems, for the time being been secured with the publication by Ecco Press of his selected stories under the title *A Distant Episode*. The volume, which covers a 50-year period and pulls together 24 stories, 9 not found in his *Collected Stories*, has been warmly welcomed. "The collection proves beyond doubt Bowles's originality and right to literary legend," *Publishers Weekly* announces in its write-up.[85] *Booklist* claims that "Bowles deserves an honored and *read* place in the canon of twentieth-century

American literature."[86] And *Kirkus Reviews* calls the book "a definitive collection by one of the more durable voices of the 20th century."[87]

Just as with Poe, with whom Bowles has many affinities, literary historians, anthologists, and critics have often had a difficult time placing Bowles's work. I hope I have gone even a short way not only in explicating stories but in suggesting how Bowles's work is tied to the essential patterns and reverberations of this century. His has been a quintessentially twentieth-century life, and his art has uniquely inscribed the tremors, fissures, and psychoses of unsettled, restless characters living in uncertain times.

Notes to Part 1

1. Gore Vidal, introduction to *Collected Stories, 1939–1976* (Santa Barbara, Calif.: Black Sparrow Press, 1980); hereafter cited in text as *CS*.

2. While my search has by no means been exhaustive, I have found Bowles represented in only one current anthology of stories: *Story*, ed. Boyd Litzinger and Joyce Carol Oates (Toronto: D. C. Heath, 1985), contains "A Distant Episode."

3. See Gilles Deleuze, "Nomad Thought," in *The New Nietzsche: Contemporary Styles of Interpretation*, ed. David B. Allison (New York: Delta, 1977), 142–49, and Gilles Deleuze and Felix Guattari, *A Thousand Plateaus: Capitalism and Schizophrenia*, trans. Brian Massumi (Minneapolis: University of Minnesota Press, 1987).

4. Steven Olson, "Alien Terrain: Bowles's Filial Landscapes," *Twentieth Century Fiction* 34, no. 3–4 (1986): 335.

5. The British publishing history of Bowles's short fiction is quite a different matter, as will be noted on occasion throughout the study.

6. Marcel Proust, *Pastiches et mélange* (Paris: Gallimard, 1970), 249.

7. Eudora Welty, "Place in Fiction" (1956), in *The Eye of the Story* (New York: Random House, 1977), 128; hereafter cited in text.

8. Preface to *A Distant Episode: The Selected Stories of Paul Bowles* (New York: Ecco Press, 1988).

9. Ross E. Dunn, in *The Adventures of Ibn Battuta: A Muslim Traveler of the 14th Century* (Berkeley: University of California Press, 1989), 13.

10. Edith Wharton, *In Morocco* (1919; reprint, New York: Hippocrene Books, 1984), 28.

11. Found in Tzvetan Todorov, "The Limits of Edgar Poe," in *Genres in Discourse*, trans. Catherine Porter (Cambridge, England: Cambridge University Press, 1990), 98–99. Todorov's note reads: "Dostoevsky's discussion of three of Poe's tales appeared in *Vremja* in January, 1861. The citation is taken from the French translation published as: Feodor Dostoevsky, *Recits, chroniques et polemiques* (Paris: Gallimard, 1969) 1091–2." The connection between Poe and Bowles has been explored at some length by Wayne Pounds in *Paul Bowles: The Inner Geography* (New York: Peter Lang, 1985); hereafter cited in text, and Catherine Rainwater, "'Sinister Overtones,' 'Terrible Phrases': Poe's influence on the Writings of Paul Bowles," *Essays in Literature* 2 (1984): 253–66.

12. Interview with Oliver Evans, *Mediterranean Review* 1, no. 2 (Winter 1971): 9. (Extended excerpts from this interview appear in part 2.)

13. Jane Bowles, from the unpublished novel *Out in the World*, notebook 2, Harry Ransom Humanities Research Center (hereafter cited as HRC), University of Texas, Austin, Texas.

14. Introduction to *A Life Full of Holes*, by Larbi Layachi (1966; reprint, New York: Grove, 1982), 9.

15. Edgar Allan Poe, "Hawthorne's *Twice-Told Tales*," in *Literary Criticism of Edgar Allan Poe*, ed. Robert L. Hough (Lincoln: University of Nebraska Press, 1965), 136.

16. Richard F. Patteson, *The World Outside: The Fiction of Paul Bowles* (Austin: University of Texas Press, 1987); hereafter cited in text.

17. Walter Benjamin, "The Storyteller," in *Illuminations*, trans. Harry Zohn (New York: Schocken Books, 1969), 87.

18. Guy Davenport, *The Geography of the Imagination* (San Francisco: North Point Press, 1981), 132.

19. Originally, Bowles had wanted the volume to be titled simply *The Delicate Prey*, but his publishers argued that such a title might suggest the book was a novel. See letter from Helen Strauss to Paul Bowles, 12 October 1950, HRC, University of Texas, Austin, Texas.

20. Taped conversation cited in Lawrence D. Stewart, *Paul Bowles: The Illumination of North Africa* (Carbondale and Edwardsville: Southern Illinois University Press, 1974), 21; hereafter cited in text as Stewart 1974.

21. *Without Stopping* (New York: Putnams, 1972; reprint, New York: Ecco Press, 1985), 128; hereafter cited in text as *WS*.

22. Michael Seidel, *Exile and the Narrative Imagination* (New Haven, Conn.: Yale University Press, 1986), x.

23. Introduction to *For Bread Alone*, by Mohamed Choukri (London: Peter Owen, 1974), 5.

24. In the early 1960s Alfred Chester wrote a story titled "Safari," in which the narrator and Gerald, a character modeled after Bowles, go scorpion hunting. The narrator says of Gerald, "You never can tell with him if he really cares about anything. I don't believe he does. I think the only thing he genuinely cares about is watching things squirm. Things and people." *Head of a Sad Angel: Stories 1953–1966*, ed. Edward Field (Santa Rosa: Black Sparrow Press, 1990), 240–241.

25. Johannes Bertens, *The Fiction of Paul Bowles: The Soul Is the Weariest Part of the Body* (Amsterdam: Costeras, n.s. 21, 1979), 199; hereafter cited in text.

26. Dedication to *The Delicate Prey and Other Stories* (New York: Random House, 1950; reprint, New York: Ecco Press, 1972).

27. The first British edition of Bowles's stories, titled *A Little Stone* (1950), omitted "A Delicate Prey" and "Pages from Cold Point." The two stories did not appear in Britain until 1968, when Peter Owen published a collection titled *Pages From Cold Point*.

28. Letter from Alice B. Toklas to Paul Bowles, 7 December 1950, HRC, University of Texas, Austin, Texas. (See part 3 for the entire text.)

29. In *Paul Bowles in the Land of the Jumblies*, a film by Gary Conklin, 1969. The film was released in England in 1971 under the title *Paul Bowles in Morocco* and has been shown in this country under the title *Paul Bowles' Morocco*.

30. *The Sheltering Sky* (New York: New Directions, 1949;reprint, New York: Ecco Press, 1978), 312.

31. Edward W. Said, *Beginnings: Intention and Method* (New York: Basic Books, 1975), 318–19.

32. Dorrit Cohn, *Transparent Minds: Narrative Modes for Presenting Consciousness in Fiction* (Princeton, N.J.: Princeton University Press, 1978), 100.

33. Norman Mailer, *Advertisements for Myself* (New York: Perigree Books, 1959), 429; hereafter cited in text.

34. Letter from Jane Bowles to Paul Bowles (East Montpelier, Vermont), December 1947, HRC, University of Texas, Austin, Texas.

35. Robert Craft, "Pipe Dreams," *New York Review of Books*, 23 November 1989, 9; hereafter cited in text.

36. Letter from Paul Bowles to Lawrence Ferlinghetti, 28 December 1961, Bancroft Library, University of California, Berkeley. Cited in Christopher Sawyer-Lauçanno, *An Invisible Spectator: A Biography of Paul Bowles* (New York: Weidenfeld & Nicolson, 1989), 357–58.

37. Letter from Bowles to Ferlinghetti, 12 January 1962, Berkeley. Cited in Sawyer-Lauçanno, p. 358; hereafter cited in text.

38. Anatole Broyard, "The Man Who Discovered Alienation," *New York Times Book Review*, 6 August 1989, 1.

39. *A Hundred Camels in the Courtyard*, 2d ed. (1962; reprint, San Francisco: City Lights Books, 1986), 57; hereafter cited in text as *HC*.

40. Interesting in this context are Bowles articles appearing in the early issues of *Kulchur* magazine dating from the same period as *A Hundred Camels*. See, in particular, his "Ketama-Taza," *Kulchur 1* (Spring 1960): 31–35, and "Kif—Prologue and Compendium of Terms," *Kulchur 3*: 35–40.) I am grateful to Abdullah Schleiffer for calling my attention to these articles and providing me with copies of them.

41. John Ryle, "Survivor of the Cold Style," review of *Unwelcome Words* and Christopher Sawyer-Lauçanno's *Invisible Spectator*, *Times Literary Supplement*, 15 September 1989, 995.

42. I have in mind Crapanzano's classic study *The Hamadsha: A Study in Moroccan Ethnopsychiatry* (Berkeley and Los Angeles: University of California Press, 1973) and his more recent book *Tuhami: Portrait of a Moroccan* (Chicago: University of Chicago Press, 1980). Rabinow's work on Morocco is recorded in *Symbolic Domination: Cultural Form and Historical Change in Morocco* (Chicago: University of Chicago Press, 1975) and *Reflections on Fieldwork in Morocco* (Berkeley: University of California Press, 1977). These works are extremely useful counterpoints to Bowles's fictional representations of Morocco.

43. *The Spider's House* (1955; reprint, Santa Barbara, Calif.: Black Sparrow Press, 1982), 187.

44. Lawrence D. Stewart writes, "Bowles submitted ' He of the Assembly' to the *London Magazine*, but John Lehmann rejected the story 'with great regret,' calling it interesting but a failure: 'The dope-dream atmosphere seems to me to become merely a confusion, and I fear that too many readers will give up

bewildered before they have got half-way' (HRC: TLS, 26 Feb. 1960). The story appeared later that year in *Big Table*" (Stewart, 1974, 129).

45. Among the 13 stories in the collection were the 4 that had earlier appeared in *A Hundred Camels in the Courtyard*, discussed in the previous section.

46. Spanish filmmaker Pedro Almodovar evidently has rights to make the story into a movie. In "Journal, Tangier [Part 2]" (*Antaeus* 64/65 [Spring/Autumn 1990]: 440–41), Bowles notes:

> June 12
> Had lunch on the Mountain with Gloria Kirby. Her guests from Madrid knew all about Pedro Almodovar, who seems to specialize in comic films. It's hard to understand, if that's the case, why he chose to take an option on *The Time of Friendship*, a story in which there's not a suggestion of a humorous situation. Unless he does the whole thing tongue-in-check. It wouldn't be difficult to satirize the crèche scene. Or making Slimane three or four years older could provide a different sort of liaison between him and Fräulein Windling. But humor? The guests at lunch suggested that Almodovar felt he had exhausted his comic vein, and intended to add a serious dimension to his work.

47. Bowles frequently offers comments on Islam, particularly its relation to Christianity. See, in particular, his North African travel essays in *Their Heads Are Green and Their Hands Are Blue: Scenes from the Non-Christian World* (London: Peter Owen, 1963; New York: Random House, 1963; reprint, New York: Ecco Press, 1984) and *Points in Time* (London: Peter Owen, 1982; reprint, New York: Ecco Press, 1985), which presents intense, fictionalized encounters at specific points in the history of relations between Islam and Christianity.

48. There is plenty of evidence of Bowles's interest in Gide, which began when he was very young. In 1925, when he was only 15, Bowles records, "[O]ne spring evening I bought my first Gide: Knopf's edition of *The Vatican Swindle*. (A later edition was called *Lafcadio's Adventures*; God knows why)" (*WS*, 67). On his transatlantic crossing on the *Rijndam* in 1929, he took along Gide's *Journal des Faux-Monnayeurs* (*WS*, 81). In his autobiography he gives a very brief account of a subsequent meeting (of little consequence) with Gide (*WS*, 108). Further, Bowles has admired Gide's North African travel book, *Amyntas*.

49. A good biography of Isabelle Eberhardt is Cecily Mackworth's *The Destiny of Isabelle Eberhardt* (New York: Ecco Press, 1975). Also available are Eberhardt's diaries: *The Passionate Nomad: The Diary of Esabelle Eberhardt*, trans. Nina de Voogd, ed. Rana Kabbani (London: Virago, 1987). Bowles's translations of some of Eberhardt's stories have been collected and published in a volume titled *The Oblivion Seekers* (San Francisco: City Lights Books, 1972).

50. See manuscript version of "The Time of Friendship" in HRC, University of Texas, Austin, Texas.

51. John Ditsky, "*The Time of Friendship*: The Short Fiction of Paul Bowles," *Twentieth Century Literature* 34, no. 3–4 (1986): 373–87; hereafter cited in text.

52. See Franz Fanon, *The Wretched of the Earth*, preface by Jean-Paul Sartre, trans. Constance Farrington (New York: Grove, 1968), for an insightful analysis of the psychological effects of colonization that remain even after liberation.

53. See Edward Said's extended treatment of the theme in *Orientalism* (New York: Pantheon Books, 1978).

54. Richard Howard's translation of the complete phrase is as follows: "Time passing here is innocent of hours, yet so perfect is our inoccupation that boredom becomes impossible" (Richard Howard, trans., *Amyntas*, by André Gide [1906; reprint, New York: Ecco Press, 1988]), 5.

55. Lawrence Stewart, "Paul Bowles and the 'Frozen Fields' of Vision," *Review of Contemporary Fiction* 2, no. 3 (1982): 64; hereafter cited in text as Stewart 1982.

56. Of interest here is Edith Wharton's *In Morocco*.

57. While Bowles chose not to include "Sylvie Ann, the Boogie Man" in American collections, it did appear in the English volume of stories, *The Hours After Noon*, brought out by Heinemann in 1959. The story was also included in Bowles's *Call at Corazón* (London: Peter Owen, 1988); hereafter cited in text as *CC*.

58. Personal interview with the author, Tangier, 18 August 1988; hereafter cited in text as personal interview.

59. Among the works of Mrabet Bowles translated during this period are *Love with a Few Hairs* (1967), *The Lemon* (1969), *M'Hashish* (1969), *The Boy Who Set the Fire* (1974), *Hadidan Aharam* (1975), *Look and Move On* (1976), and *The Beach Cafe and The Voice* (1976).

60. Mary Martin Rountree has addressed the subject of Bowles's translations in her article "Paul Bowles: Translations from the Moghrebi," *Twentieth Century Literature* 34, no. 3–4 (1986); 334–49.

61. See my treatment of irony and expatriation in "Some Versions of Ironic (Mis) Interpretation: The American Abroad," in *Alif* (Cairo) 8 (Spring 1988): 67–87.

62. Marcel Mauss, *The Gift: Forms of Exchange in Archaic Societies* (New York: Norton), 1967.

63. See Idris Shah's translations of the Nasrudin stories, for example—*The Pleasantries of the Incredible Mulla Nasrudin* (New York: Dutton, 1971), *Wisdom of the Idiots* (New York: Dutton, 1971), *Tales of the Dervishes* (New York: Dutton, 1970), and *The Dermis Probe* (New York: Dutton, 1970). See also Bowles's own translation of the Hadidan Ahaharam stories, as told by Mohamad Mrabet in *Harmless Poisons, Blameless Sins* (Santa Barbara, Calif.: Black Sparrow Press, 1976). Of Hadidan Aharam, Bowles writes in his translator's note, "He is the traditional rustic oaf who, in spite of his simplicity, and sometimes precisely

because of it, manages to impose his will upon those who have criticized and ridiculed him."

64. For an insightful analysis of the implications of this dynamic, see Pierre Bourdieu's *Outline of a Theory of Practice*, trans. Richard Nice (Cambridge, England: Cambridge University Press, 1977).

65. Loosely translated, *djinn* means "spirit" or "genie"; *djenoun* is the plural form in Arabic.

66. As an example of this position, take writer Brian Kiteley's remarks (private correspondence, April 1986):

> How far from typical Bowles was! And yet Stein was right: his type, the banal American conqueror, has spoiled the world. How hard it must be for Bowles to realize that his endless restless travelling was a perverse reflection of the terrible American disdain for the differentiation of the world's cultures. He himself recognized and relished and sought out the most unspoiled countries, and he descried the encroaching Americanization of cities and countries where ever he saw it, after the war. But he was just as much responsible for the contamination as the American businessmen who *flew* everywhere.

67. For an articulate presentation of these views, I am grateful to my Moroccan friend Dghoughi Abdellah, who for the University of Florence has written a thesis (in Italian) containing a chapter on Bowles. Dghoughi shared his insights with me in several informal conversations at El Hafa, a café on the Marshan overlooking the Straits of Gibraltar.

68. *Midnight Mass* (Santa Barbara, Calif.: Black Sparrow Press, 1981), 99; hereafter cited in text as *MM*.

69. In Michael Rogers, "Conversation in Morocco," *Rolling Stone*, 23 May 1974, 48–54 (hereafter cited in text as Rogers; portions of this interview are included in part 2 of this book), Bowles relates the story of a man whose fate is very much like Duncan Marsh's, making us believe the story has some basis in fact.

70. Joyce Carol Oates, introduction to *The Best American Short Stories* (Boston: Houghton Mifflin, 1979), xiv.

71. Letter from Paul Bowles to Millicent Dillon, 20 March 1981, HRC, University of Texas, Austin, Texas.

72. Yahyia Haqqi, *The Saint's Lamp* (*Qindil Umm Hashim*) (Cairo: Dar al-Kitab, 1973).

73. An interesting comparison here is Rifa'ah al-Tahtawi's *Takhlis al-Ibriz fi Talkhis Baris* (*An Extraction of Gold in a Summary of Paris*), which registers the influential Egyptian writer's reactions during his five-year stay in Paris (1826–31). A valuable introduction to Tahtawi and translations of

in Sandra Naddaf's "Mirrored Images: Rifa'ah al-Tahtawi and the West," *Alif* (Cairo) 6 (Spring 1986): 73–83.

74. Shannon Ravenal, ed. *The Best American Short Stories of the Eighties* (Boston: Houghton, Mifflin, 1990).

75. Jeffrey Miller, *Paul Bowles: A Descriptive Bibliography* (Santa Barbara, Calif.: Black Sparrow Press, 1986), 61–62.

76. Letter from Paul Bowles to Millicent Dillon, 5 June 1982, HRC, University of Texas, Austin, Texas. (A fuller text of this letter can be found in Part 2.)

77. John Updike, introduction to *The Best American Short Stories, 1984* (Boston: Houghton Mifflin, 1984), xix–xx.

78. Michael Wolfe, personal correspondence, 25 January 1991.

79. *Unwelcome Words* (Bolinas, Calif.: Tombouctou Press, 1988), 14; hereafter cited in text as *UW*.

80. Notebook 9, entry dated 24 July 1958, HRC, University of Texas, Austin, Texas.

81. The party described here reminds one of Bowles's descriptions of Barbara Hutton's lavish parties. See, in particular, Bowles's interview in *Rolling Stone* (23 May 1974).

82. One reads of Bowles's reaction to this phenomenon in a letter to his parents, dated 12 June 1961 (HRC, University of Texas, Austin, Texas): "The Beatniks have invaded Tangier at last. Every day one sees more beards and filthy bluejeans, and the girls look like escapees from lunatic asylums, with white lipstick and black smeared around their eyes, and matted hair hanging around their shoulders. The leaders of the 'movement' have moved their headquarters here, and direct their activities from here. Allen Ginsberg, Gregory Corso and Burroughs are all established in Tangier now, sending out their publications from here."

83. When I later went back and questioned Bowles about the status of the story, on remembering his story of Hanetta Clark the summer before, he countered, "What difference does it make who the 'real' person is? It doesn't really make a difference, does it? It's a story, after all."

84. "In Absentia" was first published in *Antaeus* (*Antaeus* 58 [Spring 1987]: 7–26) and subsequently included in *A Distant Episode: The Selected Stories of Paul Bowles*; my references are to the *Antaeus* printing of the story, hereafter cited in text as "Absentia."

85. *Publishers Weekly*, 16 December 1988, 74.

86. *Booklist*, 15 January 1989, 834.

87. *Kirkus Reviews*, 1 November 1988, 1545.

Part 2

THE WRITER

Introduction

Bowles has spoken of his writing, with varying degrees of candor, in a number of contexts. Collected here are comments the writer has made in interviews, his autobiography, letters, and prefaces, pertaining either to particular stories or, more generally, to the art of storytelling.

Interview, 1975

Daniel Halpern

HALPERN: When did you begin to write?

BOWLES: At four. I have a whole collection of stories about animals that I wrote then.

HALPERN: But it was as a poet that you first published, in *transition*?

BOWLES: I had written a lot of poetry (I was in high school) and had been buying *transition* regularly since it started publishing. It seemed to me that I could write for them as well as anyone else, so I sent them things and they accepted them. I was sixteen when I wrote the poem they first accepted, seventeen when they published it. I went on for several years as a so-called poet.

HALPERN: What ended your short career as a poet?

BOWLES: I think Gertrude Stein had a lot to do with it. She convinced me that I ought not to be writing poetry, since I wasn't a poet at all, as I just said. And I believed her thoroughly, and I still believe her. She was quite right. I would have stopped anyway, probably.

HALPERN: Were there any important early literary influences?

BOWLES: Well, I suppose everything influences you. I remember my mother used to read me Edgar Allan Poe's short stories before I went to sleep at night. After I got into bed she would read me *Tales of Mystery and Imagination*. It wasn't very good for sleeping—they gave me nightmares. Maybe that's what she wanted, who knows? Certainly what you read during your teens influences you enormously. During my early teens I was very fond of Arthur Machen and Walter de la Mare. The school of mystical whimsy. And then I found Thomas Mann, and fell into the *Magic Mountain* when I was sixteen, and that was certainly a big influence. Probably that was the book that influenced me more than any other before I went to Europe.

From Daniel Halpern, "Interview with Paul Bowles," *TriQuarterly* 33 (Spring 1975): 159–177. Used by permission.

HALPERN: Before you actually begin writing a novel or story, what takes place in your mind? Do you outline the plot, say, in visual terms?

BOWLES: Every work suggests its own method. Each novel's been done differently, under different circumstances and using different methods. I got the idea for *The Sheltering Sky* riding on a Fifth Avenue bus one day going uptown from Tenth Street. I decided just which point of view I would take. It would be a work in which the narrator was omniscient. I would write it consciously up to a certain point, and after that let it take its own course. You remember there's a little Kafka quote at the beginning of the third section: "From a certain point onward there is no longer any turning back; that is the point that must be reached." This seemed important to me, and when I got to that point, beyond which there was no turning back, I decided to use a surrealist technique—simply writing without any thought of what I had already written, or awareness of what I was writing, or intention as to what I was going to write next, or how it was going to finish. And I did that. . . .

HALPERN: To what extent does the ingestion of kif play a role in your writing?

BOWLES: I shouldn't think it has an effect on anyone's writing. Kif can provide flashes of insight, but it acts as an obstacle to thinking. On the other hand, it enables one to write concentratedly for hours at a stretch without fatigue. You can see how it could be useful if you were writing something which relied for its strength on the free elaboration of fantasy. I used it only once that way, as I say—for the fourth section of *Let It Come Down*. But I think most writers would agree that kif is for relaxation, not for work.

HALPERN: Do you revise a great deal after you've finished the rough draft?

BOWLES: No, the first draft is the final draft. I can't revise. Maybe I should qualify that by saying I first write in longhand, and then the same day, or the next day, I type the longhand. There are always many changes between the longhand and the typed version, but that first typed sheet is part of the final sheet. There's no revision.

HALPERN: Many critics like to attribute a central theme to your writing: that of the alienation of civilized man when he comes in contact with a primitive society and its natural man.

BOWLES: Yes, I've heard about that. It's a theory that makes the body of writing seem more coherent, perhaps, when you put it all together. And possibly they're right, but I'm not conscious of having such a theme, no. I'm not aware of writing about alienation. If my mind worked that way, I couldn't write. I don't have any explicit message; certainly I'm not suggesting changes. I'm merely trying to call people's attention to something they don't seem to be sufficiently aware of.

HALPERN: Do you feel trapped or at a disadvantage by being a member of Western civilization?

BOWLES: Trapped? No. That's like being trapped by having blond hair or blue eyes, light or dark skin . . . No, I don't feel trapped. It would be a very different life to be part of another social group, perhaps, but I don't see any difference between the natural man and the civilized man, and I'm not juxtaposing the two. The natural man always tries to be a civilized man, as you can see all over the world. I've never yearned to be a member of another ethnic group. That's carrying one's romanticism a little too far. God knows I carry mine far enough as it is.

HALPERN: Why is it you have traveled so much? And to such remote places?

BOWLES: I suppose the first reason is that I've always wanted to get as far as possible from the place where I was born. Far both geographically and spiritually. To leave it behind. I'm always happy leaving the United States, and the farther away I go the happier I am, generally. Then there's another thing: I feel that life is very short and the world is there to see and one should know as much about it as possible. One belongs to the whole world, not to just one part of it.

HALPERN: What is the motivation that prompts your characters to leave the safety of a predictable environment, a Western environment, for an unknown world that first places them in a state of aloneness and often ends by destroying them, as in the case of Port and Kit in *The Sheltering Sky* and Dyar in *Let It Come Down?*

BOWLES: I've never thought about it. For one thing there is no "predictable environment." Security is a false concept. As for the motivation? In the case of Port and Kit they *wanted* to travel, a simple, innocent motivation. In the case of Nelson Dyar, he was fed up with his work in America. Fed up with standing in a teller's cage. Desire for freedom, I suppose; desire for adventure. Why *do* people leave their native habitat and go wandering off over the face of the earth?

HALPERN: Many of your characters seem to pursue a course of action that often leads them into rather precarious positions, pushed

forward by an almost self-destructive curiosity, and a kind of fatalism—
for example, the night walks of Port, or the professor in *A Distant Episode.*
Could you say something about this?

BOWLES: I'm very aware of my own capacity for compulsive behavior. Besides, it's generally more rewarding to imagine the results of
compulsive than of reflective action. It has always seemed to me that my
characters act naturally, given the circumstances; their behavior is fore-
seeable. Characters set in motion a mechanism of which they become a
victim. But generally the mechanism turns out to have been operative at
the very beginning. One realizes that Kit's and Port's having left America at all was a compulsive act. Their urge to travel was compulsive.

HALPERN: Do you think that these characters have an "unconscious drive for self-destruction"?

BOWLES: An unconscious drive for self-destruction? . . . Death
and destruction are stock ingredients of life. But it seems to me that the
motivation of characters in fiction like mine should be a secondary
consideration. I think of characters as if they were props in the general
scene of any given work. The characters, the landscape, the climatic
conditions, the human situation, the formal structure of the story or the
novel, all these elements are one—the characters are made of the same
material as the rest of the work. Since they are activated by the other
elements of the synthetic cosmos, their own motivations are relatively
unimportant.

HALPERN: Why do you constantly write about such neurotic characters?

BOWLES: Most of the Occidentals I know *are* neurotic. But that's to
be expected; that's what we're producing now. They're the norm. I don't
think I could write about a character who struck me as eccentric, whose
behavior was too far from standard.

HALPERN: Many people would consider the behavior of your
characters far from standard.

BOWLES: I realize that if you consider them objectively, they're
neurotic and compulsive; but they're generally presented as integral
parts of situations, along with the landscape, and so it's not very fruitful
to try to consider them in another light. My feeling is that what is called
a truly normal person (if I understand your meaning) is not likely to be
written about, save as a symbol. The typical man of my fiction reacts to

inner pressures the way the normal man *ought* to be reacting to the age we live in. Whatever is intolerable must produce violence.

HALPERN: And these characters are your way of protesting.

BOWLES: If you call it protest. If even a handful of people can believe in the cosmos a writer describes, accept the workings of its natural laws (and this includes finding that the characters behave in a credible manner), the cosmos is a valid one.

HALPERN: Critics often label you an existential writer. Do you consider yourself an existentialist?"

BOWLES: No! Existentialism was never a literary doctrine in any case, even though it did trigger three good novels—one by Sartre (*La Nausée*) and two by Camus (*L'Etranger* and *La Peste*). But if one's going to subscribe to the tenets of a formulated belief, I suppose atheistic existentialism is the most logical one to adopt. That is, it's likely to provide more insight than another into what attitudes to take vis-à-vis today's world

HALPERN: But you do share some of the basic tenets of existentialism, as defined by Sartre.

BOWLES: He's interested in the welfare of humanity. As Port said, "What is humanity? Humanity is everybody but yourself."

HALPERN: That sounds rather solipsistic.

BOWLES: What else can you possibly know? *Of course* I'm interested in myself, basically. In getting through my life. You've got to get through it all. You never know how many years you've got left. You keep going until it's over. And I'm the one who's got to suffer the consequences of having lived my life.

HALPERN: Is this why so many of my characters seem to be asocial?

BOWLES: Are they? Or are they merely outside and perhaps wishing they were inside?

HALPERN: Do you think of yourself as being asocial?

BOWLES: I don't know. Probably very, yes. I'm sorry to be so stubborn and impossible with all this, but the point is I just don't know any of the answers, and I have no way of finding them out. I'm not equipped to dig them up, nor do I want to. The day I find out what I'm all about I'll stop writing—I'll stop doing everything. Once you know what makes you tick, you don't tick any more. The whole thing stops. . . .

HALPERN: Life seems to be inaccessible to many of your characters. By their going beyond a certain point, past which they are pulled by an unconscious force, they place themselves in a position where return to the world of man is impossible. Why are they pushed beyond that point?

BOWLES: It's a subject that interests me very much; but you've got to remember that these are all rationalizations devised after the fact, and therefore purely suppositious. I don't know the answer to the questions; all I can do is say, "Maybe," "It could be," or "It could be something else." Offhand I'd suggest that the answer has to do with the Romantic fantasy of reaching a region of self-negation and thereby regaining a state of innocence.

HALPERN: Is it a kind of testing to find out what it's like beyond that point?

BOWLES: It could be. One writes to find out certain things for oneself. Much of my writing is therapeutic. Otherwise I never would have started, because I knew from the beginning that I had no specific desire to reform. Many of my short stories are simple emotional outbursts. They came out all at once, like eggs, and I felt better afterward. In that sense much of my writing is an exhortation to destroy. "Why don't you all burn the world, smash it, get rid of everything in it that plagues you?" It is a desire above all to bring about destruction, that's certain.

HALPERN: So you don't want to change the world. You simply want to end it.

BOWLES: Destroy and end are not the same word. You don't end a process by destroying its products. What I wanted was to see everyone aware of being in the same kind of metaphysical impasse I was in. I wanted to know whether they suffered in the same way.

HALPERN: And you don't think they do?

BOWLES: I don't think many do. Perhaps the number is increasing. I hope so, if only for selfish reasons! Nobody likes to feel alone. I know because I always think of myself as completely alone, and I imagine other people as a part of something else. . . .

HALPERN: Sartre says somewhere that a man's essential freedom is the capacity to say "No." This is something your characters are often incapable of. Do they achieve any kind of freedom?

BOWLES: My characters don't attain any kind of freedom, as far as I'm aware.

HALPERN: Is death any kind of freedom?

BOWLES: Death? Another nonexistent, something to use as a threat to those who are afraid of it. There's nothing to say about death. The cage door's always open. Nobody *has* to stay in here. But people want freedom *inside* the cage. So what is freedom? You're bound by physical laws, bound by your body, bound by your mind.

HALPERN: What does freedom mean to you?

BOWLES: I'd say it was not having to experience what you don't like.

HALPERN: By the alienation that your characters go through in their various exotic settings, are they forced into considering the meaning of *their* lives, if there is meaning to life?

BOWLES: I shouldn't think so. In any case, there's not *one* meaning to life. There should be as many meanings as there are individuals—you assign meaning to life. If you don't assign it, then clearly it has none whatever.

HALPERN: In *L'Etranger*, Meursault is put in jail, which is a way of being alienated, and at that point he considers "the meaning of life."

BOWLES: Camus was a great moralist, which means, nowadays, to be preoccupied with social considerations. I'm not preoccupied in that way. I'm not a moralist. After all, he was a serious communist; I was a very unserious one, a completely negative one.

HALPERN: What was it about communism that appealed to you?

BOWLES: Oh, I imagined it could destroy the establishment. When I realized it couldn't, I got out fast and decided to work on my own hook.

HALPERN: Back to destroying the world. . . .

BOWLES: Well, who doesn't want to? I mean, look at it!

HALPERN: It's one thing to dislike something you see and another to want to destroy it.

BOWLES: Is it? I think the natural urge of every human being is to destroy what he dislikes. That doesn't mean he does it. You don't by any means get to do what you want to do, but you've got to recognize the desire when you feel it.

HALPERN: So you use your writing as a weapon.

BOWLES: Right. Absolutely. . . .

HALPERN: Has your desire to destroy the world always been a conscious one?

BOWLES: Yes. I was aware that I had a grudge, and that the only way I could satisfy my grudge was by writing words, attacking in words. The way to attack, of course, is to seem not to be attacking. Get people's confidence and then, surprise! Yank the rug out from under their feet. If they come back for more, then I've succeeded.

HALPERN: If they enjoy your work you have succeeded—in the sense that their minds have been infected.

BOWLES: Infected is a loaded word, but all right. They have been infected by the germ of doubt. Their basic assumptions may have been slightly shaken for a second, and that's important.

HALPERN: And you don't think of your goals as being negative?

BOWLES: To destroy often means to purify. I don't think of destruction as necessarily undesirable. You said "infecting." All right. Perhaps those infected will have more technique than I for doing some definite destroying. In that sense I'm just a propagandist, but then all writers are propagandists for one thing or another. It's a perfectly honorable function to serve as a corrosive agent. And there certainly is nothing unusual about it; it's been part of the Romantic tradition for the past century and a half. If a writer can incite anyone to question and ultimately to reject the present structure of any facet of society, he's performed a function.

HALPERN: And after that?

BOWLES: It's not for him to say. *Après lui le déluge.* That's all he can do. If he's a propagandist for nihilism, that's his function too.

HALPERN: To start the ball rolling?

BOWLES: I want to *help* society go to pieces, make it easy.

HALPERN: And writing about horror is your method.

BOWLES: I don't write "about horror." But there's a sort of metaphysical malaise in the world today, as if people sense that things are going to be bad. They could be expected to respond to any fictional situation which evoked the same amalgam of repulsion and terror that they already vaguely feel.

HALPERN: Are you, as Leslie Fiedler suggests, a secret lover of the horror you create?

BOWLES: Is there such a creature as a secret or even an avowed lover of horror? I can't believe it. If you're talking about the *evocation* of horror on the printed page, then that's something else. In certain sensitive people the awakening of the sensation of horror through reading can result in a temporary smearing of the lens of consciousness, as one might put it. Then all perception is distorted by it. It's a dislocation, and if it's of short duration it provides the reader with a partially pleasurable shiver. In that respect I confess to being jaded, and I regret it. A good jolt of vicarious horror can cause a certain amount of questioning of values afterward. . . .

HALPERN: Has your writing been affected by the translations you've done?

BOWLES: A little. I noticed that it had been when I wrote *A Hundred Camels in the Courtyard*. I was trying to get to another way of thinking, noncausal. . . . Those were experiments. Arbitrary use of disparate elements. . . .

HALPERN: Among your own books do you have a favorite?

BOWLES: Of published volumes I like *The Delicate Prey* the most. Naturally that doesn't mean I'd write the stories the same way now. . . .

HALPERN: What about contemporary writers? Are there any you enjoy reading?

BOWLES: Let's see, who's alive? Sartre is alive, but he did only one good novel. Graham Greene is alive. Who's alive in America? Whom do I follow with interest? Christopher Isherwood's a good novelist. They're mostly dead. I used to read everything of Gide's and Camus'.

HALPERN: Let me have some opinions on the kind of writing that's being done in America today.

BOWLES: There are various kinds of writing being done, of course. But I suspect you mean the "popular school," as exemplified by Joseph Heller, Kurt Vonnegut, John Barth, Thomas Pynchon—that sort of thing? I don't enjoy it.

HALPERN: Why not?

BOWLES: It's simply that I find it very difficult to get into. The means it uses to awaken interest is of a sort that would be valid only for the length of a short piece. It's too much to have to swim around in that purely literary magma for the time it takes to read a whole book. It fails to hold my attention, that's all. It creates practically no momentum. My mind wanders, I become impatient, and therefore intolerant.

HALPERN: Is it the content that bothers you or the style of the writing? Or both?

BOWLES: Both. But it's the point of view more than anything. The cynicism and wisecracking ultimately function as endorsements of the present civilization. The content is hard to make out because it's generally symbolic or allegorical, and the style is generally hermetic. It's not a novelistic style at all; it's really a style that would be more useful in writing essays, I should think.

HALPERN: Let me go back to the critics for a moment. Do you think they have missed the point of your writing?

BOWLES: They have, certainly, on many occasions. I've often had the impression they were more interested in my motive for writing a given work than they were in the work itself. In general, the British critics have been more perceptive; language is more important to them than it is to us. But I don't think that matters.

HALPERN: One thing that particularly interests many who meet you is the great discrepancy between what you are like as a person and the kind of books you write.

BOWLES: Why is it that Americans expect an artist's work to be a clear reflection of his life? They never seem to want to believe that the two can be independent of each other and go their separate ways. Even when there's a definite connection between the work and the life, the pattern they form may be in either parallel or contrary motion. If you want to call my state schizophrenic, that's all right with me. Say my personality has two facets. Once is always turned in one direction, toward my own Mecca; that's my work. The other looks in a different direction and sees a different landscape. I think that's a common state of affairs.

HALPERN: In retrospect, would you say there has been something that has remained important to you over the years? Something which you have maintained in your writing?

BOWLES: Continuing consciousness, infinite adaptability of human consciousness to outside circumstances, the absurdity of it all, the hopelessness of this whole business of living. I've written very little the past few years. Probably because emotionally everything grows less intense as one grows older. The motivation is at a much lower degree, that's all.

HALPERN: When you were first starting to write you were, emotionally, full of things to say. Now that that has faded somewhat, what springboard do you have?

BOWLES: I can only find out after I've written, since I empty my mind each time before I start. I only know what I intended to do once it's finished. Do you remember, in *A Life Full of Holes*, the farmer comes and scolds the boy for falling asleep, and the boys says: "I didn't know I was going to sleep until I woke up."

Interview, 1965

Ira Cohen

IC: Have you ever worked straight out of a dream state?

PB: . . . only once in fiction, in a story called "You Are Not I." It begins "You are not I. Nobody but me could possibly be. I know who I am, who I've been ever since the train went off the track down in the valley." It begins with a train wreck.

IC: And that was a direct recording of a dream then?

PB: Yes, it was, it was the result of a dream. I had a dream—I didn't know what it was, but I remember thinking I've got to get all this down. It wasn't like a dream, it was like an idea, it came in a second between waking & sleeping, or sleeping & waking & so I happened to know that I had a notebook of some sort there—I had been writing before I went to bed—something else—& I just reached down & picked it up without turning on the light—it was dark in the room. . . .

IC: Did you have any trouble staying on the paper?

PB: I wrote quite big & kept turning the pages, covered many pages with big carefully scrawled handwriting so that I could read it & then I just went on & on without moving until I was very tired & stopped & went back to sleep.

IC: Did you ever revise the story afterwards or did you keep it as it was?

PB: I kept it almost as it was. Well, I should say I changed one sentence.

Ira Cohen, Unpublished Interview 1965. Paul Bowles Papers, Rare Book and Manuscript Library, Columbia University. Used by permission.

Interview, 1971

Oliver Evans

INTERVIEWER: When did you begin to write fiction seriously?

BOWLES: After I met my wife. I had returned to the States. We met in 1937, in New York, and were married the following year.

INTERVIEWER: Did she influence you to write?

BOWLES: Well, yes. Not consciously. But her own novel—*Two Serious Ladies*—probably had some influence on me. It made me want to write, too. For some reason the book stimulated me. I suppose the first story was the one I wrote in, of all places, Brooklyn Heights in 1939: "Tea on the Mountain." It's in the collection, *The Delicate Prey*. That's the earliest one I've kept that's been published. For some reason I just wrote it one day. But I didn't write anymore. Until 1945. . . .

INTERVIEWER: Your first book, I believe was *The Sheltering Sky?*

BOWLES: Yes, and it was followed within a year by *The Delicate Prey*. Of course I had been writing the stories ever since 1945.

INTERVIEWER: I remember the dedication to *The Delicate Prey* reads, "To My Mother, Who First Read me the Stories of Edgar Allan Poe." I gather that Poe has influenced your work?

BOWLES: Undoubtedly. Anything you read over and over as a child is an influence. And she did read me the stories of Poe. What she was always doing was trying to—unconsciously, I think, make me feel exactly as she'd felt when she was sixteen, and I was only seven or eight. And they had quite a different effect, naturally. I wasn't the sort of child who admired literature because of its style; I read because I liked the story. I still do, although I can't take a style that rubs me the wrong way. . . .

INTERVIEWER: Many readers have commented on the rhythmical quality of your prose. Do you think your musical training has had anything to do with this—that there has been a carry-over from the rhythms of music to the rhythms of prose?

From Oliver Evans, "An Interview with Paul Bowles," *Mediterranean Review* 1:2 (Winter 1971): 3–15.

BOWLES: Oh, absolutely.

INTERVIEWER: And of course, as we were saying earlier, you have written poetry too.

BOWLES: And songs! I've written a great many songs. Prosody, I think, has more to do with it than anything else—the value of the spaces between words. . . .

INTERVIEWER: Could you tell me something about your writing habits? I believe you once told me you wrote lying down.

BOWLES: Yes, in bed.

INTERVIEWER: That's a curious habit. Some writers think they must be uncomfortable when they write . . . Hemingway used to write standing up.

BOWLES: I don't think it matters whether you're comfortable or uncomfortable. The important thing is to be able to leave where you are and get into the book. The quickest way of getting there is the best way, that's all. And for me the quickest way is to get there either just before I go to sleep or just after I wake up. When life itself doesn't impinge at all. I work late at night before sleeping, and again after waking up. I may work three hours in bed before going to sleep. Composing music was a much more nerve-racking thing: it made me very, very nervous. I never could sleep well during all those years. Not that I sleep too well now, but certainly much better than when I was writing music. No, I get the impression when I've finished a book that at least I've done something. When I finished a piece of music I never had the feeling that I'd *accomplished* anything, and that wasn't very satisfactory.

INTERVIEWER: Do you need seclusion as much to compose music as to write?

BOWLES: Not so much, no. Well, you do need to be alone, of course. I wrote most of my music in New York, for instance, but I never wrote any part of any book in New York. No. All the novels were written either in Asia or Africa, none of them in Europe or America—not a word of any of them. . . .

INTERVIEWER: When you're working on a book, do you make it a point to write a certain number of pages every day?

BOWLES: As many as possible—that's all I can say. Generally one.

INTERVIEWER: You don't actually count the words, I suppose, as Hemingway is said to have done?

BOWLES: Oh no, that would drive me crazy. Really, count the words! It's beyond my comprehension. He must have been paid by the word.

INTERVIEWER: I believe that with him it was a matter of conscience; he had simply committed himself to a certain quota.

BOWLES: The novel's finished when you've told the story, as far as I can see.

INTERVIEWER: All of your novels have foreign settings. Can you explain your interest in—

BOWLES: In far away places and "backward" people? Well, I don't know that. Probably some fundamental defect in my character. You find it hard to answer when someone asks you why you can't get on with your own people—and it does come back to that, certainly, that one finds oneself ill at ease in the land where one was born and brought up, among one's equals. And one finds himself *not* ill at ease among others. And it puts one in a very strange position somehow, because one is quite aware that in these countries in many respects people are definitely inferior. On the other hand, one's also aware that in other respects they're superior. And then one realizes there really is no comparison possible. And one just says, "I find it more congenial." It may or may not be rationalizing some defect in one's character, as I say—or rather in one's development, not necessarily in character.

INTERVIEWER: I think it's probably true that literary people, in particular, often find themselves ill at ease in civilized society, so-called.

BOWLES: Of course. Because they reject, at this moment in history, the mass society. I think that's it. And I do too.

INTERVIEWER: You never liked living in the States?

BOWLES: No, I hated it. No, I don't want to live there. I'll have to eventually, I suppose. The world is closing in, you know.

INTERVIEWER: Aren't there *any* places you liked in the States? Some cities you preferred over others?

BOWLES: I don't like cities anywhere. I like the country. I don't want to be with a lot of people—even backward people! Much less Americans, who are forward people. I like the world as it is, you know— the trees, the wind, the globe and whatever's on it. To take a walk in the city is to me just a waste of time, whereas to take a walk in the country is always wonderful.

INTERVIEWER: Yet the life in your Moroccan streets is very colorful. It's a constant spectacle, with something always going on.

BOWLES: Going *on* rather than going *by*. There's no metropolis here yet, thank God. Yes, I know that, because when I leave this country to go anywhere else, I feel that everywhere else is slightly dead: a certain human element is missing. Taxis always rushing by, and none of the little groups that one sees everywhere in Morocco, with just a few people standing around talking or maybe haggling over something. . . . Yes, it's wonderful that here there are those little—what shall I call them?— rocks in the brook that just stay there while everything else rushes by them in the water, people who just stand or sit all day while time goes by and people go by. That's the proof that life goes on, somehow, whereas in New York there isn't any proof. It's all going by, nothing going on.

INTERVIEWER: Do you feel that artists, generally, have a hard time of it in America? I gather you do, because you have chosen to live elsewhere and I'm sure that being an artist has had something to do with that choice. What, exactly, is the danger as you see it?

BOWLES: I don't know that there is any, to all artists. I certainly wouldn't recommend to a young writer that he leave the States just because he is a writer. Personally I felt antipathetic toward the whole set-up, but whether that was because I was a writer or not I haven't any idea. We'll say that thirty or forty years ago, when I was in my formative stage, there didn't seem to be any place for the artist there: he was considered to be an outsider. I resented that more than anything else, I suppose: the general attitude that any artist, particularly a creative artist—even more than an interpretative artist—was an outcast, a pariah. Naturally, if you were rejected, you rejected back. . . .

INTERVIEWER: What is it you look for in the fiction of other writers? Is it the story that interests you chiefly, or is it an idea or a moral message?

BOWLES: A moral message is the *last* thing I look for. I reject moral messages, unless they're my own. I don't like other people's moral messages, no! I suppose what I look for is accurate expressions, for accurate accounts of states of mind, the way in which the consciousness of each individual is reported in the book. How the author makes us believe in the reality of his characters, in the reality of his settings.

INTERVIEWER: And is this what you try to do yourself, as a writer—to create a character's state of mind so that it gives the impression of absolute reality? Or are you more interested in getting across an idea, a message? Some of your stories *are* parables.

BOWLES: Yes. Well, both. It depends on the story, really.

INTERVIEWER: And is it true, as has sometimes been charged—I believe it was Leslie Fiedler who called you a "pornographer of terror"—that you have occasionally written stories intended primarily to shock?

BOWLES: Not primarily, no.

INTERVIEWER: (INDECIPHERABLE) . . . so that the effect of shock is created [in "Pages from Cold] Point?"

BOWLES: That was not meant to shock. It's supposed to evoke a certain atmosphere, really. When I write a story I think more or less the same way as if I were writing a poem. It's quite different from writing a novel.

INTERVIEWER: What about "A Distant Episode," which I think shocks at the same time it teaches?

BOWLES: Precisely. If there's anything to teach in "A Distant Episode," it can only be taught through shock. Shock is a *sine qua non* to the story. You don't teach a thing like that unless you are able, in some way, to make the reader understand what the situation would be like to *him*. And that involves shock.

INTERVIEWER: Would you agree that the writer who *merely* shocks doesn't give his reader a vision of life?

BOWLES: I think so, yes.

INTERVIEWER: That he's concentrating solely on effect, and that this may have nothing to do with the way he feels about life?

BOWLES: Well, it does have *something* to do with it. But it's uninteresting because it has to do only with his personal neuroses, because if he's interested in shocking, it's a therapeutic thing to help himself, obviously. So he's not really free. Insofar as he wants only to shock, he's a victim. No, I can see that a lot of my stories were definitely therapeutic. Maybe they should never have been published, but they were. But they certainly had a therapeutic purpose behind them when I wrote them. For me personally. I needed to clarify an issue for myself, and the only way of doing it was to create a fake psychodrama in which I could be everybody.

INTERVIEWER: Some critics have pointed out that the quietness of your style increases the sense of horror, so that the effect of shock is created through understatement. Is this deliberate on your part?

BOWLES: Understatement is better than "enough" statement, and certainly better than too much. But I doubt that it *creates* the horror; it's just a concomitant effect.

INTERVIEWER: How do you feel about the way readers react to your books? Does it seem to you that they get out of them what you intended?

BOWLES: Some people, yes. I haven't lived in America for so long, except for the brief period in Santa Monica, when I was teaching. I don't know many literary people. And I've never discussed my books with writers I do know.

INTERVIEWER: Do you think that's a disadvantage?

BOWLES: It must be. Not having known the other, I can't say for certain. But I should think that never taking part in any literary life at all would be a disadvantage, yes.

INTERVIEWER: But you do read a great deal?

BOWLES: I read, yes. But that's not taking part. You understand, I don't want to take part in literary life, that's the whole point. On the other hand, I think you're right to ask if it is a disadvantage. It probably is. It's also a disadvantage to live out of your country.

INTERVIEWER: I imagine there are compensations.

BOWLES: Oh, yes! A great many. This house, for instance. It would be extremely difficult in the United States simply to go out in the month of May and choose an absolutely silent house and move in, occupy it for the summer, and then move out again. It would probably cost a thousand dollars a month. It would have to be miles from everything, which would mean being dependent on a car.

INTERVIEWER: You are fortunate in being able to live where you like. Many writers would envy you that. Have you never found it difficult financially?

BOWLES: Well, there's no guarantee of an annual income. I've always just trusted to luck. Have to. There's no guarantee whatever. No one has ever subsidized me or agreed to take over expenses. Fortunately I was always able to live on what I earned in the theatre. That gave me a decent living, even during the Depression—enough to travel on, but I never made a great deal. . . .

INTERVIEWER: . . . But isn't selection necessary in art?

BOWLES: Well, it's much less likely that a good work will come out of a free association than out of planning. You're taking a much greater risk, that's all. It can happen, of course. But it's almost always flawed, like most emeralds. However, I think calculation should only come in at a certain point. It's not a substitute for imagination, and it can be very dangerous—in certain work, not all.

INTERVIEWER: There is certainly a tendency among romantic writers—and I include the Beats and the Surrealists in this category—to discourage conscious control: they feel that only by ignoring external form can they be faithful to a higher or rather deeper form.

BOWLES: Organic form. Yes. But I doubt very much that with no conscious control at any point during the work it would be possible to construct that organic form. I don't think one could follow the Surrealist method absolutely, with no conscious control in the choice of material, and be likely to arrive at organic form. . . .

INTERVIEWER: . . . I believe it would be possible to argue that your story, "The Fourth Day Out from Santa Cruz," which is a parable, is universal in that sense: wouldn't the truth of that story hold good for human beings everywhere? Wouldn't what happens to your sailor in that story be just as true of a sailor on an American ship as on a Spanish ship or on any ship that sails with human beings? Isn't it a condition of human behavior everywhere?

BOWLES: Maybe not. Maybe not. Human behavior is contingent upon the particular culture that forms it. Maybe the behavior of the sailors in that story is only a condition of modern life. I don't think it would necessarily have been the same on an Indian ship, for instance. Not all cultures insist on the destruction of innocence.

Interview, 1981

Jeffrey Bailey

INTERVIEWER: For many people, the mention of your name evokes romantic images of the artist's life in exotic, far-away places. Do you see yourself as a kind of consummate expatriate?

BOWLES: I'm afraid not. I don't see myself as a consummate anything. I don't see myself, really, I have no ego. I didn't find the United States particularly interesting and once I found places that were more interesting I chose to live in them, which I think makes sense.

INTERVIEWER: Was this decision to leave the United States an early one?

BOWLES: I made it at seventeen, so I guess you'd say it was an early decision. Some people absorb things more quickly than others, and I think I had a fairly good idea of what life would be like for me in the States, and I didn't want it.

INTERVIEWER: What would it have been like?

BOWLES: Boring. There was nothing I wanted there, and once I'd moved away I saw that all I needed from the States was money. I went back there for that. I've never yet gone there without the definite guarantee of making money. Just going for the pleasure of it, I've never done.

INTERVIEWER: Since your contact with foreign places has so obviously nurtured your writing, perhaps you would never have been a writer if you had stayed in the States.

BOWLES: Quite possibly not. I might have gone on as a composer. I cut the composing cord in 1947, when I moved here, although, as I say, I went back several times to write scores for Broadway. . . .

INTERVIEWER: Did giving up an entire career because you disliked life in America leave you feeling hostile toward the place?

BOWLES: No, no. But when you say "America" to me, all I think of

From Jeffrey Bailey's interview with Paul Bowles. First published in *The Paris Review*, No. 81 (1981): 62–98. Reprinted by permission.

is New York City where I was born and brought up. I know that New York isn't America; still, my image of America *is* New York. But there's no hostility. I just think it's a great shame, what has happened there. I don't think it will ever be put right; but then again, I never expect anything to be put right. Nothing ever is. Things go on and become other things. The whole character of the country has changed beyond recognition since my childhood. One always thinks everything's got worse— and in most respects it has—but that's meaningless. What does one mean when one says that things are getting worse? It's becoming more like the future, that's all. It's just moving ahead. The future will be infinitely "worse" than the present; and in *that* future, the future will be immeasurably "worse" than the future that we can see. Naturally.

INTERVIEWER: You're a pessimist.

BOWLES: Well, look for yourself. You don't have to be a pessimist to see it. There's always the chance of a universal holocaust in which a few billion people will be burned. I don't hope for that, but it's what I see as a probability.

INTERVIEWER: Can't one also hope for things like a cure for cancer, an effective ban on nuclear arms, an upsurge of concern for the environment, and a deeper consciousness of being?

BOWLES: You can hope for anything, of course. I expect enormous things to happen in the future, but I don't think they'll be things which people born in my generation will think are great and wonderful. Perhaps people born in 1975 will think otherwise. I mean, people born in 1950 think television is great.

INTERVIEWER: Because American technology has already contributed so much to making what you regard as an inevitably undesirable future, I guess it's understandable that living outside your indigenous culture became almost a compulsion with you.

BOWLES: Not almost; it was a *real* compulsion. Even as a small child, I was always eager to get away. I remember when I was six years old, I was sent off to spend two weeks with someone—I don't know who it was or why I was sent—and I begged to stay longer. I didn't want to go home. Again, when I was nine and my father had pneumonia, I was sent off for a month or two and I kept writing letters asking, "Please, let me stay longer." I didn't want to see my parents again. I didn't want to go back into all that.

INTERVIEWER: In *Without Stopping*, you were quite frank about your feelings toward your parents in describing the fondness you had for your mother and your estrangement from your father.

BOWLES: I think most boys are fond of their mothers. The hostility involved with my father was very real. It started on his side and became reciprocated, naturally, at an early age. I don't know what the matter was. Maybe he didn't want any children. I never knew the real story of why he was so angry with me, although my maternal grandmother told me it was simply because he was jealous. She said he couldn't bear to have my mother pay attention to this third person, me. It's probably true.

INTERVIEWER: Did this negative relationship with your father affect your becoming a traveler and an artist?

BOWLES: Probably, I don't know. I've never really gone over it in my mind to see what caused what. I probably couldn't. It's obvious that a shut-in childhood is likely to make an introverted child and that an introverted child is more likely to be "artistic." . . .

INTERVIEWER: Were you running away from something?

BOWLES: No, I was running toward something, although I didn't know what at the time.

INTERVIEWER: Did you ever find it?

BOWLES: Yes, I found it over the years. What I was ultimately running toward was my grave, of course: "The paths of glory lead but to the grave." . . . Of course, I've never been a thinking person. A lot seems to happen without my conscious knowledge.

INTERVIEWER: Has it always been that way, or has it developed over the years?

BOWLES: It was always like that. All through my late teens, from sixteen on, I was writing surrealist poetry. I read André (Breton) who explained how to do it, and so I learned how to write without being conscious of what I was doing. I learned how to make it grammatically correct and even to have a certain style without the slightest idea of what I was writing. One part of my mind was doing the writing, and God knows what the other part was doing. I suppose it was bulldozing the subconscious, dredging up ooze. I don't know how those things work, and I don't want to know.

INTERVIEWER: It sounds as though Breton served to inspire your early writing. Did you have many "inspiration" writers?

BOWLES: Not really. During my early years in Europe, I was very much taken with Lautréamont. I carried him with me wherever I went, but I got over that and didn't supplant him with anyone else. You may have such enthusiasms when you're very young, but you don't usually have them when you get older, even a few years older. There were many writers whom I admired, and if they were living I tended to seek them out: Stein, Gide, Cocteau, many others. . . .

INTERVIEWER: How do you write?

BOWLES: I don't use a typewriter. It's too heavy, too much trouble. I use a notebook, and I write in bed. Ninety-five percent of everything I've written has been done in bed.

INTERVIEWER: And the typing?

BOWLES: The typing of a manuscript to send out is another thing. That's just drudgery, not work. By work I mean the invention of something, the putting down, the creation of a page with words on it. . . .

INTERVIEWER: You don't seem to have a particularly high regard for your talent as a writer.

BOWLES: No, no. I haven't.

INTERVIEWER: Why not?

BOWLES: I don't know. It doesn't seem very relevant.

INTERVIEWER: Haven't people encouraged you along the way, telling you that you were good?

BOWLES: Oh, yes. Of course.

INTERVIEWER: You just didn't believe them?

BOWLES: I believed that they believed it, and I wanted to hear them say they liked this or disliked that, and why. But I was never sure of their viewpoint, so it was hard to know whether they understood what they were liking or disliking. . . .

INTERVIEWER: In reading your work, one doesn't expect to be led to some conclusion through a simple progression of events. One has the sense of participating in a spontaneous growth of events, one on top of another.

BOWLES: Yes? Well, they grow that way. That's the point, you see. I don't feel that I wrote these books. I feel as though they had been written by my arm, by my brain, my organism, but that they're not necessarily mine. The difficulty is that I've never thought anything belonged to me. At one time, I bought an island off Ceylon and I thought that when I had my two feet planted on it I'd be able to say: "This island is mine." I couldn't; it was meaningless. I felt nothing at all, so I sold it. . . .

INTERVIEWER: Was writing, for you, a means of alleviating a sense of aloneness by communicating intimately with other people?

BOWLES: No. I look on it simply as a natural function. As far as I'm concerned it's fun, and it just happens. If I don't feel like doing it, I don't do it.

INTERVIEWER: One is struck by the violence in your work. Almost all the characters in *The Delicate Prey*, for example, were victimized by either physical or psychological violence.

BOWLES: Yes, I suppose. The violence served a therapeutic purpose. It's unsettling to think that at any moment life can flare up into senseless violence. But it can and does, and people need to be ready for it. What you make for others is first of all what you make for yourself. If I'm persuaded that our life is predicated upon violence, that the entire structure of what we call civilization, the scaffolding that we've built up over the millenia, can collapse at any moment, then whatever I write is going to be affected by that assumption. The process of life presupposes violence, in the plant world the same as the animal world. But among the animals only man can conceptualize violence. Only man can *enjoy* the *idea* of destruction.

INTERVIEWER: In many of your characterizations, there's a strange combination of fatalism and naiveté. I'm thinking in particular of Kit and Port Moresby in *The Sheltering Sky*. It seemed to me that their frenetic movement was prompted by an obsessive fear of self-confrontation.

BOWLES: Moving around a lot is a good way of postponing the day of reckoning. I'm happiest when I'm moving. When you've cut yourself off from the life you've been living and you haven't yet established another life, you're free. That's a very pleasant sensation, I've always thought. If you don't know where you're going, you're even freer.

INTERVIEWER: Your characters seem to be psychologically alienated from each other and from themselves, and though their isolation may be accentuated by the fact that you've set them as foreigners in exotic places, one feels that they'd be no different at home; that their problems are deeper than the matter of locale.

BOWLES: Of course. Everyone is isolated from everyone else. The concept of society is like a cushion to protect us from the knowledge of that isolation. A fiction that serves as an anaesthetic.

INTERVIEWER: And the exotic settings are secondary?

BOWLES: The transportation of characters to such settings often acts as a catalyst or a detonator, without which there'd be no action, so I shouldn't call the settings secondary. Probably if I hadn't had some contact with what you call "exotic" places, it wouldn't have occurred to me to write at all. . . .

INTERVIEWER: What is life like for you in Tangier these days?

BOWLES: Well, it's my home. I'm settled here and I'm reasonably content with things as they are. I see enough people. I suppose if I had been living in the States all this time I'd probably have many more intimate friends whom I'd see regularly. But I haven't lived there in many years, and most of the people I knew are no longer there. I can't go back and make new acquaintances at this late date.

INTERVIEWER: All those trunks you've got stacked in your entryway bear testament to your globe-trotting days. Don't you miss traveling?

BOWLES: Not really, surprisingly enough. And Tangier is as good a place for me to be as any other, I think. If travel still consisted of taking ships, I'd continue moving around. Flying to me isn't travel. It's just getting from one place to another as fast as possible. I like to have plenty of luggage with me when I start out on a voyage. You never know how many months or years you'll be gone or where you'll go eventually. But flying is like television: you have to take what they give you because there's nothing else. It's impossible.

INTERVIEWER: Tangier is nothing like the booming international city it once was, is it?

BOWLES: No, of course not. It's a very dull city now. . . .

INTERVIEWER: What was Tangier like back then [early 1960s]?

BOWLES: By the Sixties, it had calmed down considerably, although it was still a good deal livelier than it is these days. Everyone had much more money, for one thing. Now only members of the European jet-set have enough to lead amusing lives, and everyone else is poor. In general, Moroccans have a slightly higher standard of living than they did, by European criteria. That is, they have television, cars and a certain amount of plumbing in their houses, although they all claim they don't eat as well as they did thirty years ago. But nobody does, anywhere.

INTERVIEWER: Moroccan life seems to be so incongruously divided between Eastern and Western influences—the *medinas* and *nouvelles villes*, *djellabas* and blue jeans, donkey-carts and Mercedes—that it sometimes seems downright schizophrenic. I wonder where the Moroccan psyche really is.

BOWLES: For there to be a Moroccan psyche there'd have to be a national consciousness, which I don't think has yet come into being. The people are much more likely to think of themselves as members of a subdivision: I'm a Soussi, I'm a Riffi, I'm a Filali. Then there are those lost souls who privately think of themselves as Europeans because they've studied in Europe. But the vast majority of Moroccans have their minds on getting together enough money for tomorrow's meal.

INTERVIEWER: Through the years that you've been here, have you ever had feelings of cultural estrangement, or even superiority?

BOWLES: That wouldn't be very productive, would it? Of course I feel apart, at one remove from the people here. But since they expect that in any case, there's no difficulty. The difficulties are in the United States, where there's no convention for maintaining apartness. The foreigners who try to "be Moroccan" never succeed, and manage to look ridiculous while they're trying. It seems likely that it's this very quality of impenetrability in the Moroccans that makes the country fascinating to outsiders.

INTERVIEWER: But isn't there a special psychological dimension to the situation of a foreigner living in Morocco? It seems to me that a foreigner here is often looked upon automatically as a kind of victim.

BOWLES:: Well, he *is* a victim. The Moroccans wouldn't use the word. They'd say "a useful object." They believe that they, as Moslems, are the master group in the world, and that God allows other religious groups to exist principally for them to manipulate. That seems to be the average man's attitude. Since it's not expressed as a personal opinion but is tacitly accepted by all, I don't find it objectionable. Once a thing like that is formulated you don't have to worry about the character of the person who professes it. It's no longer a question of whether or not he agrees with it as part of his personal credo.

INTERVIEWER: Doesn't this rather limit the nature of a relationship between a Moroccan and a non-Moslem?

BOWLES: It completely determines the nature of a relationship, of course, but I wouldn't say that it limits it, necessarily.

INTERVIEWER: You've never met a Moroccan with whom you felt you could have a Western-style relationship in terms of depth and reciprocity?

BOWLES: No, no. That's an absurd concept. Like expecting a boulder to spread its wings and fly away. . . .

INTERVIEWER: What do you know about Moroccan witchcraft?

BOWLES: Witchcraft is a loaded word. To use it evokes something sinister, a regression to archaic behavior. Here it's an accepted facet of daily life, as much as the existence of bacteria is in ours. And their attitude toward it is very much the same as ours is toward infection. The possibility is always there, and one must take precautions. But in Morocco only what you'd call offensive magic is considered "witchcraft." Defensive magic, which plays the same game from the other side of the net, is holy, and can only be efficacious if it's practiced under the aegis of the Koran. If the *fqih* uses the magician's tricks to annul the spell cast by the magician, it doesn't necessarily follow that the *fqih* believes implicitly in the existence of the spell. He's there to cure the people who visit him. He acts as confessor, psychiatrist, and father image. Obviously some of the *fouqqiyane* must be charlatans, out to get hold of all the money they can. But the people get on to the quacks fairly fast.

INTERVIEWER: One hears a lot about the legend of Aicha Qandicha. Who is she?

BOWLES: You mean who do I think she really is? I'd say she's a vestigial Tanit. You know when a new faith takes over, the gods of the previous faith are made the personification of evil. Since she was still here in some force when Islam arrived, she had to be reckoned with. So she became this beautiful but dreaded spirit who still frequented running water and hunted men in order to ruin them. It's strange; she has a Mexican counterpart, La Llorona, who also lives along the banks of streams where there's vegetation, and who wanders at night calling to men. She's also of great beauty, and also has long tresses. The difference is that in Mexico she weeps. That's an Indian addition. In Morocco she calls out your name, often in your mother's voice, and the danger is that you'll turn and see her face, in which case you're lost. Unless, unless. There are lots of unlesses. A series of formulas from the Koran, a knife with a steel blade, or even a magnet can save you if you're quick. Not all Moroccans consider Aicha Qandicha a purely destructive spirit. Sacrifices are still made to her, just as they are to the saints. The Hamadcha leave chickens at her sacred grotto. But in general she inspires terror.

INTERVIEWER: The Moroccans have had an extremely violent history, and even now it seems that there's an innate belligerence in their character; a constant undercurrent of violence. Do you think that's true?

BOWLES: As far as I can see, people from all corners of the earth have an unlimited potential for violence. . . .

INTERVIEWER: One also feels, don't you think, that the concept of time is completely different here?

BOWLES: Well, yes, but it's partially because one lives a very different life. In America or Europe the day is divided into hours and one has appointments. Here the day isn't measured; it simply goes by. If you see people, it's generally by accident. Time is merely more or less, and everything is perhaps. It's upsetting if you take it seriously. Otherwise it's relaxing, because there's no need to hurry. Plenty of time for everything.

INTERVIEWER: What are your future plans, as regards writing?

BOWLES: I don't think much about the future. I've got no plans for future books. The book of stories I'm writing at present takes up all my attention. More tales about Morocco. If an idea were to come to me which required the novel form, I'd write a novel. If it happens it happens. I'm not ambitious, as you know. If I had been, I'd have stayed in New York.

Interview, 1974

Michael Rogers

Q: Did you ever smoke [kif] when you were trying something creative?

A: Theater scores, yes, but serious music, no.

Q: How about writing?

A: Oh, I wrote with it a great deal. In fact, I used it consciously in most of the books. In *The Sheltering Sky*, I got to the death scene and I didn't feel up to tackling it, so I ate a lot of majoun and just lay back that afternoon and the next day I had it resolved. . . .

Q: Mrabet is quite a storyteller.

A: It starts at night; he tells five or six stories in a row, one right after the other, and each one you wish you could put down. I always say, don't tell it now, I'd like to record it—but he tells it anyway and it gets lost. He can never remember them.

Q: He makes them up on the spot?

A: I don't whether he makes them up or synthesizes them. I don't think he knows. The Moroccans don't make much distinction between objective truth and what we'd call fantasy.

Q: Power to the perceiver.

A: That's what they say, strangely enough. What do you want to believe? What do you want to think? There's a truth for everyone, and no one truth carries away all the others. Statistical truth means nothing to them. No Moroccan will ever tell you what he thinks, or does, or means. He'll tell you some of it and tell you other things that are completely false and then weave them together into a very believable core, which you swallow, and that's what's considered civilized. What's the purpose of telling the truth? It's not interesting, generally. It's more interesting to doctor it up a bit first of all, so it's more decorative and hence more civilized. And besides, how could anyone be so idiotic as to open himself to the dangers involved in telling the

From "Conversations in Morocco" by Michael Rogers, from *Rolling Stone* Issue #161, May 23, 1974, pp. 48–54. Reprinted by permission.

unadorned truth to people? You even have two pockets in your kif pouch—one for the kif you smoke yourself and one for the less good you give your friends.

Q: But everyone knows that, right?

A: Oh sure, but they're not sure which part you keep the good in and which you keep the bad in. You change from day to day.

Q: Lord.

A: Well, the Moroccans can read each other's lies pretty well, so it's a whole art of pulling the pieces together and trying to get the truth from the other's invention. Europeans have the reputation of swallowing everything, because they're too polite to say, "Well, I don't believe that." They say, "Oh, really?" and perhaps some of them really do believe what the Moroccans tell them. I don't know . . . they must think we're pretty foolish people. I think they look upon us with a certain amount of pity and some tolerance. There's a popular song which begins, "Our love was so nice at the beginning and then it turned Christian. . . ."

Q: Which means?

A: Which means it became . . . ah—messed up, not straight. They'll say, "Now you're talking like a Christian," and that means, now you're saying what you don't believe.

On the other hand, they trust us. If you say, I'll take your wrist watch and give it back tomorrow, they would certainly rather give it to you than to a Moroccan. They'd rather work for you than for a Moroccan, because they believe you'll more likely pay them their wages. If you ask them why we exist, they will explain immediately that Allah made the Christians for us to live on. The Christians are for the Moslems to live off of, by milking. That's what life is all about.

They used to capture us, of course, and carry us off and make slaves of us, for centuries. The Barbary pirates—all Morocco was pirates, the whole coast of the Mediterranean, at least. . . .

Q: Morocco is changing very quickly.

A: The country is in such a state of transition you can't even use the present tense, really. The impact of technology on the culture, for example. Television, automobiles, gas pumps—they know how to make them work, but they have no idea why they work. Several years ago there was a student at Meknes military school who was explaining something to Brion Gysin and he said, "It works by magic—just like an airplane."

And everyone realized that, God, here he is just about ready to go to St. Cyr in Paris, a man of 18 or 19 who's studied geometry and all the rest, but says it works by magic like an airplane.

And that means, of course, at any moment it might not work—and they're delighted when the machine breaks. Since it's magic, it's obvious that when you break it, then you've really won, you've proven that it doesn't exist. They love to see machines fail, or medicines fail, and then say, see—man can't do anything, only Allah can do it. All these things we think are so important are just toys and one day they'll all break and then we'll have to live in front of Allah without toys. But, of course, as long as the toys are here. . . .

Q: I've noticed that in your fiction you like to set up situations with the civilized man—the faintly decadent European—who deals with a less civilized culture and loses disastrously.

A: Yes, the degenerate European who feels able to cope with his own culture and therefore imagines he can cope with any culture, imagines wrongly.

Q: It's a common fantasy among travelers of my generation that it's possible to shed, say, one's Americanism, go barefoot and wear a djellabah and thus be part of a native system.

A: Well, that's a recurrent fantasy. Rousseauesque.

Q: True.

A: But there is no such thing as going backwards, really. You can't identify with a culture that is several centuries behind what you know. If you were able to become part of a truly archaic culture, it would imply something wrong with the psychic organism, I'm afraid. If a Westerner encounters an archaic culture with the idea of *learning* from it, I think he can succeed. He wants to absorb the alien for his own benefit. But to lose oneself in it is not a normal desire. A romantic desire, yes, but actually to try and do it is disastrous.

Q: What does it take to be considered crazy in this country?

A: Well, a bit more than by our standards. The place is full of what we would call lunatics. As long as they don't hurt anybody, it's all right. When they do hurt someone, they either put them away or they don't.

Q: I'd imagine there are some incredible kinds of mental conditions here.

A: Well, there's one very strange phenomenon here that I don't know of anywhere else. Perhaps in someplace like Malaysia . . . it's a mass psychosis around a character called Aicha Qandicha. You ever heard of it?

Q: Aicha Qandicha.

A: She's a woman—a spirit in the form of a woman. Practically every Moroccan has had contact with her some way or another. She's legion, she's manifold, like Santa Claus. I have a book that says, about 25 years ago, there were 35,000 men in Morocco married to her. A lot of the people in Ber Rechid—the psychiatric hospital—are married to her.

Q: She appears to people?

A: She appears to men, yes, never to women. Women don't need to worry about her. Except that they're even more afraid of her. I don't know why—you say her name and they go to the corners of the room and whisper a prayer to clean the room of her name. Especially when they've just come from the country, the women are terrified of Aicha Qandicha.

If you're a man, it's always late at night that she calls you, when you're walking, and it has to be by running water. With a certain amount of vegetation. She will call you from behind, and of course you know better than to turn around. She often calls you in the voice of your mother. If you turn around, you're lost, because she's the most beautiful woman in the world and once you look at her you have no power against her at all. You must never see her, keep going, and if possible, have a piece of steel in your hand. Anything made of steel, plus the right prayers, and so on.

Q: What exactly happens if you look at her?

A: Then you're married to her and that's that. You begin behaving very strangely. There are several well-known husbands of Aicha Qandicha around Tangier. They walk along brooks and river beds, hoping to hear her voice—you see them wandering. They'll come into cafes and sit down and be quite normal, but if anybody mentions Aicha Qandicha, they very quietly get up and leave. Most people know better than to mention it. But they all know when the man comes in.

Q: A contagious psychosis. . . .

A: Right. And when they find Aicha Qandicha again, they may make love to her right there, doesn't matter who's there. What you see is they're sort of screwing the ground, that's all. Children standing around, watching, laughing. Of course, then the police catch them and take them away. They don't beat them, just shut them up. Then they ship them to Ber Rechid.

Q: Amazing. . . .

A: Mental illness is very different in Morocco from in Europe or America. Based on different things. There was an American here who decided to set himself up as a psychiatrist in Casablanca, taking both Moslems and Christians, but his interest was in Moslems. And all he could discover in 13 years of practice was that everything was undifferentiated for the Moroccans. And Freudian therapy had nothing at all to do with it. You want a cup of tea? . . .

Q: Magic and poison.

A: Well, that's part of everyday life. I'm not afraid of magic, but I'm afraid of poison.

Q: The Moroccans make nasty poisons?

A: Oh, horrible. Because they don't work right away. Little by little. There was a man here, an Englishman, two years ago, who was poisoned. When he woke up in the mornings, he would find incisions, designs cut into his feet. During the night someone came in and carved these cabalistic designs with a penknife on his feet. He couldn't even walk, they were so cut up. Obviously, he must have been very drugged, and every morning he would find these new tic-tac-toe sorts of things on his soles. He finally died.

Q: How did he get himself in such a situation?

A: I have no idea. . . .

Q: What's the future for the expatriate population here in Tangier?

A: Oh, the population itself is diminishing. The tens of thousands of little European artisans and shopkeepers and so on, are leaving—and have already left, most of them. This year there was a big Moroccanization program, and now all companies have to be controlled at least 51% by Moroccans. If you have a bakery, a cobbler's shop, you have to turn half of it over to Moroccans. Of course, you don't—what you do is sell out cheap. About 60,000 French have left Morocco in the last four months.

Q: That's a big change.

A: Certainly. Who will want to live here, after a few years, when there's no way of eating properly, or having anything done? No—it would be impossible. What will come of it, I don't know. Eventually maybe Europeans and Americans won't be able to visit countries like this. Practically no Arab country receives tourists any more.

Q: The Tangier way of life is disappearing fast.

A: Very fast. But then it is all over the world, too.

Q: If you had to leave Morocco, where would you go?

A: Where would you go?—that's the point. I don't know whether one would have a choice. If one had to leave here, I'm sure one would be taken willy-nilly to the United States. If someone, say, should happen to make Hassan dead, things could change very quickly. As the American consul says, one small bag down at the dock at dawn and we'll have boats to get you out. But you won't be able to take anything with you. You'd have to start out again from the United States, and decide where to go, but with nothing . . . you'd have to buy everything all over again. It'd be a job.

Q: And there's no place like Tangier, or the Tangier of ten years ago?

A: I don't know of any place in the world like it. There were, but now. . . .

Interview, 1986
Paula Chin

CHIN: Most of your writings are stories of horror and violence set in Africa, Asia and Latin America. Why have you felt compelled to write on these subjects in these places?

BOWLES: Precisely because of the fact that I am afraid of [violence] and hope it won't happen to me. Writing is, I suppose, a superstitious way of keeping the horror at bay, of keeping the evil outside. As for where they take place, it's probably easier to believe such stories happen in Latin America, North Africa or Sri Lanka than in Europe or the United States.

CHIN: How much of your writing is based on actual events?

BOWLES: Oh, not very much. Some of them are based on tales told by other people, some are accounts of real events people have related to me—and sometimes they are pure invention. Fiction, you know, can grow like a weed. . . .

CHIN: You have expressed an intense dislike for "the modern world"—was that part of the reason you chose to settle in Morocco?

BOWLES: I detest modern gadgets—planes, television, big cities, airports, crowds. The world has changed enormously, and what used to be pleasure is now an ordeal. If I hadn't traveled a lot when I was younger, perhaps I wouldn't have been content to stay put. Now I don't want to be anywhere I've been before because I know I'll be disappointed. . . .

CHIN: With your work, your travels and the artistic coterie to which you belonged, you have lived a very unconventional life. Was there an element of rebellion in this?

BOWLES: I traveled to see places I didn't know. To a certain extent I did it to shock my parents, mostly my father. It's a Freudian story. If I hadn't had parents, I would never have joined the Communist Party.

(Bowles joined only briefly during the 1930s.) But they were so horrified, it seemed worthwhile at the time. . . .

CHIN: Forty years after the publication of your first novel, what is your view of the world?

BOWLES: The world has gone to pieces in a moral sense. No one is honest anymore the way they were 60 years ago. There was a concept of what is a gentleman; it was a valued attribute of our Western culture. Now no one gives a hoot. There is also an enormous emphasis on money. The concept of women in the United States—being married, having children and working all day—is ghastly. How can children have moral standards instilled in them? I can be accused, at my age, of being senile and in love with the past, and there is some truth in these allegations. I can't regret that the world's a mess, save that I think it's too bad for everybody.

Talk with Paul Bowles

Harry Breit

The question of music and prose, it's a tricky one to answer. . . . If I had ever known I was going to write the latter seriously, I should have taken another name. I wrote a short story, and then another, and then others, and very quickly I found myself writing a novel, by which time of course it was too late to pretend to be another person. I must admit, however, that I still think it would be fun to have a *nom de plume*. Yet perhaps it would be bad psychologically: one might feel less implicated, less responsible toward one's self. I don't know.

[On music and prose] For one thing, I had always felt extremely circumscribed in music. It seemed to me there were a great many things I wanted to say that were too precise to express in musical terms. Writing music was not enough of a cathartic. Nor, perhaps, would writing words be if I should do it exclusively. The two together work very well. As to the influence, I think there is a considerable one. I am extremely conscious of the sound of the word, the phrase and the sentence. Not so much the paragraph; it's probably nonsense to speak of the sound of the paragraph anyway. The truth is that I've never thought of any of this until this moment. Since this is an interview I suppose it won't matter if I occasionally produce a bit of nonsense. One usually does in conversation, but then one cleverly covers it up with word or gesture.

In "The Sheltering Sky" I did think of the three parts as separate 'movements' but I can see that was an error. A novel is not a symphony or a sonata. If it's anything that can be compared to music, it's a melody.

I have no political ideas to speak of. I don't think we're likely to get to know the Moslems very well, and I suspect that if we should we'd find them less sympathetic than we do at present. And I believe the same applies to their getting to know us. At the moment they admire us for our technique; I don't think they could find more than that compatible. Their culture is essentially barbarous, their mentality that of a purely predatory people. It seems to me that their political aspirations, while emotionally understandable, are absurd, and any realization of them will have a disastrous effect on the rest of the world.

The critics who refer to what I have written as "decadent" would be likely to be the same people who take it for granted that the U.S. has the highest moral standard in the world, and that the "outlook" of its inhabitants is automatically "healthier" than elsewhere. I don't think either of those hypotheses needs discussion. The xenophobe will always find the alien unhealthy; even the rustic does the urbanite. I'm afraid of you, thus I must find you inferior. Unhealthiness is one of a hundred ways of being inferior. It's the obvious one in my case, because I am writing about disease. Why? Because I am writing about today . . . not about what happens today, but about today itself.

You ask what decadence is. I should think in art and literature nothing is decadent but incompetence and commercialism. If I stress the various facets of unhappiness, it is because I believe unhappiness should be studied very carefully; this is certainly no time for anyone to pretend to be happy, or to put his unhappiness away in the dark. (And anyone who is not unhappy now must be a monster, a saint or an idiot.) You must watch your universe as it cracks above your head.

Interview, 1988

Allen Hibbard

AH: What is the motive for writing a story? Why do you bother to sit down and work out a story that has been told, or work out an idea that has just popped into your head?

PB: I suppose a lot of it is the desire to make a pattern, an order out of what is more chaotic than it should be—to give it form.

AH: Do you imagine a kind of audience out there?

PB: No. I'm my own audience. I assume that something that satisfies me will satisfy the audience that I write for—whoever that is. I don't think that it will satisfy the great public, but that is something else. They have other books to satisfy them.

AH: Indeed, they do! You do the same thing, I bet, with your music. Simply listening and seeing what works and when you were content with the sound you got, that was it.

PB: Yes. In music it's the form and the sound, of course.

AH: Sometimes I get a strong sense in the stories that they were formed, fashioned, almost as though they were miniature musical compositions. There's a real sense of counterpoint, of balance; a sense of when to bring in background, when to introduce dialogue. Again, the analogy which springs to mind is music.

PB: It could be. I'm not conscious of it. People have said it, so therefore it is probably true.

AH: What in your mind stands out as being a major difference between the novel and the story? What can the story do that the novel can't? Which genre do you feel more comfortable with? It seems as though you have been writing more stories recently. . . . They do, of course, take less time to write.

PB: Well, yes, of course. But I enjoy them more.

AH: You don't have to keep up such a sustained effort, and stay with characters so long.

This interview was conducted by Allen Hibbard in Tangier on 17–18 August 1988. It was commissioned especially for this volume and is used here by permission of Mr. Hibbard © Copyright 1988 Allen Hibbard.

PB: It seems as though the writing of a novel isn't over for such a long time.

AH: There seem to be similarities between the internal progress of your characters in stories and those in your novels. Take Port in *The Sheltering Sky*, and Dyar in *Let it Come Down*, for example, and compare them to the protagonists in stories such as "Tapiama" and "Pastor Dowe at Tacaté." They are all characters who enter the unknown, move about in it a while, become uncomfortable, then set out in another direction. The stories seem to be based on some kind of journey—like the novels.

PB: You're simply contrasting some of the stories with novels. . . . I don't know what the connections are. I don't see any. I'm not a critic. I don't analyse these kinds of things. . . . It's all right to pull things apart, to see what the strands are, the fibers.

AH: What kind of sensation did you have upon finishing "Tea on the Mountain," the first story in *The Collected Stories*?

PB: Nostalgia. I was in New York, in Brooklyn Heights, that's where I was writing, in 1939. I wished I was back there to relive what Tangier was like in those days.

AH: You often write about places other than where you are when you are writing.

PB: Uhm, yes. Well, it's natural.

AH: Does it sometimes take a little distance before we can absorb the place?

PB: I never like writing about the place I'm in. I can do it sometimes, if I have to. When I was in my traveling days, I would always write about other places I had been. That's because one has to invent the atmosphere. That is, remember. When writing about the place one is in, it becomes journalism.

AH: There are too many details. They don't have a chance to filter out. When you remember, you leave a lot out.

PB: Also, you remember that which is important for the atmosphere, and that which isn't is forgotten.

AH: In a story like "At Paso Rojo," for example, you wrote at Oche Rios in Jamaica . . . and yet it seems to be set somewhere in Costa Rica. Do sometimes likenesses of the places you are in creep in, even though you may be writing about a place other than you are in, such as in that story?

PB: No, it doesn't do that in that story. It *did* in *The Sheltering Sky*, but that was because it was part of the aesthetic, but it doesn't happen by itself. I made it happen. I made lists of things I saw on my walks, then put them in. I never did it after that. . . .

AH: It's been interesting to look at the various collections of your stories which have come out, and what stories are included in each. One of the stories which caught my eye in *Call at Corazón* [Peter Owen, 1988] which I hadn't seen before was "Sylvie Ann, the Boogie Man."

PB: Yah, that wasn't in any other collection. Oh, yes, it was. Years ago. '59. It came out and was published by Heinemann in London, but nowhere else.

AH: Why was it left out of the *Collected*?

PB: It came just at the time there was a lot of trouble with blacks, and I thought I don't know what to write. Whatever you write, they won't like it; so I thought I'd better not write anything. . . . I don't know if blacks would object to it or not. It does show the black as being illiterate and a laundress.

AH: Also in the *Call at Corazón* collection we have "An Inopportune Visit," not found elsewhere. The conceit there is marvelous—to have a saint come back so that you can show a unique perspective on the modern world. . . . Where did the idea come from?

PB: I don't know. I have no idea. I think I was sitting one day thinking what a shame it was that nobody was singing Gregorian chants, and that's because they don't do anything in Latin anymore. And I thought, "What would it be like if someone came back and realized what was going on?" They'd be horrified!

AH: It of course comes out in the end; Santa Rosenda rushes to the altar and begins to attack the priest. . . . I realize that my Black Sparrow edition of *Midnight Mass* doesn't have "In the Red Room."

PB: The reason for that is that a publisher in L.A. wrote me sometime in the late seventies, asking me for a story. They wanted to publish it by itself, and they did. But there was a proviso in the contract saying that I couldn't sell it to anyone else or have it published for a year after the original publication; so the first edition of *Midnight Mass* was just coming out, and I couldn't send it to them. Once the year was over, I sent it and they put out a second edition, with the story in it.

AH: In the story "Midnight Mass," you always have the suspicion that Madame Dervaux had something to do with the appropriation of the house, and the artist moving in, but there is never any proof of that.

PB: No, probably not. I imagine the Moroccan family did that by themselves and she, knowing that, would immediately say, "Ah, then. I want the tower." She was probably willing to pay a good price.

AH: That leads to suspicions in the end, when she is there entrenched in the house.

PB: Yah, but I don't know.

AH: Well, there is no way of telling in the story.

PB: It doesn't matter, really.

AH: One of my favorite stories in that volume is "Here to Learn." You said that you liked it, too. Is it your favorite, or do you have any favorites?

PB: Not really.

AH: Not any that you like more than others?

PB: Some I like less than others.

AH: One thing which is evident in a story like "Ahmed and Madame" is that, like so many of your stories, it involves a chain of deception.

PB: Ah!

AH: I suppose the first deception is the bringing of the plants by the gardener under false pretenses.

PB: And the second one was the real gardener cutting them and ruining them.

AH: Right.

PB: Killing them.

AH: And then the . . .

PB: . . . third big deception was when the ones who had originally supplied the hot plants come back and he goes to the door and tells them that she is going to get the police. Then when he comes back, Madame says, "Oh, what did you tell them?" and he said, "No Moslem would take advantage of a woman without a husband." . . . Then he says, "You can't trust anyone."

AH: I suppose the reader of "Kitty" is apt to draw a connection to Kafka's "Metamorphosis." I'm sure that you didn't have that in mind when you wrote it.

Part 2

PB: It's a well-known story of metamorphosis.

AH: You have a number of other stories which involve metamorphosis. "Allal," for instance.

PB: Yah . . . but he didn't mean to. He didn't start out wanting to become a snake, but Kitty started out wanting to be a cat. A woman was here last week from London, a woman with a difficult name. I've known her for many years. She has a daughter, about eight or so, and her mother read her "Kitty" a year or so ago and she decided that she was going to become a cat, and her mother would say, "Where are your hands?" and the daughter would say, "I have no hands. I have claws."

AH: So, life does imitate art.

PB: Then her mother wrote and asked, "Couldn't you publish it by itself?" But I said, "No. No. Because I don't think it is really a child's story." . . . I wrote it as a child's story.

AH: You did?

PB: For a collection called *Wonders*, put out by Simon and Schuster. It is supposed to be a child's story, by adults. But, someone else had the same idea of publishing it in a book by itself. She got in touch with one or two publishers and they said, "Oh, no. It's much too gruesome for small children." The Americans thought it was too gruesome, so I wrote this back to . . . you know who and she wrote me that she had read my letter to her little girl and the little girl, when she heard what the Americans had said, she stamped her foot and said, "Rubbish!" It's very funny. I can't imagine any other small child saying "Rubbish."

AH: A lot of these later stories seem to have a little more wit or slyness.

PB: There're not so . . . Gothic.

AH: Then, too, you seem to get a little more involved in some of these later stories. In "Unwelcome Words" you even appear as the writer of these letters.

PB: The protagonist.

AH: The reader's never really sure about how many of the attitudes expressed in the letters coincide with your own.

PB: Oh, no. It's not about me at all.

AH: It's interesting to come across the story of Valeska, because last summer when I was here you told it in its real form, using her real name . . . and now it pops up in the story.

PB: More or less as it happened . . . *exactly* as it happened!

AH: In that story and some of these other later ones, you get a sense of being cramped in more. The man the narrator is writing to is immobile, but the person who is writing the letter also seems to be feeling hemmed in by Tangier, talking about the villas around, and the increasing crowds and Tangier being a less livable kind of city. I suppose it does seem a lot less exotic than it did.

PB: Well, it is.

AH: A lot of memory comes through in these stories, too. It seems as though the narrators are continually delving back into the past and pulling up little bits and pieces of things. There's that story about the mosquito netting that the writer tells, becoming drunker and drunker. . . . It seems to have taken place in Latin America or somewhere. Is that something out of an imagined past? Or a real one?

PB: No. It was out of a real past. Absolutely.

AH: In Mexico?

PB: In Mexico. It's all in the story. I took a train and the train went as far as the railroad had been built down into the state of Guerrero. There's nothing there. I don't know why they built it that far. But they came to an arroyo above which they couldn't build a decent bridge so the railroad just stopped on the side of the arroyo. . . . There's no reason for it to go anywhere.

AH: And that's where you stopped?

PB: Yah! That's where I stopped.

AH: You like places at the end of the tracks, don't you.

PB: Well, yes, they're more interesting.

AH: At the end of "Unwelcome Words," there's this bit about rewriting the end of *Huckleberry Finn*. There's a suggestion that you think in some way Twain's ending was twisted to make it acceptable to the American public. Do you think that a muzzle has been placed on a lot of American writers, even unconsciously?

PB: I don't think any muzzle was placed on Mark Twain . . . except by himself. I think that he was afraid he had written such a lyrical novel. . . . He had wanted it to be popular, so he had to make a farce. . . . I never did understand just what he was aiming at. . . . You didn't have tea?

187

AH: I did have tea. Mrabet kindly fixed me a cup when I first came in. . . . The first story in *Unwelcome Words*—"Julian Vreden"—that's a recent story as well?

PB: That was written in 1984.

AH: I presume that it happened as it was told. You begin by noting there was a newspaper account, and this is what had happened.

PB: I read it in a paper in New York.

AH: In *Unwelcome Words*, too, one of the things which is rather obvious, is the shift in style, not only the epistolary, but the monologue. Why the monologue, especially the monologue with no punctuation? You do it in "Afternoon with Antaeus" . . .

PB: . . . but not without punctuation.

AH: Yah. Without punctuation you get a lot of enjambments which carry one from one sentence to another.

PB: You think so? You think they could apply to one sentence as well as to another?

AH: Sometimes you go a little further and you get the beginning of the next before you stop, then you go back and you stop and you begin again. . . . In "New York 1965" neither of these women, the one telling nor the one being told about, is very likable. You get these two positions. The one is a moralist commenting on how awful the other's life is—how she's taking care of her son and living her life in Tangier. They're both equally repulsive.

PB: Yes, I think they are. The poetess isn't very likable.

AH: When you first begin, you think that the storyteller might have some redeeming virtue, but as you move through, you get a sense that her words are motivated by jealousy and a whole lot of other emotions. After all, her friend has become a rather famous poet.

PB: Yes, and Kathleen thinks that's a lot of nonsense.

AH: And she hasn't read any of the poetry!

PB: *No*! Of course she hasn't. She says, "Thank God, I don't have to read it." When the poet says, "I've been writing a lot of poetry," she says, "I'll *bet* you have!"

AH: What takes you back to the New England setting in "Massachusetts 1932"?

PB: What takes me back anywhere?

AH: The difference between that one and the New York monologue—at least a key difference—is that the man whom the narrator is talking to is right there in the room, apparently, and in the first one you don't have a sense of exactly to whom it is being told. The other person never surfaces and she isn't being offered drinks or anything.

PB: No. And the last one also . . .

AH: Although in the last one, the one set in Tangier, you get more of a sense of the motive of the telling. . . . The place I had in mind as I was reading the story was somewhere up on the hill just between the Marshan and the Old Mountain.

PB: Well, that's where it was.

AH: Of course, what seems to happen in that story is that as one moves through the story it becomes less and less obvious who is to blame for what has gone wrong. It seems as though the motive for telling the story is some kind of guilt.

PB: Well, partially. She's not sure. . . . No, I don't think she really believes that the woman was screaming and she heard her. She kept thinking it might have been so. She didn't do anything. She couldn't really have.

AH: You also get the piece of information right here at the end that the people who have come in and beaten her while her boyfriend's been away came in the first time when they had left their guardpost.

PB: Except that you felt they were justified in leaving, because the Countess had told them two hours and it had been five hours. So they had done more than their share.

AH: But it is one of those situations where you just can't determine who is to blame.

PB: No. . . . She couldn't help thinking maybe it would have been different if she had stayed on another half-hour. Who knows?

AH: What pulled you in the direction of using monologue in the later stories, or why you decided to use that means of telling?

PB: Well, it's hard to say. I don't know. I heard the voice of the woman telling about the peacocks [in "Tangier 1975"], and heard it very strongly in my ear, and so I started writing what she would say, and what she did say, in her kind of speech. Once I had written one, I found it fun to become someone else and write what words I heard in my head—rather like writing music.

189

AH: You stick with one voice.

PB: Yes, all are in one voice.

AH: If you began with the sound of peacocks, that would have been toward the end.

PB: Well, they're there, in the woods. . . . They sound like lost souls [sound] . . . and then it comes down [continues sound] in a long arc of sound, coming down.

AH: The other few stories in *Unwelcome Words* seem to have been based on reminiscences of particular characters—"Hugh Harper," "Dinner at Sir Nigel's." I remember you told me once that Hugh Harper was based upon a real character. Was Sir Nigel as well?

PB: Oh, yah! The whole business.

AH: Who was the person on which it was based?

PB: I don't see any point in connecting up fiction with fact. It doesn't tell anything about the fiction, just to recount the facts, does it? It might have come from many different sources. In that one, though, it didn't. It all came from one source, the dinner I had with him—Sir Cyril.

AH: Things change, of course, in the writing. You can never get it down the way it happened.

PB: No.

AH: Nor do you want to.

PB: No, because it isn't journalism. You're inventing. There's less invention in that [story] than in most.

AH: Do you want to stop? Have you had enough?

PB: I don't know. What time is it?

AH: Twenty-five before five.

PB: It's not so late.

Preface to *A Hundred Camels*

Moroccan kif-smokers like to speak of "two worlds," the one ruled by inexorable natural laws, and the other, the kif world, in which each person perceives "reality" according to the projections of his own essence, the state of consciousness in which the elements of the physical universe are automatically rearranged by cannabis to suit the requirements of the individual. These distorted variations in themselves generally are of scant interest to anyone but the subject at the time he is experiencing them. An intelligent smoker, nevertheless, can aid in directing the process of deformation in such a way that the results will have value to him in his daily life. If he has faith in the accuracy of his interpretations, he will accept them as decisive, and use them to determine a subsequent plan of action. Thus, for a dedicated smoker, the passage to the "other world" is often a pilgrimage undertaken for the express purpose of oracular consultation.

In 1960 I began to experiment with the idea of constructing stories whose subject matter would consist of disparate elements and unrelated characters taken directly from life and fitted together as in a mosaic. The problem was to create a story line which would make each arbitrarily chosen episode compatable with the others, to make each one lead to the next with a semblance of naturalness. I believed that through the intermediary of kif the barriers separating the unrelated elements might be destroyed, and the disconnected episodes forced into a symbiotic relationship. I listed a group of incidents and situations I had either witnessed or heard about that year.

A. had an old grudge against B. When B. was made a policeman, A. sent money to him, seeing to it that B.'s superior was made aware of the gift. B. was reprimanded and given a post in the Sahara.

C. acquired an old pair of shoes from D. When he had them resoled he discovered that he could no longer get them on. As a result he quarreled with D.

In another personal feud, E. consulted with a witch to help him deal with his enemy F.

Finding his kitten dead with a needle in its stomach, G. decided that it had been killed because he had named it Mimí.

H. slipped a ring over the head of a stray bird, and the bird flew away with it.

I. although brought up as a Jilali, hated and feared the Jilali.

J. ate so many cactus fruit that the peelings covered his gun and he was unable to find it.

K. frightened a Jewish woman by leaving the ingredients of magic on her doorstep.

This constitutes the bulk of the factual material I gave myself to work with. To get three stories out of it, I combined A., B., G. and K. (for *A Friend of the World*); and C., D., and H. (for *The Story of Lahcen and Idir*; and E., F., I. and J. (for *The Wind at Beni Midar*). No one of the actual situations had anything to do with kif, but by providing kif-directed motivations I was able to use cannabis both as solvent and solder in the construction.

He of the Assembly has no factual anchors apart from three hermetic statements made to me that year by a kif-smoker in Marrakech: "The eye wants to sleep, but the head is no mattress," "The earth trembles and the sky is afraid, and the two eyes are not brothers," and "A pipe of kif before breakfast gives a man the strength of a hundred camels in the courtyard." He uttered these apocalyptic sentences, but steadfastly refused to shed any light on their meanings or possible applications. This impelled me to invent a story about him in which he would furnish the meanings. Here the content of each paragraph is determined by its point of view. There are seven paragraphs, arranged in a simple pattern: imagine the cross-section of a pyramidal structure of four steps, where steps 1 and 7 are at the same level, likewise 2 and 6, and 3 and 5, with 4 at the top. In paragraphs 1 and 7 He of the Assembly and Ben Tajah are seen together. 2 and 6 are seen by Ben Tajah, and 3 and 5 by He of the Assembly, and 4 consists of He of the Assembly's interior monologue.

Preface to A Distant Episode

The stories in this volume were written during a period which covers approximately forty years. Many are the result of nostalgia for places left behind; the composition of these began with an evocation of the *ambiance* of the locale, a general atmosphere out of which the protagonists were born. It seems a practical procedure to let the place determine the characters who will inhibit it.

Often the settings used are precise descriptions of actual places: "At Paso Rojo" on a ranch in Guanacaste, Costa Rica, "The Time of Friendship" at a hotel which existed during colonial times in Taghit, Algeria, and "He of the Assembly" is the streets of the Medina of Marrakech. Characters, being determined by the backdrop, are of necessity entirely improvised, as is the action in which they become involved. For me the pleasure of writing stories, as opposed to novels, lies in the freedom to allow protagonists to invent their own personalities as they emerge from the landscape.

As we know, creativity is an eruption of the unconscious. Exposed to the light of reason, this subterranean material ordinarily discovers the uses to which it will be put, and the form it will assume. The author, aware of what he is doing, gives it an argument and a voice. The end product is man-made. Most of the tales in the collection adhere to this formula.

There is, however, another way of treating this basic element, which is to use it "raw," without questioning its sense, allowing it to cool and harden into its own natural shape. Here the author remains ignorant of what he has written, and is not likely to be able to assign a "meaning" to it, inasmuch as that consideration did not occur to him during its composition. "Tapiama" is an example of this approach.

—PAUL BOWLES
TANGIER, MOROCCO
JANUARY, 1989

From Without Stopping

I had been reading some ethnographic books with texts from the Arapesh or from the Tarahumara given in word-for-word translation. Little by little the desire came to me to invent my own myths, adopting the point of view of the primitive mind. The only way I could devise for simulating that state was the old Surrealist method of abandoning conscious control and writing whatever words came from the pen. First, animal legends resulted from the experiments and then tales of animals disguised as "basic human" beings. One rainy Sunday I awoke late, put a thermos of coffee by my bedside, and began to write another of these myths. No one disturbed me, and I wrote on until I had finished it. I read it over, called it "The Scorpion," and decided that it could be shown to others. When *View* published it, I received compliments and went on inventing myths. The subject matter of the myths soon turned from "primitive" to contemporary, but the objectives and behavior of the protagonists remained the same as in the beast legends. It was through this unexpected little gate that I crept back into the land of fiction writing. Long ago I had decided that the world was too complex for me ever to be able to write fiction; since I failed to understand life, I would not be able to find points of reference which the hypothetical reader might have in common with me. When *Partisan Review* accepted "A Distant Episode," even though I had already sold two or three other tales to *Harper's Bazaar*, I was triumphant: it meant that I would be able to go on writing fiction. . . .

That autumn [1957], in the course of a London epidemic, I caught Asian flu. During the nine days I spent in bed, I ran a high fever which prompted me to write a story about the effects of an imaginary South American drink, the *cumbiamba*. It was called "Tapiama" and was something of an experiment for me, being the only fever-directed piece I had written. On the tenth day, when the story was finished and typed in

From *Without Stopping: An Autobiography* by Paul Bowles. (c) by Paul Bowles 1972. First published by the Ecco Press in 1985. Reprinted by permission.

duplicate, my thermometer showed ninety-eight and six-tenths. I got up, dressed, and went to Harrod's. A few hours later I was delirious. The next morning they plumped me onto a stretcher and removed me to a hospital. Pleurisy set in, and I spent a bad two weeks in a ward with fifty other pneumonia cases, too sick to notice the oxygen tanks being wheeled in or to watch those who had not been saved by them being wheeled out.

Notebook Entries

I.

1. It is not a foregone conclusion when you ask an author the "meaning" of one of his works that you are going to be given the whole meaning and nothing but the meaning.

2. The classical childhood fantasy of invisibility serves as a springboard to assist the reader in imagining a kind of consciousness which is as yet undifferentiated, not dependent upon the human condition.

3. If you are looking for a category for the story, I'd suggest making one in the vicinity of science fiction rather than allegory.

II.

1. The Atlajala is not meant as a symbol. Let us say it is a detached scrap of consciousness, parasitical in the sense that for its sensations it depends upon living organisms. . . .

2. The Atlajala has no other purpose than consciousness itself has; it repudiates extinction.

3. "Evil intent" being a human concept, the Atlajala remained unaware of its existence. It hoped only to continue to savor the phenomenological world through the medium of the woman's psychic organism. The fact that, as seen from the limitations of the human social structure it was committing murder, clearly could not be of any importance to it.

Paul Bowles, comments on "Atlajala," Notebook 18 (seemingly a draft of a letter). Harry Ransom Humanities Research Center. The University of Texas at Austin. Used by permission.
Paul Bowles, comments on "Atlajala," Notebook 19. Harry Ransom Humanities Research Center. The University of Texas at Austin. Used by permission.

[Christianity]

Religion seems to me the most practical of all the sciences invented by man. Whether this is a basically "C[hristian]" viewpoint or not, I am too ignorant of C. orthodoxy to know. Since I am a product of C. society (New England–Unitarian forbears) I assume that I am to be counted among the Christians. I admit I was astonished to hear that there existed someone who thought of me as a fundamentally "C" writer. All I can say is that you are in a better position than I am to know such a thing. If I am ever able to arrive at a point of view which expresses the Ch. ethos despite the corrosive effect [of] my own ignorance and weakness, I shall be supremely happy.

Paul Bowles, comments on Christianity, Notebook 19 (seemingly a draft of a letter). Harry Ransom Humanities Research Center. The University of Texas at Austin. Used by permission.

Excerpts from Letters to Millicent Dillon

I.

I'm glad to hear that the publishers kept their word and sent you a copy of IN THE RED ROOM. Also glad to hear you liked it. I wrote it in 1980; it's the most recent piece of fiction. After that I went to Points in Time, as you know. The story came in a letter from Leonardo de Arrizabalaga, who had had the experience in Baguio, filipinas, when he was traveling with his parents. Immediately I knew it was for me, and merely transposed the setting from Baguio to Gintota, substituting my own parents for his. When the dedication to Leonardo. (I couldn't write about the Philippines, having spent only one week there, and in any case, the place was unimportant. The only important difference between the actuality and the fiction is the son's decision not to tell his parents the story behind the red room. In reality the parents as well as the son heard it, after they got back to Manilla.)

II.

I got into a run of work two or three weeks ago and began to write stories in the form of monologues; it was a change, and therefore fun. So far I've got three, but I'm hoping to mine the vein while there's anything there.

III.

It's interesting that you imagined the Monsieur Ducros [in "Rumor and a Ladder," *Midnight Mass*] had been "manipulating" from the beginning. I don't know from which part of the tale you got that impression; I thought I had arranged it logically. The reason I say it's interesting is that in reality "Monsieur Ducros" denounced himself anonymously after breaking his leg, thus making certain he'd be detained and examined.

5/6/82 Paul Bowles to Millicent Dillon. Harry Ransom Humanities Research Center. The University of Texas at Austin. Used by permission.
7/11/82 Paul Bowles to Millicent Dillon. Harry Ransom Humanities Research Center. The University of Texas at Austin. Used by permission.

Part 2

Then when nothing was discovered in the cast, he made a great geschrei and got the French Ambassador in to complain, again making certain that when he took the money out he wouldn't be bothered. He got the money out safely. The only difference is that in my story there are paintings, and Monsieur Ducros is not premeditating anything; it's his mistreatment that causes him to make his decision.

IV.

Perhaps I told you the story of *Rumor and a Ladder* as it actually happened, and it remained in your consciousness. That could account for your suspicions regarding M. Ducros's honesty.

20/3/81 Paul Bowles to Millicent Dillon. Harry Ransom Humanities Research Center. The University of Texas at Austin. Used by permission.
16/4/81 Paul Bowles to Millicent Dillon. Harry Ransom Humanities Research Center. The University of Texas at Austin. Used by permission.

Part 3

The Critics

Introduction

Since the appearance of Bowles's first volume of stories, *The Delicate Prey and Other Stories*, editors of the literary sections of major newspapers and magazines have judged the writer's work worthy of mention and discussion. Respected writers (often friends), such as Tennessee Williams, Gore Vidal, and Joyce Carol Oates, have taken up Bowles's case, arguing eloquently and forcefully for the aesthetic merits and cultural value of his stories. In the following section I have culled what I hope is a representative sampling of these initial critical responses, including personal responses from Alice B. Toklas and Jane Bowles.

While the consensus among readers is that Bowles is a consummate storyteller, the more lurid or Gothic elements in his fiction have provoked responses ranging from unbrooked outrage to unqualified appreciation and praise. Among the first readers of *The Delicate Prey*, Alice B. Toklas, in private correspondence to the author, pronounced, "Your delicacy is perfect—precise and poignant—but the macabre fate—though inevitable that overtakes most of your prey is not to my taste." Along similar lines, Leslie Fiedler invented an epithet—"pornographer of terror"— that has stuck to Bowles; Fiedler went on to suggest that Bowles was "a secret lover of the horror he evokes." Countering Fiedler's attacks, Ihab Hassan has placed Bowles in the context of a time "stigmatized by a passion for violence and negation," seeing his work acting "both as the choice proof and refutation of modern defections." Bernard Bergonzi, in the *New York Review of Books* in 1967, charged that Bowles had "a taste for gamey, melodramatic situations and not much liking for humanity." A year later, in *Partisan Review*, Maureen Howard wrote that Bowles depicts "a bleak modernity which has worn thin." In 1989 Anatole Broyard, in the *New York Times Book Review*, called Bowles "the grand panjandrum of paranoid expatriation."

Bowles has always had a faithful following, however. Norman Mailer has called Bowles's themes "adventurous and pure." Reviewing *The Delicate Prey*, Tennessee Williams wrote that Bowles is a master at depicting the separateness of the human psyche. Vidal lets out all the stops in his introduction to Bowles's *Collected Stories*, claiming Bowles has had few equals in the later half of the twentieth century. Vidal goes on to discuss the merits of the stories and offer an explanation for the writer's neglect.

An overview of the contemporary journalistic responses shows differing reactions to each volume. *The Delicate Prey* seems to have generated the most interest at the time of its publication in 1950, with critics referring almost without fail to the castration in the title story. Reviewers of *The Time of Friendship* tended to make favorable though qualified judgments, with nearly universal praise of the title story. *Things Gone and Things Still Here* has generally been viewed as a weak volume. With the publication of the *Collected Stories* by Black Sparrow in 1980 came a fresh wave of reviews, more comprehensive and on the whole favorable. While the most recent two volumes, *Midnight Mass* and *Unwelcome Words*, have not individually generated much criticism (perhaps because of their publication by small presses), Ecco's release of *The Selected Stories* in 1989 provoked a handful of serious essays, such as the one by Robert Craft in the *New York Review of Books*.

Perhaps as influential as the reviews in creating Bowles's distinctive, alluring persona have been the various visual images reproduced in the media. Familiar is the picture of a well-groomed Bowles, sporting a charming smile, cigarette holder in hand, standing in front of an Arab archway; reclining, odalisque fashion, on a Moroccan carpet; posing in front of palm trees or the whitewashed houses of the *medina*; or sitting in a local café with Mohammed Mrabet. Jay McInerney's "Paul Bowles in Exile" (*Vanity Fair*, September 1985), with its obligatory photos, promotes the Bowles legend, as does the *New York Times Magazine* article (20 May 1990) on Bertolucci's film version of Bowles's novel *The Sheltering Sky*. No less, Bowles himself makes a cameo appearance in the movie, according to Bertolucci, "to evoke the pain of memory." A thinly disguised Bowles persona (Tom Foster, in the film) figures prominently in David Cronenberg's film rendition of William Burroughs's *Naked Lunch*. Bowles is also at the heart of Michelle Green's journalistic, gossipy *The Dream at the End of the World: Paul Bowles and the Literary Renegades in Tangier*, brimming with outrageous anecdotes and photos. All these popular pieces attest to the power of the Bowles legend, aid in creating an image of the writer, and keep his name before the public.

This collection of criticism does not contain excerpts from any of the full-length books devoted to Bowles's literary output, largely because of the difficulty in carving out a slice to serve that would give a full sense of the argument in each. To date, four full-length critical studies have been published. The most comprehensive of these, as I have argued elsewhere (*Partisan Review*, Fall 1991, 736–39), is Richard F. Patteson's *The World Outside: The Fiction of Paul Bowles*. Patteson analyzes the structures of Bowles's fiction—both novels and stories—and develops the notion of story as shelter, both necessary and inevitably fragile and vulnerable. Lawrence D. Stewart's early study *Paul Bowles: The Illumination of North Africa* provides useful material concerning the genesis of many of Bowles's early stories. Johannes Bertens, in *The Fiction of Paul Bowles: The Soul Is the Weariest Part of the Body*, seems most interested in the writer's nihilism and possible connections to a Calvinist tradition, while Wayne Pounds, in *Paul Bowles: The Inner Geography*, explores Bowles's fiction in light of psychological theory, particularly that of Freud and R. D. Laing. Finally, Christopher Sawyer-Lauçanno's biography of Bowles, *An Invisible Spectator*, while not wholly reliable, at least usefully directs attention to the writer.

The history of Bowles's critical reception is still in the making. It is hoped that accounting for and pulling together various public commentary will aid readers and critics in forming, refining, and redefining their own views.

Norman Mailer

Paul Bowles opened the world of Hip. He let in the murder, the drugs, the incest, the death of the Square (Port Moresby), the call of the orgy, the end of civilization; he invited all of us to these themes a few years ago, and he wrote one short story, *Pages from Cold Point*, a seduction of a father by a son, which is one of the best short stories ever written by anyone. Yet, I am not ready to think of Bowles as a major novelist—his characters are without life, and one does not feel that the author ever lived with them. He does not love them and certainly he does not hate them—he is as bored with his characters as they are bored with each other, and his boredom, the breath of Bowles' work, is not the boredom of the world raised to the cool relations of art, but rather is a miasma from the author. One can never disregard Paul Bowles, however, for whatever his lacks, his themes have been adventurous and pure.

Advertisements for Myself by Normal Mailer used by permission of the author and his agents, Scott Meredith Literary Agency, Inc., 845 Third Avenue, New York, New York 10022.

Tennessee Williams

Paul Bowles is preoccupied with the spiritual isolation of individual beings. This is not a thing as simple as loneliness. Certainly a terrible kind of loneliness is expressed in most of these stories and in the novel that preceded them to publication, but the isolated beings in these stories have deliberately chosen their isolation in most cases, not merely accepted and endured it. There is a singular lack of human give-and-take, of true emotional reciprocity, in the groups of beings assembled upon his intensely but somberly lighted sets. The drama is that of the single being rather than of beings in relation to each other. Paul Bowles has experienced an unmistakable revulsion from the act of social participation. One may surmise in him the social experience of two decades. Then the withdrawal is logical. The artist is not a man who will advance against a bayonet pressed to his abdomen unless another bayonet is pressed to his back, and even then he is not likely to move forward. He will, if possible, stand still. But Mr. Bowles has discovered that the bayonet is pointed at the man moving forward in our times, and that a retreat is still accessible. He has done the sensible thing under these circumstances. He has gone back into the cavern of himself. These seventeen stories are the exploration of a cavern of individual sensibilities, and fortunately the cavern is a deep one containing a great deal that is worth exploring.

Nowhere in any writing that I can think of has the separateness of the one human psyche been depicted more vividly and shockingly. If one feels that life achieves its highest value and significance in those rare moments—they are scarcely longer than that—when two lives are confluent, when the walls of isolation momentarily collapse between two persons, and if one is willing to acknowledge the possibility of such intervals, however rare and brief and difficult they may be, the intensely isolated spirit evoked by Paul Bowles may have an austerity which is frightening at least. But don't make the mistake of assuming that what is

Tennessee Williams's review of Paul Bowles's "The Delicate Prey" from the December 23, 1950 issue of *Saturday Review*. Permission by Omni International, Ltd.

frightening is necessarily inhuman. It is curious to note that the spirit evoked by Bowles in so many of these stories does *not* seem inhuman, nor does it strike me as being antipathetic.

Even in the stories where this isolation is most shockingly, even savagely, stated and underlined the reader may sense an inverted kind of longing and tenderness for the thing whose absence the story concerns. This inverted, subtly implicit kind of tenderness comes out most clearly in one of the less impressive stories of the collection. This story is called "The Scorpion." It concerns an old woman in a primitive society of some obscure kind who has been left to live in a barren cave by her two sons. One of these deserters eventually returns to the cave with the purpose of bringing his mother to the community in which he and his brother have taken up residence. But the old woman is reluctant to leave her cave. . . .

Here is a story that sentimentality, even a touch of it, could have destroyed. But sentimentality is a thing that you will find nowhere in the work of Paul Bowles. When he fails, which is rarely, it is for another reason. It is because now and then his special hardness of perception, his defiant rejection of all things emollient have led him into an area in which a man can talk only to himself.

The volume contains among several fine stories at least one that is a true masterpiece of short fiction—"A Distant Episode," published first in *Partisan Review*. In this story Paul Bowles states the same theme which he developed more fully in his later novel. The theme is the collapse of the civilized "Super Ego" into a state of almost mindless primitivism, totally dissociated from society except as an object of its unreasoning hostility. It is his extremely powerful handling of this theme again and again in his work which makes Paul Bowles probably the American writer who represents most truly the fierily and blindly explosive world that we live in so precariously from day and night to each uncertain tomorrow.

Charles Jackson

The natural creativity of the artist who is Paul Bowles finds its fullest expression, it seems to me, in his music, which I have known and admired for many years and which has given delight to untold thousands as "background" music for this or that theatre-piece, not to speak of his distinguished and independent musical works. Yet as a story-teller he leaves—for my taste, at least—much to be desired. Last year we all admired his first novel, "The Sheltering Sky," as a piece of good writing: crystal-clear, economical, unrhetorical, sophisticated, evocative of far places and atmospheres but not adding up to much by way of actual story, action, characterization, and hence credibility. All we took away from a reading of the novel was a series of brilliantly graphic, even poetic, descriptions of Algerian towns and stopping places in the vastnesses of an intensely hypnotic Sahara Desert, with its changing moods, winds, lights, nomads. This was beautifully done, but was little more than background for a "story" whose characters we did not know enough about to believe in, and therefore a story that we could not take part in ourselves, as one inevitably takes part when one is absorbed and held.

So, it seems to me, is this new collection of Mr. Bowles' short stories. They are less story and characterization than scenes and places described with great originality, bearing, let us say, the same relation to dramatic fiction that Mussorgsky's "Pictures at an Exhibition" bears to the same composer's "Boris Godunov." The latter is all character, action, drama; the former, though charming and expert, is anybody's guess as to content. . . .

There is hardly a story among the seventeen without a Latin-American, Mexican, Spanish, Algerian, Arabian or other foreign name or setting; but this connotation of romantic and far places by no means proves to be "escape" literature. Far from it. Many readers like the remote, the strange, the untypical; but I, for one, look forward to the day when such a forthright and honest writer as Paul Bowles returns to his

Excerpts from Charles Jackson's review of Paul Bowles's *The Delicate Prey*, December 3, 1950. Copyright (c) 1950 by the New York Times Company. Reprinted by permission.

native scene and gives us personal, intimate, and, shall we say, down-to-earth stories or glimpses of the small town in which he was brought up. For it is the native, and the personal, reflections or refractions of every-day living—particularly American adolescence, never a tired theme when well done—that are universal that will prove to be the stuff of our literature, and that Paul Bowles could do so well.

Plainly, he is a gifted writer, intense, simple, saying exactly what he means and no more and no less—the kind of writing that writers, especially, enjoy and admire and that is even easier on the general reader. For all their violence, these tales are actionless, which is to say characterless, and vice versa.

John J. Maloney

One feels that Mr. Bowles needs exotic and perilous places in which to house his gallery of grotesques. Most of his people are wanderers on the face of the earth: like Port and Kit Moresby in *The Sheltering Sky* they are lost and rootless, searching for something nameless (perhaps a quick and sensible death) but finding only slow disintegration and senseless destruction. The insane shriek of a parakeet, the dry scurrying click of monstrous sun-spawned insects, the steady quiet lisp of nameless rivers roping black and swift through the jungle, the thin wail of an Arab flute—all of these are woven by the musically minded Mr. Bowles into a weird obbligato, a kind of dissonant accompaniment for these splintered people, which seems so inevitable that it is difficult to think of them as existing without it.

Maloney, John J. "Skillful Tales From Exotic Gardens of Evil." Rev. of *The Delicate Prey*. *New York Herald Tribune Book Review* 3 December 1950: 4.

The *New Yorker*

The Americans Mr. Bowles presents in these short stories are a dislocated, ingrown group whose most significant sign of life is an occasional pleasurable sigh of despair. His non-Americans, all olive-skinned residents of hot climates, need not be considered, since they are merely ambulating extensions of a general atmosphere of ominous mystery, and not really people. In all this passivity and menace, not a spark of human feeling lives, although at times the tension is broken, but not illuminated, by a sudden, reasonless flare of violence. Where such a flare occurs, passivity changes to defeat, but some of the stories lack even that much development. However, the writing—steady, melancholy, and colloquial—is an excellent conveyor of the atmosphere within an atmosphere in which Mr. Bowles' creatures exist, and emphasizes by its monotony the inexplicable acts of violence with which he is mostly concerned.

"*The Delicate Prey.*" (A review) *The New Yorker* 26: 167, 9 Dec., 1950: 167–8.

Letters from Alice B. Toklas

To Paul Bowles from Alice B. Toklas

7–12–50

Dear Freddie.

Someone has sent me The Delicate Prey—reading them so speedily—In a late sitting the memory this morning is that your delicacy is perfect—precise and poignant—but the macabre fate—though inevitable that overtakes most of your prey is not to my taste. I'll be reading them shortly more quietly and will write you then.

22–3–51

Dear Paul—one might as well conform—

A letter from Brion tells me mine to you has not turned up. The only thing in it that would have interested you was that your explanation of your stories—as on a previous occasion—cleared some small confusion one reader had created for herself [—] the seduction of following the way you so admirably solved your technical difficulties instead of discovering that your construction was based on each of your characters [*sic*] response to the bottom nature as Gertrude used to call it. So that the story is often a mystery until near the end to the hero himself—which makes it a really modern mystery story—So once again my thanks and felicitations—You always so abundantly justify my instinctive confidence in you—please dont be bored with—a hazy old head.

9–1–51

Dear Freddie—

It was kind of you to write to me. You told me what—I wanted to hear—that The Delicate Prey was written before The Sheltering Sky (What a perfect sense for telling you have). All reservations are withdrawn. I am rereading it—as if your second book wasnt yet read and I am

Harry Ransom Humanities Research Center, The University of Texas at Austin.

astonished at what you have done— (It should have been said on the jacket that it was your first book, instead of this foolish Gothic violence— which isnt violent to us today—) And you are so right in calling them detective stories.

Letter from Jane Bowles
[East Montpelier, Vermont]
[December 1947]

I *loved* your story ["How Many Midnights"]. Everything that happened in it was perfect down to the man who was looking for Riley and her dismal return to her own apartment house (the janitor having to bring the elevator up from the basement!). You write wonderfully about this country I think, as well as you do about any other country. In fact I am convinced that you are a writer down to the marrow of your bone. Certainly I should never have expected this kind of story out of you. It is even more surprising than the one about Prue and the other two women ["The Echo"]. This is besides *sumamente* saleable I should say. The tension as usual is terrific. It seems like an innocent enough little story when it begins and the way in which you have shaded it so that it becomes steadily more somber, almost as imperceptibly to the reader as to the girl herself, is I should say masterful. I read it twice because I could not quite encompass it. The effect was so much as though it were almost that night itself and not just something written about a night that I had to reread it to see how on earth you did it, and if you really did. Of course I still don't see how, even now, except through the expert and naturally instinctive choice of the detail. The candles, the sound of the log breaking in two, the melting ice cubes, and some perfect word you use concerning her fingers in the ice bowl. I can't think of such a word *even* after reading it. It was simple enough but so accurate. The drawer and her running to the buzzer, and not pushing it, going back again to the drawer and then to the buzzer again and finally the man called "Riley," were so terrible and exciting somehow that I almost threw up. I think the artistry there was her not answering the buzzer the first time it rang, which started the suspense at just the right pitch. It is an exhausting story

Harry Ransom Humanities Research Center, The University of Texas at Austin. (Published in *Out in the World: Selected Letters of Jane Bowles, 1935–1970*, ed. Millicent Dillon. Santa Barbara: Black Sparrow, 1985, p. 69.)

and the morning was really wonderful. It is even better reading the second time, too, because one notices little indications about the boy's character in the beginning which should actually be just as lightly drawn as they are or the suspense would be ruined and one would expect him not to return or at least expect some calamity. The whole thing is very wily and real short story writing, I should say. (We don't have to go in to your talent and originality because that has never been questioned.) Perhaps writing *will* be a means to nomadic life for you, but I hope you won't slowly stop writing music, altogether. I think you will do both. You have always wanted to go back to writing anyway and I remember your discussing it very solemnly once at the Chelsea.

Leslie A. Fiedler

It is Paul Bowles who does for the intellectuals what STF has done for the pulp-reader, compels from us the shocked, protesting acceptance of terror as an irreducible element of being. The whole impact of his work is the insistence on the horrible, and his stories seem only literary by accident, despite their having appeared in very little magazines, and despite the astonishing ease and rhythmical beauty of the style. Like the tales of the science-fictionist, his work denies the world of our everyday living for landscapes more easily allegorized for his purposes; his mythic North Africa and Latin America has its reality in the nightmare, like the trans-galactic worlds of space fiction. He suffers from two basic faults, however, which keep him from achieving the effect upon us he seems always on the verge of attaining. The first arises out of his speaking to intellectuals; driven to deal with ideas, he soon reveals his total inability to make intellectual notions as real as feelings, to specify men thinking as convincingly as he can specify men undergoing castration. The second is a fault endemic to this whole new enterprise; like Chandler and the writers of STF, with their endlessly sapped heroes and their victims stripped of all skin and screaming forever in a saline solution, he is a pornographer of terror, a secret lover of the horror he evokes. It seems to me that he suffers in this latter respect because of the breakdown of a tradition.

Fiedler, Leslie A. "Style and Anti-Style in the Short Story." *Kenyon Reivew*. Winter (1951): 171.

Ihab Hassan

Few writers have, after the Lost Generation, succeeded in engaging serious and continued attention. For we are told that the age is one of transition, that our current literature is stigmatized by a passion for violence and negation, and that Arnold would have found little indeed to point at on our scene. I consider it fortunate that authors have taken upon themselves the risks which critics have refused.

It is precisely such a risk that Paul Bowles has assumed. His work acts both as the choice proof and refutation of modern defections. And yet it would seem that the promise, the firmness of talent, and the intrinsic significance of Bowles' fiction should have won him a different quality of interest, an interest, nonetheless, that would embrace his particular historical position no less than his singular limitations. . . .

Some of his stories were first published, between 1945 and 1950, in such magazines as *Harper's Bazaar, Horizon, Partisan Review, Zero, Life and Letters, Mademoiselle, Penguin New Writing, World Review*, and *Wake*. In these stories and novels Bowles reveals an exceptional sensibility at work on the central and unifying problem of man's existential status in a world of apparently dissociating values—and by existential here I mean nothing more special than the private, the personal, in man's nature interacting with its surroundings. It is by approaching this area of meaning in Bowles' work that we can understand the role of terror and negation so often imputed to him, a role which implicitly questions Leslie Fiedler's idea that terror must be based on a real sense of evil, and John Aldridge's belief that negation should refer to an established hierarchy of values.

For the characters of Bowles are seldom preys or pilgrims, though more often they are both at once. Their quest, a quest vague as it is obsessive, has for goal the traditional self-affirmations in a world that has ceased to be traditional. But the paradox is deeper still: when these characters attempt to salvage a personal meaning or a basic human

Hassan, Ihab. "The Pilgrim as Prey: A Note on Paul Bowles." *The Western Review*. 19 (1954):23–36.

relationship from life, they only manage to accelerate their doom with a terror that is real if somewhat sensational. Nor does Bowles allow us to attribute the sinister transformation from pilgrim into prey to a mythic inherence of evil, for the latter is nowhere hinted as such, nowhere evolved from the lives of his protagonists. Yet the pilgrimage is genuine enough, a pilgrimage from incipient decay to total regression. And as in the Black Mass the initiates painted crosses on the soles of their feet, the black pilgrims of Bowles anoint themselves with the secretions of their most festering depths. But unlike Macbeth, unlike Dostoevsky's Svidrigailov, and unlike the heroes of Existentialism, who nakedly face, and sometimes assert, the demonic elements of their selves, the characters of Bowles move in a world from which choice and regeneration are absent. Their peculiar fate brings neither liberation nor self-discovery. (This is equally true of Kit and Port Moresby in *The Sheltering Sky*, Nelson Dyar in *Let It Come Down*, the linguistics professor in "A Distant Episode," and even the predatory Moungari of "The Delicate Prey"). But it is necessary to recognize that violence in Bowles' work is exercised as a technique, is in effect a mode of artistic license. As such, it cannot be ruled gratuitous till we have either satisfied ourselves that it achieves no purpose in the author's vision of reality; or, that by achieving such a purpose, it leaves us in doubt as to the validity of his vision. The work of Bowles proves itself more vulnerable on the second of these counts, for it suggests an ironic determinism, a sort of cosmic flaw, that is a gesture in the direction of Naturalism. . . .

In the stories of *The Delicate Prey*, 1950, the medium's limitation seems to enhance the basic virtue of Bowles, his tight control of savage and baleful situations, and to foreshorten his main weakness, the inability to conceive and develop characters dramatically. These stories may share Tennessee Williams' and Truman Capote's explorations of the sombre, the primitive, and the destructive in human nature; but in them lyricism is muted, the grotesque harsh, and the point of view distant. All but two of the stories, "You Are Not I" and "How Many Midnights," are set in North Africa and Latin America. The themes of isolation, of anxiety, of lovelessness, all of the cruelty and perversions which they can induce, are spun in hard, brilliant tones, tones that can sometimes be garish as in "The Delicate Prey" and murky as in the psychopathic "You Are Not I," where a certain arbitrariness of conception is in both stories apparent. But in the plights of Pastor Dowe who can only bring Christianity as Jazz to his Indian congregation, "Paster Dowe at Tacate;" of the child forced into the sinister world of dope peddling, "Senor Ong and Senor Ha;" of the girl supplanted in her mother's affection by a lesbian friend, "The Echo;" of the boy who can only win the acceptance of his shipmates by an act of cruelty, "The Fourth Day Out From Santa Cruz;" of the retired professor incapable to restrain or even communicate with his homosexual son, "Pages From Cold Point;" of the American woman novelist who discovers her utter alienation in the amorous company of a handsome Arab schoolboy, "Tea On The Mountain;" and of the linguist brutalized into the role of a speechless clown by the wild Reguiba, "A Distant Episode;" in these plights there is nothing false or precious: they belong to man, man between two civilizations, "one dead, the other waiting to be born." The range of Bowles is perhaps nowhere better delimited than in this collection, his techniques nowhere better illustrated. One feels that whatever development Bowles will undergo—and his ultimate importance depends greatly on such a development—the starting point will remain in these stories. . . .

For cruelty and perversion, dominant as they are in so many contacts of Bowles' characters, seem the dramatic proof of a radical impossibility, the impossibility of love. Human relationships are, with scarcely a few exceptions, shown as sterile or intolerable, though at times also implausible. Rape, incest, lesbianism, homosexuality, adultery, and simple betrayal, with all their attending virulence, betoken the most complete negation of human love to which a novelist may refer. Estrangement and loneliness—of Kit and Port, of Dyar, of Thami, of the couple in "Call at Corazon," of the native in "Under the Sky," of the father and son in "Pages From Cold Point," and of the mother and daughter in "The Echo"—express a situation in which fear and meaninglessness compel each character to entrench himself in the narrowest corner of his selfhood. In that corner no hope of intercourse can subsist. Nor can there even be hope for the palliative of amenities—Eunice Good and the Lyles truly carry unpleasantness to a point of rare refinement. Hence the age is an Age of Monsters (as Bowles entitles a section of *Let It Come Down*) and "monsters," like Iago, cannot be reconciled to the existence of good in humanity. Even Chalia, who is no Iago, succeeds, in the story "At Paso Rojo," in wantonly "framing" the Indian boy Roberto because her uncle's faith in the honesty of his ranch Indians is intolerable to her. Bowles' questioning of human relationships becomes yet more intense when the most traditionally close of these relationships, conjugal and familial ties, are shown to be the least adequate—those whom we generally consider nearest to each other turn out to be the most alienated. Stories like "Pages From Cold Point," "The Echo," and even

"The Scorpion," challenge the sentimental complacencies that hide a real evil and insist on a revaluation of all relationships.

But it is perhaps Bowles' style, inclusive of manner as of perception, that converts terror and negation to form and meaning. Occasionally the Gothic element asserts its presence, as in the dinner scene at the Valverde house, high on a cliff overlooking the sea, with cuttlefish in the dining room aquarium, cats, syringes, and the smell of a zoo pervading the interior, and a branch clawing at the windowpane. Yet Bowles is far less indebted, if at all, to William Beckford, Anne Radcliffe, or Horace Walpole than he is to a later tradition now absorbed beyond recognition: the tradition of Poe, his first idol, and of Hoffmann, of Novalis, Lautréamont, and the French Symbolists, writers to whom it would be as difficult explicitly to annex Bowles as it would be to annex the Kafka of "Metamorphosis" and "In the Penal Colony" or the James of *The Turn of the Screw*. Different as they are, what James and Kafka do that Poe does not is to relate horror, in action and incident, to a more significant range of human values and experiences. And while Bowles does not in this respect equal James or Kafka—"The Delicate Prey," for instance, is more akin to "The Cask of Amontillado" and "The Pit and the Pendulum" than it is to anything else—in his best work terror, constantly subject to the discipline of style, acquires inescapable reference.

Nor is the discipline of Bowles' style only created by a parity of adjectives, or a hard, crystalline vividness of imagery, or a stark rhythm and presence of simple constructions, or a semblance of externality, distance, and objectivity in point of view. . . . The discipline of style, rather, is to be found in that larger understatement which allows terror or irony to develop from character and situation with the minimum of commentary, as in "Senor Ong and Senor Ha" and "Under the Sky." It is also to be found, more specifically, in the implication of verbal understatement. Unlike Hemingway's style, which conveys a constant shimmer of emotions restrained, radiating from a sensitive core, Bowles' communicates a sense of rigidity, a bludgeoning of sensibility, a determination not to feel, or escape, or claim pity, a determination which is itself the final source of terror. Its implication is not "the courage of despair," but inner death and corruption.

That in Bowles' world terror and violence are not rooted in a Christian view of Evil or a theological conception of Sin, and that his "negations" do not depend on a traditional hierarchy of judgment or belief, neither cancels his meaning nor makes his techniques superfluous. It is through these techniques that Bowles has attempted to discover man's status in existence and the reality of human personality in a manner that psycho-analysis or ethics can hardly discover, and it is through these same techniques that he has questioned human relationships, isolation, and the condition of lovelessness in a way sociology is helpless to question. I should think that Santayana's criterion would be far more applicable to a novelist: "For the sad, the ridiculous, the grotesque, and the terrible, unless they become esthetic goods, remain moral evils."

Oliver Evans

Bowles is an obsessionist, and his obsession may be simply stated: that psychological well-being is in inverse ratio to what is commonly known as progress, and that a highly evolved culture enjoys less peace of mind than one which is less highly evolved. This is of course a romantic attitude, going back at least as far as Rousseau by way (in English literature) of Samuel Butler, D. H. Lawrence, and E. M. Forster. Lawrence is probably Bowles's strongest single influence, and it seems curious that none of the newspaper reviewers have noted this connection: Faulkner and McCullers, with much less justification, are usually pointed to, and such unlikely and dissimilar antecedents as Henry James, Frederic Prokosch, Jean Genêt, and even Elinor Glynn have all been suggested.

It is no accident that the three novels and that fifteen of the seventeen stories in *The Delicate Prey* have a foreign setting. Nor is it true, as has sometimes been charged, that Bowles is merely indulging in a pointless exoticism, for not only are the settings foreign, they are usually primitive as well. For this reason he chooses such remote locales as a small town in the Sahara, a Columbian jungle, a river boat winding painfully through the interior of an unidentified Latin-American country. And in nearly all of his work the tension arises from a contrast between alien cultures: in a typical Bowles story, a civilized individual comes in contact with an alien environment and is defeated by it. The United States is not without primitives of its own, and Bowles could perhaps have achieved something of the same effect by going to the mountains of East Tennessee or the sheep ranches of Montana—or, for that matter, by doing a little social work in his native Manhattan. The contrast, however, would not have been so great: it is important for his purpose that the language, beliefs, and psychology of his natives be as different as possible from those of his travelers, the victims of modern civilization.

Evans, Oliver. "Paul Bowles and The 'Natural' Man." *Critique*. No. 1, 3 (1959): 43–59. Reprinted with permission of the Helen Dwight Reid Educational Foundation. Published by Heldref Publications, 1319 18th Street, N.W., Washington, D.C. 20036–102. Copyright 1959.

There is still another reason for Bowles's choice of remote locales. Deserts and jungles are places in which people can easily get lost, and Bowles believes that modern man, if not already lost in a spiritual and moral sense, is in serious danger of becoming so. It is symbolically fitting that his civilized traveler should suffer defeat at the hands of a nature, or of a "natural" (*i.e.*, primitive) society which he has insisted upon "improving." In *The Sheltering Sky*, one is tempted to equate the Sahara with Dante's *selva selvaggia* and with Eliot's Waste Land. There is, indeed, a certain correspondence, but the difference—and an important one—is that in Dante's poem there is no connection between the symbolic forest, which has only a malevolent aspect, and a natural one; and Eliot's Waste Land has only a negative relation to nature. Bowles's desert on the other hand, is neutral—malevolent only insofar as it is prepared to destroy those who are out of tune with nature itself, of which it is the real as well as the merely formal symbol. There is nearly always a symbolic level present in Bowles's work, and he has suffered considerable injustice at the hands of popular reviewers who have insisted upon reading him at a single level. . . .

It was his second book, a collection of short stories entitled *The Delicate Prey*, that gained for Mr. Bowles the reputation of being a specialist in horror, a "pornographer of terror, a secret lover of the horror he evokes," as Leslie Fiedler put it in *Kenyon Review* (Winter, 1951, p. 170). "The whole impact of his work is his insistence on the horrible," wrote Mr. Fiedler, who went on, incredibly enough, to place Bowles in the tradition of science fiction.

There is no denying it: the stories, many of them, *are* terrible, and their horror is intensified by the manner in which they are written: they are told quietly, gently, almost tenderly, in a style as pure and as polished as any in modern English. But granting the horror, it is reasonable to inquire whether the stories are *merely* horrible—that is, whether other intentions may not be involved; and if so, whether the horror may not be essential to these intentions; and, finally, whether some beauty may not exist even in the midst of the horror.

Even in this collection, Bowles does not usually indulge in horror for its own sake; it is nearly always related, as a careful reading of the stories proves, to his central obsession—an effect through which he strives to dramatize a thesis. They are most of them highly moral tales in the sense that *The Sheltering Sky* is moral—and in the sense that Faulkner's "A Rose for Emily" is not. . . . In "A Distant Episode," an American (or European) pedant, a professor of languages, is captured by a tribe of desert bandits who cut out his tongue and retain him as a kind of performing clown: he is dressed in a suit of tin cans, made to dance, grimace and turn handsprings, and is kept in a cage like an animal. The professor reminds us at once of Port, in *The Sheltering Sky*: "He came down out of the high, flat region in the evening by bus, with two small overnight bags full of maps, sun lotions and medicines." Prim and over-civilized, he is an ideal candidate for defeat and degradation at the hands of a primitive people, and there is terrible irony in the circumstance of a linguist's losing his tongue. One reason this story seems so horrible is that the reader is not made to feel that the author sympathizes with the professor: this, however, is purely a matter of implication, not of statement nor even overt suggestion, for Mr. Bowles realizes that for his story to be effective dramatically it has to be told with the utmost objectivity. The skill with which he creates in the first few pages an atmosphere of danger and impending disaster is remarkable, and reminds one of the beginning of *Benito Cereno*. . . .

To my mind, the least successful stories are those in which the horror does constitute an end in itself, like the title story and "Pages from Cold Point," which last, a study of homosexual incest, is a brilliant *tour de force* written in Bowles's very best manner but without any apparent root in the author's fundamental convictions: in this respect, as also in the cumulative horror of its situation and its technical perfection, it reminds us of *The Turn of the Screw*. The most pessimistic story in the book is "The Fourth Day Out from Santa Cruz," a fable with a terrible message: that it is cruelty which holds men together; it is the leveling influence, the lowest common denominator of human behavior. The story is remarkable for its delicate balancing of narrative and allegory: on both levels it is completely coherent. . . .

Mr. Bowles emerges as a champion for religious orthodoxy, albeit of an exotic variety. . . . It is not surprising to encounter an anti-Christian bias in Bowles—the reader will remember "Pastor Dowe at Tacaté"—but there is an important difference, for in that story Bowles is writing as a sociologist concerned with the relativity of all religions to the particular needs which they serve rather than as the champion of any specific creed: Metzabok and Hachakyum are no better and no worse than the Christian deity; they are just different, like the people who worship them. It is possible that Mr. Bowles has not yet resolved this problem in his own mind, and that we may expect a more definitive attitude from him in his future work.

Ned Rorem

In 1949, with the publication of his very successful *Sheltering Sky* at the age of forty, Paul Bowles became the author-who-also-writes-music, after having long been the composer-who-also-writes-words. That success brought more than a re-emphasis of reputation; from the musical community's standpoint it signaled the permanent divorce of a pair of careers. During the next two decades Paul Bowles produced fourteen books of various kinds, but little more than an hour's worth of music. Did he feel that one art, to survive, needed to swallow and forget the other? Surely he received in a year more acclaim for his novel than he had received in a lifetime for his music. This need not imply a superior literary talent; indeed, if history recalls him, it will be for musical gifts. It's just that ten times more people read books than go to concerts. Someday Bowles may fully release the underestimated musician who doubtless still sings within him. Meanwhile, perhaps chagrined by the underestimation, he coolly enjoys an international fame based solely on his books.

Composer-authors generally compartmentalize their two vocations, allotting parts of each year, if not each day, to each profession. But as authors their subject is inevitably music (as witness Berlioz, Schumann, Debussy, or today, Boulez, Thomson, Sessions), whereas Paul Bowles is a fiction-writing composer, the only significant one since Richard Wagner, and even Wagner's fiction was at the service of his operas. Except during the war years when he functioned as music critic for the *New York Herald Tribune*, Bowles's prose has been antithetical to his music. Whatever resemblance exists between the working procedures for each craft, the difference between his results is like day and night.

Paul Bowles's music is nostalgic and witty, evoking the times and places of its conception—France, America and Morocco during the twenties, thirties and forties—through langourous triple meters, hot jazz and Arabic sonorities. Like most nostalgic and witty music that works,

Bowles's is all in short forms, vocal settings or instrumental suites. Even his two operas on Lorca texts are really garlands of songs tied together by spoken words. . . .

Paul Bowles's fiction is dark and cruel, clearly meant to horrify in an impersonal sort of way. It often bizarrely details the humiliation and downfall of quite ordinary people, as though their very banality was deserving of punishment. Bowles develops such themes at length and with a far surer hand than in, say, his sonata structures. His formats in even the shorter stories are on a grander plan than in his music; at their weakest they persuasively elaborate their plots (albeit around ciphers, and in a style sometimes willfully cheap); at their best they transport the reader through brand-new dimensions to nightmare geographies. Bowles communicates the incommunicable. But even at their most humane his tales steer clear of the "human," the romantic, while his music can be downright sentimental. Indeed, so dissimilar are his two talents that it is hard to imagine him composing backgrounds to his own dramas.

Lawrence D. Stewart

Knowing what we do of Bowles's upbringing, we inevitably look for correspondence between the facts of his life and the events in his fiction. But Bowles himself resists the correlation. "I don't ever want to be in them [the fictional works] at all. I am *not* in them. That's why I object when people say 'That's you!' or also, 'What was your idea in writing this; what was your method?' Well, I didn't have any idea or method— not that I'm aware of—so I can't answer these questions." Nevertheless, if we look at some of the chronicled events, as well as his announced intentions, we can see where small bridges have been built between his personal activities and the dramatic action in his stories. . . .

Unlike most composer-authors, Bowles insists that he is preeminently a writer of words. His primary interest is the sentence. (As his mentor, Gertrude Stein, said of Scott Fitzgerald: he writes naturally in sentences, and that is a comfort.) When Bowles first met Gertrude Stein she was insisting that paragraphs are emotional, and, if not misleading, at least troubling to the development of ideas. A sentence, however, is a self-contained entity: as she told Fitzgerald, it has good plumbing and does not leak. Bowles believes that a sentence does more than merely contain itself: it generates a successor-sentence. His practice has always been to work over a sentence in all its possible structures and forms until he settles for the particular casting that serves best. (To serve, a sentence must not only express an idea clearly but generate that necessary successor-sentence.) Incremental inspiration often denies him, he feels, an over-view or general plan for work-in-progress, and the process can lead into dullness or desiccation. But Bowles cautiously feels his way through the rhetorical maze and is uncommonly successful in avoiding wrong-turnings.

Lawrence D. Stewart's "Paul Bowles and 'The Frozen Fields' of Vision" published in *The Review of Contemporary Fiction* vol. 2, no. 3, 1982. Reprinted by permission.

Time

The pieces that make up Paul Bowles's first collection of stories in 17 years [*The Time of Friendship*] read like obituaries of the soul. His characters, robbed of purpose, their spirits rubbed flat, move zombielike through exquisitely desolate landscapes—Moroccan ghettos, Algerian deserts, New York subway tunnels. Displaced in the present, they have vague pasts and menacing futures; sighing despair, they search for something unnameable.

Perhaps their quest is for what they find: hostility, hallucination, more intense dislocation, the last retreat of death—Bowles doesn't say. After several novels, books of stories and essays, he is still the inscrutable artist. He fixes his characters in his own hopeless wastelands and in the reader's shocked consciousness. His warped people are beyond help because they will not help themselves. They have surrendered, and Bowles, the devil's advocate, grinds them further into defeat. He is American fiction's leading specialist in melancholy and insensate violence.

At his best, Bowles has no peer in his sullen art. . . . For his terrifying, black penetration of the heart, Paul Bowles commands cold admiration. Living in Africa, corresponding with America in a kind of code, he uses the same metaphors of loneliness and abandon that signaled his leap from music to the novel with *The Sheltering Sky* in 1949. His work is art, a minor art, mirroring a part truth—that man is alone. The other part of the truth is that man has the power to break out of his loneliness through two forces: love and art. Bowles knows the second, not the first.

R. G. G. Price

Pages From Cold Point is a slight handful of stories, mostly set in North Africa, though the best is Caribbean. Smoothly admitting the tedium, sleaziness and brutality of native life, they show a guest's unwillingness to criticise, or is it abdication of judgment disguised as objectivity? The fascinated observation of racial habits and tensions has a slight tinge of the pre-1914 spinster who fell in love with the Italians or the Irish or others of nature's children. Good as the stories are, easy to read without being facile, they do not seem to have extended Mr. Bowles's talent.

R. G. G. Price's review of Paul Bowles's *Pages From Cold Point* first appeared in *Punch* May 1, 1968, p. 652 and is reproduced by permission of *Punch*.

Times Literary Supplement

The best and most interesting of these stories are terse, pregnant narratives set in North Africa—gnomic, almost veiled compositions which strike the eye rather as an outlandish dress seen suddenly and sharply on a street. The outline is lucid, proper and almost intimidatingly functional, but meaning, origin and context are scrupulously undisplayed. The entire experience is impeccably clear yet an enigma intacta.

Mr. Bowles is thoughtful enough to ease us gradually into this opaque but luminous world. The first two tales in the book are transitional. They are orientated—if precariously—in a familiar culture and their point of view is that of the puzzled, vulnerable exile. . . .

Violence and counter-violence, magic, the rule of the strong and canny, the spell of kif smoke, tribal solidarity, ritual vengeance. Mr. Bowles's success here is that his restraint is indeed of the firmest and rarest kind. For his most stringent loyalty as a writer is to the context of that part of the Arab world in which he has for so long been absorbed. So tenacious is that world's grip on him that he can resist entirely the temptation to explain it to an alien and maybe imperceptive readership. The thing, if shaded and puzzled, remains superbly true to itself.

Review of Paul Bowles's *Pages from Cold Point and Other Stories*. Originally published in the *Times Literary Supplement*, May 1968. Reprinted by permission.

Bernard Bergonzi

Critics have already placed Mr. Bowles as a writer of Gothic tendency with a taste for gamey, melodramatic situations and not much liking for humanity. This is a fair enough description of his short stories; still one must insist on his extreme verbal skill, while finding what he does with it very limited and ultimately monotonous. He places his characters before us and then destroys them in an unerring way: it is a remarkable performance, but one expects something more from literature.

Maureen Howard

Reading *The Time of Friendship*, Paul Bowles's new collection of stories, I was aware of a career honest in its aims but only occasionally swinging free of a steady performance. Unlike Tennessee Williams' attempts at unmanageable forms, Bowles sticks with what he can do. Here are the gothic tales with their meaningless violence and seedy Arab settings which repeat the formula established in *The Delicate Prey* seventeen years ago. Here are the macabre Saki endings and the landscapes beautifully tuned to an indefinable melancholy. The stories are always carefully written but, for the most part, they are too self-contained and seldom have anything to match the atmosphere of frenzied desolation that drives through *The Sheltering Sky* to make it Bowles's masterpiece. He is still involved with his ideas of twenty years ago but he has lost his passion for them. The existential experience of *The Sheltering Sky* can never seem dated, but many of the empty exotic scenes in *The Time of Friendship* depend upon a bleak modernity which has worn thin even for Bowles.

This is not true of the story entitled *The Time of Friendship*—a wonderful exploration of the limits of love between a Swiss spinster and an Arab boy. Significantly, it gains from its concerns with society. The woman's yearly retreat to the peace of the desert is based on a travel-poster conception of tranquillity that screens out most of the picture. She can never stop teaching, in an enlightened colonial spirit, the little boy whom she grows to love. Polite friendship is the only possible arrangement for these two because she will always give in the wrong way and he will always use her. Her European morality, his devious Arab practicality will make them blind to the other's needs. The Swiss woman is forced to leave the desert because of the Algerian War, the sort of historic occasion which is rare in Bowles. It is not an intrusion upon the tenderness of the story, but a fact which makes *The Time of Friendship* more than a delicate tale. Only the war will set the spinster and the boy free of each other—each to live with his own disappointment and his own possibilities. . . .

Maureen Howard's "Other Voices" first published in *Partisan Review*, Winter 1968. Reprinted by permission.

In another story, "The Hours After Noon," the shoddy morality of a British matron is played off against a real, though decadent, sensuality of one of the guests at her pension. Again Bowles lets us get hold of some easy associations and then with great artistry proceeds to transform the familiar setup into a real horror for which we must find a fresh response. . . .

Another splendid story in the collection, "The Frozen Fields," centers on the dreamlike quality of a child trying to piece together the terrible world of adults. It is set on an American farm at Christmas time, almost exotic territory for Bowles, but he knows it thoroughly—all the cruelty and pain rooted in the definable past—and I felt once more that the ordinary should be more central to his vision. His voice need only break through a distracting patter of accomplishment to be heard again.

Gore Vidal

"Carson McCullers, Paul Bowles, Tennessee Williams are, at this moment at least, the three most interesting writers in the United States." A quarter century has passed since I wrote that sentence in a piece on contemporary American writing.

Six years ago when I reprinted those words in *Homage to Daniel Says*, I felt obliged to add: "This was written in 1952. McCullers was a good and fashionable novelist of the day (I cannot say that I have any great desire to read her again). Paul Bowles was as little known then as he is now. His short stories are among the best ever written by an American. Tennessee Williams, etc. . . ." All in all, I still see no reason not to support my youthful judgment of Paul Bowles. As a short story writer, he has had few equals in the second half of the twentieth century. Obvious question: If he is so good, why is he so little known?

Great American writers are supposed not only to live in the greatest country in the world (the United States, for those who came in late), but to write about the greatest of all human themes: *The American Experience.* From the beginning of the Republic, this crude America First-ism has flourished. As a result, there is a strong tendency to misrepresent or under-value our three finest novelists: Henry James (who lived in England), Edith Wharton (who lived in France), Vladimir Nabokov (who lived in Switzerland, and who wasn't much of an American anyway despite an unnatural passion for our motels, so lyrically rendered in *Lolita*).

Paul Bowles has lived most of his life in Morocco. He seldom writes about the United States. On the other hand, he has shrewd things to say about Americans confronted with strange cultures. . . .

I suspect that Bowles's apparent foreignness has limited the number of doctoral theses that ought by now to have been devoted to one whose art far exceeds that of . . . well, name the great American writers of our day (a list that was as different yesterday as it will be tomorrow). For the

Gore Vidal, "Introduction," *Collected Stories 1939–1976* by Paul Bowles, Santa Barbara, Black Sparrow Press, 1980.

American Academic, Bowles is still odd man out; he writes as if *Moby Dick* had never been written. Odder still, he is also a distinguished composer of music. In fact, he supported himself for many years by writing incidental music for such Broadway plays as *The Glass Menagerie*. It is curious that at a time when a number of serious critics have expressed the hope that literature might one day take on the attributes of the "highest" of all the arts, music, Bowles has been composing music as well as writing prose. I am certain that the first critic able to deal both with his music and his writing will find that Bowles's life work has been marvelous in a way not accessible to those of us who know only one or the other of the two art forms.

In the spring of 1945, Charles Henri Ford asked Bowles to edit an issue of the magazine *View*. The subject was Central and South American culture. Bowles translated a number of Spanish writers; and wrote some texts of his own. In the course of "reading some ethnographic books with texts from the Arapesh or from the Tarahumara given in word-for-word translation . . . the desire came to me to invent my own myths, adopting the point of view of the primitive mind." He resorted to "the old Surrealist method of abandoning conscious control and writing whatever words came from the pen." The first of these stories was written "one rainy Sunday"; it is called "The Scorpion."

The story was well received, and Bowles went on writing. "The subject matter of the myths soon turned from 'primitive' to contemporary. . . . It was through this unexpected little gate that I crept back into the land of fiction writing. Long ago I had decided that the world was too complex for me ever to be able to write fiction; since I failed to understand life, I would not be able to find points of reference which the hypothetical reader might have in common with me." He did not entirely proceed through that small gate until he wrote "A Distant Episode" and found that if life was no more understandable to him than before, prose was. He now possessed the art to depict his dreams.

During the next thirty years Paul Bowles wrote the thirty-nine short stories collected in this volume. They were published originally in three volumes: *The Delicate Prey*, 1950; *The Time of Friendship*, 1967; *Things Gone and Things Still Here*, 1977. Even before the first collection was published, three of the stories caused a great stir in the literary world. "Pages from Cold Point," "The Delicate Prey" and "A Distant Episode" were immediately recognized as being unlike anything else in our literature. I have just re-read the three stories, with some nervousness. After all these years, I wondered if they would still "work." In my youth I had admired

D. H. Lawrence's novels. Now, I deeply dislike them. I was relieved to find that Bowles's art is still as disturbing as ever. I was surprised to note how the actual stories differ from my memory of them. I recalled a graphic description of a sixteen-year old boy's seduction of his father on a hot summer night in Jamaica. Over the years, carnal details had built up in my memory like a coral reef. Yet on re-reading "Pages From Cold Point," nothing (and everything) happens. In his memoirs Bowles refers, rather casually, to this story as something he wrote aboard ship from New York to Casablanca: "a long story about a hedonist. . . ." It is a good deal more than that. Both "The Delicate Prey" and "A Distant Episode" create the same sense of strangeness and terror that they did the first time I read them. "The Delicate Prey" turns on a Gidean *acte gratuit*: the slicing off of the boy's penis is not only like the incident on the train in *Les Caves du Vatican* but also presages the driving of a nail through a skull in Bowles's novel *Let It Come Down*. "A Distant Episode" seems to me to be more than ever emblematic of the helplessness of an over-civilized sensibility (the Professor's) when confronted with an alien culture. Captured by North African nomads, his tongue cut out, he is made into a clown, a toy. He is used to make his captors laugh. He *appears* to accept his fate. Something harsh is glimpsed in the lines of a story that is now plainer in its reverberations than it was when written. But then it is no longer news to anyone that the floor to this ramshackle civilization that we have built cannot bear much longer our weight. It was Bowles's genius to suggest the horrors which lie beneath that floor, as fragile, in its way, as the sky that shelters us from a devouring vastness.

The stories fall into rough categories. First: locale. Mexico and North Africa are the principal settings. Landscape is all-important in a Bowles story. Second: how the inhabitants of alien cultures regard the creatures of our civilized world, as in "Under the Sky." Bowles goes even further in a beautiful story called "The Circular Valley" where human life is depicted as it must appear to the anima of a place. This spirit inhabits at will those human beings who visit its valley; feeds on their emotions; alters them during its occupancy. Third: the stories of transference. In "You Are Not I" a madwoman becomes her sane sister. In "Allal," a boy exchanges personality with a snake. The intensity of these stories makes them more like waking dreams than so many words on a page. Identity is transferred in such a way that one wonders which, finally, is which? and what is what? The effect is rather like the Taoist story of the man who dreamed that he was a butterfly. When "he woke up with a start, he did not know whether he was Chuang Chou who had dreamed that he was a butterfly, or whether he was a butterfly dreaming that he was Chuang Chou. Between Chuang Chou and the butterfly there must be some distinction. This is what is called the transformation of things."

There are a number of more or less realistic stories that deal with the plain incomprehension of Americans in contact with the natives of Mexico, North Africa, Thailand. One of the most amusing is "You Have Left Your Lotus Pads on the Bus." An American goes on an excursion with some Buddhist priests. The day is filled with splendid misunderstandings. There is the man at the back of a crowded bus who never stops screaming. He is ignored by everyone except the American who wonders why no one shuts him up. At the end, the priests tell him that the "madman" is an employee of the bus company giving necessary warnings and advice to the driver.

In several stories white ladies respond not-so-ambiguously to dark-skinned youths. Bowles notes the sadism that sexual frustration can cause ("At Paso Rojo"). But where the ordinary writer would leave it at that, Bowles goes deeper into the human case and, paradoxically, he achieves his greatest effects when he concentrates entirely on surfaces. Although he seldom describes a human face, he examines landscape with the precision of a geologist. Bowles himself seems like one of those bright sharp-eyed birds that flit from story to story, staring with eyes that do not blink at desert, hills, sky. He records weather with all the solemnity of a meteorologist. He looks closely at food. As for his human characters, he simply lets them reveal themselves through what they say or do not say. Finally, he is a master of suggesting anxiety (are all the traveller's cheques lost or just mislaid?) and dread (will this desert prove to be the setting for a very special death?). Story after story turns on flight. It is no accident that Bowles called his memoir (with pride?) *Without Stopping.*

Four stories were written to demonstrate that by using "kif-inspired motivations, the arbitrary would be made to seem natural, the diverse elements could be fused, and several people would automatically become one." These pieces strike me as entirely uninhabited, and of no interest. Yet in other stories (inspired perhaps by smaller doses of kif) he does demonstrate the essential one-ness of the many as well as the interchangeability not only of personality but of all things. As Webster saw the skull beneath the skin, so Bowles has glimpsed what lies back of our sheltering sky . . . an endless flux of stars so like those atoms which make us up that in our apprehension of this terrible infinity, we experience not only horror but likeness.

Joyce Carol Oates

Thirty-nine stories, coldly and impeccably crafted, the work of four decades: tales set, for the most part, in Morocco, Mexico, and South America, in landscapes of a superlunary authority. (Even Bowles's Manhattan is not our Manhattan.) To state that the intensely evoked settings of Bowles's disturbing stories are usually hostile to his people— natives as well as hapless North Americans—is perhaps misleading, for the setting of a typical Bowles story possesses more life, more identity, than the human beings who find themselves trapped in it, succumbing to fates that read more like ominous parables than "stories" in the usual sense of the word. In one of his poems D. H. Lawrence speaks of a creature whose origins predate not only man, but God—a creature born "before God was love"—and it is precisely this sense of a natural world predating and excluding consciousness that Paul Bowles dramatizes so powerfully in his fiction. It is not an accident that the doomed professor (of linguistics) of the notorious story "A Distant Episode" loses his tongue before he loses his sanity, and his humanity, a captive of an outlaw tribe of the Sahara; nor is it chance that the American girl Aileen, visiting her mother and her mother's Lesbian-companion in Colombia, in "The Echo," succumbs to an irrational violence more alarming than any she has witnessed, and, while attacking her mother's lover, "uttered the greatest scream of her life"—pure sound, bestial and liberating.

Too much has been made, perhaps, of the dreamlike brutality of Bowles's imagination, which evokes a horror far more persuasive than anything in Poe, or in Gide (whom Bowles peripherally resembles). But the stories, like fairy tales, tend to dissolve into their elements because so little that is "human" in a psychological sense is given. The reader is usually outside Bowles's characters, even in those stories—"You Are Not I," "Pages from Cold Point," "Reminders of Bouselham"—in which a first-person narrator speaks. Most of the stories are terrible without being terrifying, as if the events they delineate take place outside our customary human world. A young boy is tortured and castrated in the desert by a maddened hashish smoker ("The Delicate Prey"); an Amazonian woman, living in a squalid ruin in Mexico, captures infants in order to devour their hearts and thereby gain supernatural power ("Doña Faustina"); the soul of a kif-besotted boy passes into a snake who has "the joy of pushing his fangs" into two men before he is killed ("Allal"); a sensitive young Mexican girl succumbs to the atmosphere of sadism about her, and accepts a kinship with "monstrous" spiders who live in the crevices of her bedroom wall ("At Paso Rojo"). In "Call at Corazón" a traveler abandons his alcoholic wife to an unimaginable fate in the South American jungle; in "The Hours After Noon" a child molester is driven by a fellow European into the Moroccan hills, where his fate (a few twists of wire about the neck) is inevitable, once he approaches an Arab child. The last we see of the North American professor of linguistics he has become sheer animal: ". . . Bellowing as loud as he could, he attacked the house and its belongings. Then he attacked the door into the street. . . . He climbed through the opening . . . and still bellowing and shaking his arms in the air . . . he began to gallop along the quiet street toward the gateway of the town. A few people looked at him with great curiosity." A soldier shoots at him, idly, and he runs in terror out into the desert, into "the great silence out there beyond the gate." The insight of Conrad's Kurtz—"The horror! The horror!"—strikes a reader fresh from Bowles's fiction as supremely romantic, even sentimental. Conrad's Africa remains comfortingly European: its terrors can be verbalized.

Even those stories in which nothing explicitly violent occurs, stories which would probably not offend the average genteel reader—"The Frozen Fields," "The Time of Friendship"—create an unnerving suspense by virtue of Bowles's masterly craft. He has learned from Hemingway as well as Lawrence; even his descriptions are wonderfully dramatic. Nothing is extraneous, nothing is wasted. If one wants, at times, more humanity—more "consciousness"—surely this is a naïve prejudice, a wish that art affirm our human vantage point, as if the brute implacable *otherness* of the natural world were no more threatening than a painted backdrop for an adventure film. Though Bowles's marvelous landscapes call to mind another twentieth-century master of short fiction, D. H. Lawrence, it is misleading to read Bowles in the light of Lawrence. Even in Lawrence's coldest, most "legendary" tales, where landscape overcomes humanity—"The Man Who Loved Islands,"

"The Woman Who Rode Away"—one confronts and, to some extent, lives within recognizable human beings whose personalities are always convincing; and this is not true in Bowles. Lawrence's people are like us, Bowles's people tend to be our very distant kin, shadowy and remote, unclaimable. One cannot imagine Bowles creating a Constance Chatterly or a Mellors, trembling with apprehension of each other, or a Gerald (of *Woman in Love*), so susceptible to erotic passion that he chooses death rather than a life without the woman he desires. Desire in Bowles's fiction—in "Under the Sky," for instance, where a Mexican peasant rapes an American woman—is no more articulated than the emotion of the deranged professor of linguistics. Bowles does not write of sexual love in order to challenge its mythology, like many contemporary writers; he does not write about it at all. His interests lie elsewhere.

This collection, a companion to *The Thicket of Spring* (1972), which brought together four decades of Bowles's poetry, should strengthen Paul Bowles's position in American literature. Austere, remorseless, always beautifully crafted, the best of these stories are bleakly unconsoling as the immense deserts about which Bowles writes with such power, and they linger in the memory—disturbing, vexing—literally for decades. The reader is advised to approach them with caution, however, limiting himself to one or two at a sitting. For these are stories set in an epoch "before God was love," and beside them most acclaimed fiction of our time—brightly and nervously ironic, or dutifully attuned to the latest "moral" problems— seems merely shallow.

Stephen Koch

Bowles is an artist of landscape; Stein was right to advise him to find a place. His characters at times are vague; his landscapes vivid, to the last rock, puddle, bush. Whether set in Morocco, Mexico, or the New York subway, the Bowles scene is invariably ominous with secret terrors. Familiar comforts are delusions. Awful things are going to happen: I can think of no other writer who induces that impression so often, so convincingly. Even in such relatively genteel pages as those of "The Echo," hairline cracks are everywhere in the smooth surface of decency, sanity, reasonableness. A pleasant American college girl waits for her nice American mother. But the place is an unnameable Mexican dive; the mother, for some reason, is not there. Mute Indians stare at her, knowing but not telling. The girl slips, falls.

And so the essential Bowles format consists of a westerner—i.e., a rationalist, therefore a naif—disoriented in some seductive, alien Elsewhere. In a way, it is yet another version of the familiar romantic obsession with the mysterious East, and one can't help thinking of recent attacks on that fantasy—notably Edward Said's *Orientalism*. But this is a hard romanticism. The stories are wonderfully crafted; yet, despite their elegant order, one senses a contempt for all appearance of order. One even senses—20 years before Main Street's head shops mimicked Tangier—a certain pre-'60's taste for mind-blowing. One character speaks of "that unpardonable mechanism, the intellect." It is all here—the Casbah, the kif dens, the mazes of slums, the hurt, lurking, imperialized Arab boys. Bowles has lived this murky Western dream, brought his formidable artistic intelligence to it. Its paradoxes and possibilities find expression here.

Terror can be a kind of ecstasy. Except for William Burroughs— Bowles' friend and admirer—I know no modern writer who can produce quite Bowles' impression of an almost charnel horror of the flesh. There are agonies, there are mutilations. Bowles' stories are more polished,

Stephen Koch's "Paul Bowles: The High Stylist of Tangier" first appeared in *The Washington Post Book World* August 9, 1979. (c) 1979. The Washington Post. Reprinted with permission.

more "conventional" than Burroughs' wild dissociations, but at moments his pages are almost too much to bear. Even reading through his more benign moments, I have rarely felt so often the classic shiver of anticipation at the thought of plain mortality. The mind holds still. No matter what, it—*It*—will come. Later. Sooner. Maybe even now.

Michael Krekorian

This Bowles retrospective, *Collected Stories*, represents the work of an innovator in American literature who seeks to debunk apparent order residing deep within nature and to dismiss man's reasoning power over the world as irrelevant hallucination. As with the finest of contemporary works, the thrust of the Bowles story rests in the disjointed ambiguity of human activity rather than the germ of order in a world, as Kosinski put it, where identity cannot exist, only situations. Paul Bowles mixes disharmonious elements of reality, the jungles working within the imaginative framework of human-like impulses and actions, to create a character of chaotic situation, rather than a stable identity. This personification of the setting, in the end, meshes with the violent jungle of human situation—posing as human identity.

Thus, Bowles' *Collected Stories* take the arguable position that rationality and pragmatism, the hallmarks of contemporary Western Civilization—our "rage for order"—appear to be hollow gestures in the face of the jungles that appear before us or within us.

"Paul Bowles, Collected Stories, 1939–1976," by Michael Krekorian. First appeared in *Fiction International* 12 (1980): 188–189. Reprinted by permission.

Conger Beasley, Jr.

Bowles' ability to project himself into the primitive mind is extraordinary. It is a risky thing for any Western writer to attempt, the result quite often being pure sentimental hash, a cloying recloaking of dusky skins in familiar spiritual garb, reminiscent of the best (worst?) of Rudyard Kipling—the "Gunga Din syndrome," it might be called, which is responsible for that most outrageous of all colonial violations, the remaking of a human identity exclusively in the conqueror's terms.

Fortunately, Bowles is too skilled and honest a writer to permit this to happen. His *indigenes* are without compromise, and frequently without mercy. They don't behave like white people because they aren't white people; they act impulsively, whimsically, even brutally on occasion. Within the context of their own lives, they behave with impeccable logic.

Conger Beasley Jr.'s "Some Places and Ways to Live" from *The North American Review* number 1, 1981. Reprinted by permission.

Gilbert Sorrentino

Nowhere in Bowles do we find any hint of the exotic. His Arabs don't think of themselves as such, but as people who live the lives that have been given them. The brilliance of Bowles' work is rooted in the fact that his prose takes his non-western world for granted, and this matter-of-fact attitude is tacitly held in subtle opposition to what might be called the reader's expectations. We bring our great bag of *idées fixes* to Bowles' Morocco, and he calmly proceeds to empty it in front of us. Furthermore, Bowles' western characters are often seen to be carrying that same bag in the stories in which they appear: their reward for this cultural error is usually disaster.

It should be noted that those stories that deploy only western characters are handled in the same way by Bowles, so that the reader has the eerie feeling that he is reading about people that he *should* be able to recognize, but does not. The author's attitudes toward Western culture and Western people are very hard on the ideas of the marketplace. This technical ability has grown, as I have suggested, from Bowles' refusal to follow the fictional path of least resistance. He does what the good artist everywhere does: solves the problems he has created for himself with the same tools used to create the problems. He is responsible to his work and not to the dim flickerings of "taste."

Gilbert Sorrentino's article "Paul Bowles: The Clash of Cultures" first appeared in *The Washington Post Book World* August 2, 1981. (c) 1981. The Washington Post. Reprinted with permission.

Wendy Lesser

The most essential aspect of Bowles's stories—the way in which things *don't* get said explicitly—is inevitably lost in any discussion of their content. Yet these stories must be talked about, because it is rare for any writer's "Collected Works" (and this one spans 47 years of writing) to present the kind of uniform perfection that this book does.

"Uniform" is a misleading word here, in that it suggests lack of variety. Certainly the 39 stories in this collection could not be more various. They range in setting from South American jungles to mountainous villages to African deserts to the subways of Manhattan. They deal with virtually every imaginable intimate human relationship: husband to wife, parent to child, sister to sister and brother to brother, employee to employer, pastor to congregation, killer to victim, human to animal, lover to lover, and stranger to stranger. Even their narrative technique varies widely, from the first-person distorted reality of the mad narrators in "You Are Not I" and "If I Should Open My Mouth," to the removed, neutral, folk-myth-like telling of "The Scorpion" and "The Waters of Izli." Yet there *is* something common to all these stories, and I think that sameness has to do with tone, or what Bowles himself—in the introductory note to his recent edition of five Moroccan story-tellers, published by Black Sparrow Press as *Five Eyes*—calls the "voice" of a story. In all of the stories Bowles has written, that voice is shaped by one particular effort—the strenuous withholding of judgment.

Not that the strain shows in the stories themselves: if anything, their language seems at first glance to be as fluid and straightforward as the language of folk tales and fireside stories. The narrative voice itself never suggests that judgment is in any way called for. Yet a brief look at the kind of stories Bowles *seems* to borrow from—for instance, the oral tales he translates in *Five Eyes*—reveals that authorial opinions are pervasive in those stories: the narrators think nothing of saying "This was good" or

Excerpts from Wendy Lesser's review of Paul Bowles's *Collected Stories* published in *The American Book Review* May 1980. Reprinted by permission.

247

"She was ugly" whenever they feel like it. Bowles, on the other hand, has consciously excised such narrative judgments from his own stories, leaving a gap that creates strong tension between the seemingly traditional form and the far-from-traditional voice. Moreover, the events in Bowles's stories are the sort that cry out for judgment: enormous cruelty, bizarre and inexplicable behavior, psychological and cultural conflict. Yet judgment is consistently suppressed, and therefore the events never fully take shape as "bizarre" or "cruel"—they are simply events.

If I have given the impression that Bowles is a sort of Robbe-Grillet who writes on action-packed topics, this is a false impression. Whereas Robbe-Grillet and other writers who experimented in that manner were interested in the photographic, "objective" look of things, Bowles is at least as much concerned with internal states. Even the stories which are written from a third-person viewpoint frequently focus on a single character's perceptions, and all of Bowles's landscapes seem tinged by human response to them. But such distinctions—internal/external, subjective/objective, alien/familiar, willed/fated, and even cruel/kind— begin to seem pointless in relation to Bowles's work. His stories, if they are uniformly about anything, are about the annihilation of such barriers—and yet he depends on us to remember these barriers, and thereby to give the stories something solid to work against. Bowles's stories about the loss of distinctions are written for an audience that believes in the necessity of distinctions.

Catherine Rainwater

The works of Bowles suggest Poe's influence in three major areas: characterization, architectonics, and notions about language. Like Poe, Bowles develops characters who suffer an imbalance between rational and nonrational forces of mind; such characters attempt to transcend or escape the limits of personality, often to find themselves inhabiting nightmarish psychological realms from which there is no exit. Also like Poe, who develops a single mythopoetic vision which informs almost all of his works, Bowles devises a system of spatial symbols that remains constant throughout the majority of his stories and novels. And finally, both Poe and Bowles raise similar questions about the relationship between the deterioration of personal identity and of linguistic ability. Despite the affinities between Poe and Bowles, however, Bowles's is consistently the darker vision. The complex and mostly disillusioning array of twentieth-century discoveries and philosophies has darkened the vision of most contemporary writers, and Bowles numbers among the most cynical of this already pessimistic generation. Drawing ideas and techniques from Poe's art, Bowles inevitably concentrates upon the "modern" features of Poe's fiction; he emphasizes as basic principles of existence paradox, despair, and nihilism, which Poe only part of the time entertains as possibilities. Whereas Poe searches for an elusive center of meaning in the universe, Bowles's fiction reduces the significance of human existence by disclosing only a center of meaninglessness. . . .

Bowles continues to develop Poe-esque characters in the stories of *The Delicate Prey*. Like several of Poe's stories such as "The Fall of the House of Usher" and "Ligeia" which involve unreliable, irrational narrators (or narrators such as those in "The Tell-Tale Heart" and "The Cask of Amontillado" who are so exaggeratedly rational that they appear deranged), "Pages From Cold Point" lends itself to interpretation as psychomachia. Similar to "The Fall of the House of Usher," "Ligeia,"

Catherine Rainwater's article " 'Sinister Overtones,' 'Terrible Phrases': Poe's Influence on the Writings of Paul Bowles" first appeared in *Essays in Literature* Fall, volume 2, 1984. Permission to quote from *Essays in Literature* is given by Western Illinois University.

"The Tell-Tale Heart" and perhaps especially "William Wilson," Bowles's story presents a constellation of characters symbolically suggesting a battle between flesh and spirit, and between intellect and emotion. Another portrayal of the "war between reason and atavism," "Pages From Cold Point" includes a narrator who desires to lapse into unconsciousness and atavistic behavior; it also includes the narrator's brother, Charles, who represents consciousness and rational (socially sanctioned) behavior, and the narrator's son, Racky, a homosexual adolescent who must soon choose between the former men's modes of existence.

Publishers Weekly

Bowles is convinced "that the human world has entered into a terminal period of disintegration and destruction." His pessimism is manifested in the common themes of these seven short stories—insanity and death, both of which reflect "the decay of civilization." Despite their different settings, the tales are all obsessed with the deviant side of human behavior, be it torture, poisoning, vampirism, suicide, murder. Five of these pieces are set in Morocco and Tangiers, where a racist attitude toward the indigenous populations is apparent. Clearly, in Bowles's view, to these "uncivilized" people, death by violent means is the norm. European and American foreigners are at the mercy of the natives unless, as Bowles implies, they create their own separate enclaves apart from the Moslems. Insanity is the basis for most of these stories and, interestingly, is confined to women. Ten out of his 12 female characters are nagging, hysterical, mentally ill or suicidal, the doomed victims of weak psyches. Finally, it is noteworthy that three of the stories are compelling stream-of-consciousness monologues, a pleasant change from Bowles's (*Points in Time*, etc.) otherwise bland observations.

Unwelcome Words (a notice), *Publisher's Weekly*, March 25, 1988, p 60. Reprinted by permission.

Chronology

1910   Paul Frederic Bowles born 30 December in Jamaica, Long Island, New York, to Rena Winnewisser Bowles and Claude Dietz Bowles, a dentist.

1928   Poem "Spire Song" appears in volume 12 of the Paris-based experimental journal *transition*; the following issue features "Entity." Enrolls in the University of Virginia, Charlottesville.

1929   Boards *Rijndam* on 30 March without his parents' knowledge, Paris his ultimate destination; returns to New York in July.

1930   Meets Henry Cowell and, through him, Aaron Copland; returns to the University of Virginia in fall.

1931   Sets out for Europe again, in March, anticipating the arrival of Copland soon after; meets Gertrude Stein, Cocteau, Pound, and Gide; travels to Berlin with Copland; meets Kurt Schwitters in Hannover, goes to Holland, then returns to Paris, where Stein and Alice B. Toklas invite him to accompany them to their country home in Bilignin; with Copland, makes his first trip to Morocco that summer; returns to Paris after visits to Fez, Spain, London, and the Italian Alps.

1932   Returns to Tangier and travels for several months in Morocco before returning to Paris in early May, having contracted typhoid; in Monte Carlo works at musical compositions, including music to St. John Perse's *Anabase*; leaves for Algeria late in December.

1933   Travels in Sahara, returns to Tangier, then heads back to North America by spring, short on cash.

1934   Leaves Manhattan for Morocco, to act as secretary to Colonel Charles Williams in Fez; returns by ship, via Puerto Rico and Colombia, to arrive in California.

1935   Back in New York.

1936   Composes music for *Horse Eats Hay*, directed by Orson Welles for the Federal Theater Project.

1937   Meets Jane Auer; composes music for ballet *Yankee Clipper*, travels to Mexico.

1938   Marries Jane Auer 21 February in Manhattan, then embarks for Central American honeymoon, ending up in Europe, before returning to New York.

1940   Composes score for *Twelfth Night* and a U.S. Department of Agriculture film, *Roots in the Soil*; travels to Mexico and meets Tennessee Williams.

1941   Composes score for *Liberty Jones*; receives Guggenheim fellowship and again escapes to Mexico; meets Ned Rorem.

1943   Composes score for *'Tis a Pity She's a Whore* and for *South Pacific*, as well as an opera, *The Wind Remains*, based on a Lorca play; Knopf publishes Jane Bowles's *Two Serious Ladies*.

1944   Composes score for Tennessee Williams's *The Glass Menagerie*; writes "The Scorpion."

1945   Writes "By the Water" and "A Distant Episode" in New York.

1947   After securing book advance, leaves for Morocco; on board ship writes "Pages from Cold Point"; buys house in Tangier's Casbah, with Oliver Smith.

1948   Composes score for Williams's *Summer and Smoke*.

1949   *The Sheltering Sky* published; sets sail for Indian Ocean, Ceylon in particular.

1950   Returns to Morocco and develops friendship with young artist, Ahmed Yacoubi; *The Delicate Prey and Other Stories*, Bowles's first volume of stories, published; composes score for *The Tempest*.

1952   *Let It Come Down* published; travels to India and Ceylon with Yacoubi; buys Taprobane, island off coast of Ceylon.

1953   Composes score for Jane Bowles's play, *In the Summer House*.

1954   Travels to Ceylon with Jane, Yacoubi, and Temsamany, their driver.

1955   *The Spider's House* published.

1956   Travels to Ceylon with Yacoubi.

1957   Returns to Tangier; Jane suffers stroke.

1958   Bowleses travel to Portugal, then New York; *Yerma*, an opera based on the Lorca play, produced.

1959   Composes music for *Sweet Bird of Youth*; receives Rockefeller grant for collection of indigenous Moroccan music.

1962   *A Hundred Camels in the Courtyard* published.

1964   *A Life Full of Holes*, by Larbi Layachi, taped and translated by Bowles.

1966   *Up Above the World* published; travels to Thailand.

1967   *The Time of Friendship* published; with *Love with a Few Hairs*, begins collaboration with Mohammed Mrabet.

1968   Teaches at San Fernando State College in California.

1972   *Without Stopping*, Bowles's autobiography, published.

1973   Jane Auer Bowles dies in Malaga, Spain.

1977   *Things Gone and Things Still Here* published.

1978   Composes score for *Caligula*.

1980   *Collected Stories* published.

1981   *Midnight Mass* published.

1982   *Points in Time* published.

1988   *Unwelcome Words* and *A Distant Episode: The Selected Stories* published.

1990   Celebrates eightieth birthday.

1991   *Tangier Journal: 1987–1989* published.

Selected Bibliography

Primary Works

Published Collections of Short Stories

Call at Corazón and Other Stories. London: Peter Owen, 1988.
Includes "Call at Corazón," "At Paso Rojo," "Doña Faustina," "Under the Sky," "The Echo," "An Inopportune Visit," "Tea on the Mountain," "The Successor," "The Hours After Noon," "The Frozen Fields," "Sylvie Ann, the Boogie Man," "Monologue, Tangier 1975," "Monologue, New York 1965," "Monologue, Massachusetts 1932," "In Absentia," "Hugh Harper," "Dinner at Sir Nigel's."

Collected Stories, 1939–1976. Santa Barbara, Calif.: Black Sparrow Press, 1980.
Includes "Tea on the Mountain," "The Scorpion," "By the Water," "A Distant Episode," "The Echo," "Call at Corazón," "Under the Sky," "Pages from Cold Point," "How Many Midnights," "The Circular Valley," "At Paso Rojo," "Pastor Dowe at Tacaté," "You Are Not I," "The Delicate Prey," "Señor Ong and Señor Ha," "A Thousand Days for Mokhtar," "The Fourth Day Out from Santa Cruz," "Doña Faustina," "The Hours After Noon," "The Successor," "If I Should Open My Mouth," "The Frozen Fields," "Tapiama," "The Hyena," "A Friend of the World," "The Story of Lahcen and Idir," "He of the Assembly," "The Wind at Beni Midar," "The Time of Friendship," "The Garden," "Afternoon With Antaeus," "Mejdoub," "The Fqih," "The Waters of Izli," "Reminders of Bouselham," "You Have Left Your Lotus Pods on the Bus," "Istikhara, Anaya, Medagan and the Medaganat," "Things Gone and Things Still Here," "Allal."

The Delicate Prey and Other Stories. New York: Random House, 1950. Reprint: New York: Ecco Press, 1982.
Includes "At Paso Rojo," "Pastor Dowe at Tacaté," "Call at Corazón," "Under the Sky," "Señor Ong and Señor Ha," "The Circular Valley," "The Echo," "The Scorpion," "The Fourth Day Out from Santa Cruz," "Pages from Cold Point," "You Are Not I," "How Many Midnights," "A Thousand Days for Mokhtar," "Tea on the Mountain," "By the Water," "The Delicate Prey," "A Distant Episode."

A Distant Episode: The Selected Stories. New York: Ecco Press, 1988.
Includes "A Distant Episode," "The Echo," "Call at Corazón," "Pages from Cold Point," "The Circular Valley," "The Delicate Prey," "At Paso Rojo,"

"Pastor Dowe at Tacaté," "Señor Ong and Señor Ha," "The Frozen Fields," "He of the Assembly," "The Time of Friendship," "Mejdoub," "Allal," "Tapiama," "The Little House," "Here to Learn," "Rumor and a Ladder," "In the Red Room," "The Eye," "An Inopportune Visit," "In Absentia," "Tangier 1975," "Unwelcome Words."

The Hours After Noon. London: Heinemann, 1959.

Includes "Doña Faustina," "Tapiama," "The Frozen Fields," "Sylvie Ann, the Boogie Man," "How Many Midnights," "If I Should Open My Mouth," "Tea on the Mountain" "A Thousand Days for Mokhtar," "The Successor," "The Hours After Noon."

A Hundred Camels in the Courtyard. San Francisco: City Lights Books, 1962.

Includes "A Friend of the World," "He of the Assembly," "The Story of Lahcen and Idir," "The Wind at Beni Midar."

A Little Stone. London: John Lehmann, 1950.

Includes "Call at Corazón," "Pastor Dowe at Tacaté," "The Echo," "At Paso Rojo," "The Scorpion," "Señor Ong and Señor Ha," "The Circular Valley," "Under the Sky," "A Spring Day," "The Fourth Day Out from Santa Cruz," "By the Water," "A Distant Episode."

Midnight Mass. Santa Barbara, Calif.: Black Sparrow Press, 1981. Reprint: London: Peter Owen, 1985.

Includes "Midnight Mass," "The Little House," "The Dismissal," "Here to Learn," "Madame and Ahmed," "Kitty," "The Husband," "At the Krungthep Plaza," "The Empty Amulet," "Bouayad and the Money," "Rumor and a Ladder," "The Eye."

Pages from Cold Point and Other Stories. London: Peter Owen, 1968.

Includes "Pages from Cold Point," "The Time of Friendship," "The Hyena," "He of the Assembly," "The Garden," "The Story of Lahcen and Idir," "The Delicate Prey," "A Friend of the World," "The Wind at Beni Midar."

Things Gone and Things Still Here. Santa Barbara, Calif.: Black Sparrow Press, 1977.

Includes "Allal," "Mejdoub," "You Have Left Your Lotus Pods on the Bus," "The Fqih," "Istikhara, Anaya, Medagan, and the Medaganat," "The Waters of Izli," "Afternoon with Antaeus," "Reminders of Bouselham," "Things Gone and Things Still Here."

Three Tales. New York: Frank Hallman, 1975.

Includes "Afternoon with Antaeus," "The Fqih," "Mejdoub."

The Time of Friendship. New York: Holt, Rinehart & Winston, 1967.

Includes "The Time of Friendship," "The Successor," "The Hours After Noon," "A Friend of the World," "He of the Assembly," "The Story of Lahcen and Idir," "The Wind at Beni Midar," "The Hyena," "The Garden," "Doña Faustina," "Tapiama," "If I Should Open My Mouth," "The Frozen Fields."

Unwelcome Words. Bolinas, Calif.: Tombouctou Books, 1988.

Includes "Julian Vreden," "New York 1965," "Hugh Harper," "Massachusetts 1932," "Dinner at Sir Nigel's," "Tangier 1975," "Unwelcome Words."

Uncollected Story Published in Periodical

"Bluey." *View* 3 (October 1943):81–82.

Novels

Let It Come Down. London: John Lehmann, 1952; New York: Random House, 1952. Reprints: Santa Barbara, Calif.: Black Sparrow Press, 1980; London: Peter Owen, 1984.

"A Novel Fragment," *Library Chronicle of the University of Texas at Austin* n.s. 30 (1985):67–71.

The Sheltering Sky. London: John Lehmann, 1949; New York: New Directions, 1949. Reprints: New York: Ecco Press, 1978; London: Peter Owen, 1981.

The Spider's House. New York: Random House, 1955; London: Macdonald, 1957. Reprint: Santa Barbara, Calif.: Black Sparrow Press, 1986.

Up Above the World. New York: Simon & Schuster, 1966; London: Peter Owen, 1967. Reprints: New York: Ecco Press, 1982; London: Peter Owen, 1982.

Poetry

Next to Nothing: Collected Poems, 1926–1977. Santa Barbara, Calif.: Black Sparrow Press, 1981.

Nonfiction

"The Ball at Sidi Hosni." *Kulchur* 2 (1960):8.

"The Challenge to Identity." *Nation*, 26 April 1958, 360.

Points in Time. London: Peter Owen, 1982. Reprint: New York: Ecco Press, 1984.

Tangier Journal: 1987–1989. London: Peter Owen, 1989. Reprint: New York: Ecco Press, 1991 (under title *Days: Tangier Journal: 1987–1989*).

Their Heads Are Green and Their Hands Are Blue: Scenes from the Non-Christian World. London: Peter Owen, 1963; New York: Random House, 1963. Reprint: New York: Ecco Press, 1984.

Without Stopping. New York: Putnam, 1972; London: Peter Owen, 1972. Reprint: New York: Ecco Press, 1985.

Yallah. New York: McDowell, Obolensky, 1957.

Secondary Works

Interviews

Bailey, Jeffrey. Interview with Paul Bowles. *Paris Review* 81 (1981):62–98.

Breit, Harvey. "Talk with Paul Bowles." *New York Times Book Review*, 9 March 1952, 19.

Evans, Oliver. "An Interview with Paul Bowles." *Mediterranean Review* 1 no. 2 (Winter 1971):3–15.

Halpern, Daniel. Interview with Paul Bowles. *TriQuarterly* 33 (Spring 1975):159–77.

Rogers, Michael. "Conversation in Morocco." *Rolling Stone*, 23 May 1974, 48–54.

"Stories of Violence." Interview. *Newsweek* (International), 4 August 1986, 48.

Books

Bertens, Johannes Willem. *The Fiction of Paul Bowles: The Soul Is the Weariest Part of the Body.* Amsterdam: *Costerus*, n.s. 21 (1979).

Briatte, Robert. *Paul Bowles, 2117 Tanger Socco.* Paris: Plon, 1989.

Green, Michelle. *The Dream at the End of the World: Paul Bowles and the Literary Renegades in Tangier.* New York: Harper Collins, 1991.

Patteson, Richard F. *A World Outside: The Fiction of Paul Bowles.* Austin: University of Texas Press, 1987.

Pounds, Wayne. *Paul Bowles: The Inner Geography.* New York: Peter Lang, 1985.

Rochat, Joyce Hamilton. "The Naturalistic-Existential Rapprochement in Albert Camus' *L'Etranger* and Paul Bowles' *Let It Come Down*: A Comparative Study in Absurdism." Diss., Michigan State University, 1971.

Sawyer-Lauçanno, Christopher. *An Invisible Spectator: A Biography of Paul Bowles.* New York: Weidenfeld & Nicholson, 1989.

Stewart, Lawrence D. *Paul Bowles: The Illumination of North Africa.* Carbondale and Edwardsville: Southern Illinois University Press, 1974.

Articles and Reviews

Amster, Leonard. "In No Country." Review of *Let It Come Down. Saturday Review*, 15 March 1952, 21.

Beasley, Jr., Conger. "Some Places and Ways to Live." Review of *Collected Stories. North American Review* 266, no. 1 (1981):56–57.

Bergonzi, Bernard. "Not Long Enough." Review of *The Time of Friendship. New York Review of Books*, 9 November 1967, 33.

Broyard, Anatole. "The Man Who Discovered Alienation." Review of *An Invisible Spectator*, by Christopher Sawyer-Lauçanno. *New York Times Book Review*, 6 August 1989, 3.

Cooke, Judy. "You Don't Forget." Review of *A Thousand Days for Mokhtar* (published by Peter Owen in London, 1989). *Listener*, 23 February 1989, 32–33.

Craft, Robert. "Pipe Dreams." *New York Review of Books*, 23 November 1989, 6+.

Dagel, Gena. "A Nomad in New York: Paul Bowles, 1933–48." *American Music* (Fall 1989): 278–314.

Review of *The Delicate Prey*. *New Yorker*, 9 December 1950, 167–68.

Ditsky, John. "*The Time of Friendship*: The Short Fiction of Paul Bowles." *Twentieth Century Literature* 34, no. 3–4 (1986):373–87.

Drabelle, Dennis. "Paul Bowles: The Outsider of the Avant-Garde." *Washington Post Book World*, 11 June 1989, 3.

Eisinger, Chester E. "Paul Bowles and the Passionate Pursuit of Disengagement," in *Fiction of the Forties*. Chicago: University of Chicago Press, 1963.

Evans, Oliver. "Paul Bowles and the 'Natural' Man." *Critique* 1, no. 3 (1959):43–59.

Fiedler, Leslie A. "Style and Anti-Style in the Short Story." *Kenyon Review* (Winter 1951):155–72.

Fost, Michelle. Review of *Unwelcome Words*. *Small Press* 5 (August 1988):29.

Friend, James. "No More Rapport." Review of *The Time of Friendship*. *Saturday Review*, 26 August 1967, 32.

Gray, John. "Indefinite Futures." Review of *News from Cold Point*. *Books and Bookmen*, June 1968, 34.

———. "Steps off the Beaten Path." Review of *Collected Stories*. *Time*, 27 August 1979, 73–74.

Handlin, Oscar. Review of *The Time of Friendship*. *Atlantic Monthly*, 27 September 1967, 130–31.

Harris, Oliver. "City of Dreams and Nightmares." Review of *Call at Corazón, Without Stopping*, and *M'Hashish*. *New Statesman*, 15 April 1988, 39–40.

Hassan, Ihab. "The Pilgrim as Prey: A Note on Paul Bowles." *Western Review* 19 (1954):23–36.

Hibbard, Allen. "Expatriation and Narration in Two Works by Paul Bowles." *West Virginia Philological Papers* 21 (1986): 61–71.

Horvath, Brooke K. Review of *A Distant Episode: The Selected Stories*. *Review of Contemporary Fiction* 10 (Spring 1990):297.

Howard, Maureen. "Other Voices." Review of *The Time of Friendship*. *Partisan Review* (Winter 1968): 141–52.

Hunter, Frederic. "Bowles: A Master of Bizarre Exotica, Irony." Review of *Collected Stories*. *Christian Science Monitor*, 10 August 1981, B9.

"In Exile." Review of *Pages from Cold Point and Other Stories* (published by Peter Owen, 1968). *Times Literary Supplement*, 9 May 1968, 473.

Jackson, Charles. "On the Seamier Side." Review of *The Delicate Prey*. *New York Times Book Review*. 3 December 1950, 6.

Keegan, Paul. "Americans in Foreign Parts." *Times Literary Supplement*, 13–19 May 1988, 526.

Koch, Stephen. "Paul Bowles: The High Stylist of Tangier." Review of *Collected Stories. Washington Post Book World*, 9 September 1979, 11.

Krekorian, Michael. "Paul Bowles, *Collected Stories, 1939–1976*." *Fiction International* 12 (1980):288–89.

Lehan, Richard. "Existentialism in Recent American Fiction: The Demonic Quest." *Texas Studies in Literature and Language* (Summer 1959):181–202.

Lerner, Bennett. "Paul Bowles: Lost and Found." In *Perspectives on Music: Essays on Collections at the HRC*, edited by Dave Oliphant and Thomas Zigal, Austin, Texas: Humanities Research Center 1985, 149.

Lesser, Wendy. "*Collected Stories*: Paul Bowles." *American Book Review* 2 (May 1980):24. Reprinted in *Review of Contemporary Fiction* 2, no. 3 (1982):32–41.

Lewis, Tom J. Review of *A Distant Episode: The Selected Stories. World Literature Today* 2 (Autumn 1989):681.

McInerney, Jay. "Paul Bowles in Exile." *Vanity Fair*, September 1985, 68+.

Maddox, Melvin. "Brilliant Hobbyist of Modern Infernos." *Life*, 21 July 1967, 8.

Malin, Irving. "Drastic Points." *Review of Contemporary Fiction* 2, no. 3 (1982):30–32.

———. "*The Time of Friendship*, by Paul Bowles." *Studies in Short Fiction* 4, no. 3 (1968):311–13.

Maloney, John J. "Skillful Tales from Exotic Gardens of Evil." Review of *The Delicate Prey. New York Herald-Tribune Book Review*, 3 December 1950, 4.

Mottram, Eric. "Paul Bowles: Staticity and Terror." *Review of Contemporary Fiction* 2, no. 3 (1982):6–30.

Oates, Joyce Carol. "Bleak Craft." Review of *Collected Stories. New York Times Book Review*, 30 September 1979, 9. Reprinted in Oates's collection of essays, under the title "Before God Was Love," *The Profane Art*, 128–31. New York: E. P. Dutton, 1983.

Olson, Steven, E. "Alien Terrain: Paul Bowles's Filial Landscapes." *Twentieth Century Literature* 34, no. 3–4 (1986):334–49.

Patteson, Richard F. "Paul Bowles: Two Unfinished Projects." *Library Chronicle of the University of Texas at Austin* n.s. 30 (1985):57–65.

Pounds, Wayne. "Paul Bowles and *The Delicate Prey*: The Psychology of Predation." *Revue Belge de Philologie et d'Histoire* 59, no. 3 (1981):620–33.

Price, R. G. G. "New Fiction." Review of *Pages from Cold Point. Punch*, 1 May 1968, 652.

Rainwater, Catherine. "'Sinister Overtones,' 'Terrible Phrases': Poe's Influence on the Writings of Paul Bowles." *Essays in Literature* 2 (Fall 1984):253–66.

Rorem, Ned. "Paul Bowles." *New Republic*, 22 April 1972, 24. Reprinted in Rorem's *Setting the Tone*, 355. New York: Limelight Editions, 1984.

Rountree, Mary Martin. "Paul Bowles: Translations from the Moghrebi." *Twentieth Century Literature* 34, no. 3–4 (1986):388–401.

Ryle, John. "Survivor of the Cold Style." Review of *Unwelcome Words*, by Paul Bowles, and *An Invisible Spectator*, by Christopher Sawyer-Lauçanno. *Times Literary Supplement*, 15 September 1989, 995–96.

261

St. Louis, Ralph. "The Affirming Silence: Paul Bowles's 'Pastor Dowe at Tacaté.'" *Studies in Short Fiction* 24, no. 4 (Fall 1987):381–86.

Samuels, Charles T. "What's That in the Tank." Review of *The Time of Friendship*. *Nation*, 4 September 1967, 183–84.

Solotaroff, Theodore. "The Desert Within." Review of *The Time of Friendship*. *New Republic*, 2 September 1967, 29. Reprinted in Solotaroff's book of essays, *The Red Hot Vacuum*, 254–60. New York: Atheneum, 1970.

Sorrentino, Gilbert. "Paul Bowles: The Clash of Cultures." Review of *Midnight Mass*. *Washington Post Book World*, 2 August 1981, 3, 6.

"Specialist in Melancholy." Review of *The Time of Friendship*. *Time*, 4 August 1967, E4.

Stern, Daniel. "Encounters East and West." Review of *The Time of Friendship*. *New York Times Book Review*, 6 August 1967, 4.

Stewart, Lawrence. "Paul Bowles and 'The Frozen Fields' of Vision." *Review of Contemporary Fiction* 2, no. 3. (1982):64–71.

Williams, Tennessee. "The Human Psyche—Alone." Review of *The Delicate Prey*. *Saturday Review of Literature*, 23 December 1950, 19–20.

Bibliographies

McLeod, Cecil R. *Paul Bowles: A Checklist, 1929–1969*. N.p.: Apple Tree Press, 1970.

Miller, Jeffrey. *Paul Bowles: A Descriptive Bibliography*. Santa Barbara, California: Black Sparrow Press, 1986.

Index

The Author

Allen Hibbard is currently an assistant professor at Middle Tennessee State University, where he teaches American literature and literary theory. Before moving to Tennessee, he taught at the University of Washington in Seattle, where he received his Ph.D., and at the American University in Cairo. He has written a study of the American expatriate novel and published articles on irony, fictional employment of exotic settings, narrative strategies in Paul Bowles's fiction, and Jane Bowles's unfinished novel, *Out in the World*. He also writes fiction. For 1992–93 he was chosen to be a Fulbright lecturer in American literature at Damascus University.

The Editor

General Editor Gordon Weaver earned his B.A. in English at the University of Wisconsin-Milwaukee in 1961; his M.A. in English at the University of Illinois, where he studied as a Woodrow Wilson Fellow, in 1962; and his Ph.D. in English and creative writing at the University of Denver in 1970. He is author of several novels, including *Count a Lonely Cadence*, *Give Him a Stone*, *Circling Byzantium*, and most recently *The Eight Corners of the World* (1988). Many of his numerous short stories are collected in *The Entombed Man of Thule*, *Such Waltzing Was Not Easy*, *Getting Serious*, *Morality Play*, *A World Quite Round*, and *Men Who Would Be Good* (1991). Recognition of his fiction includes the St. Lawrence Award for Fiction (1973), two National Endowment for the Arts Fellowships (1974, 1989), and the O. Henry First Prize (1979). He edited *The American Short Story, 1945–1980: A Critical History*, and is currently editor of *Cimarron Review*. He is professor of English at Oklahoma State University. Married, and the father of three daughters, he lives in Stillwater, Oklahoma.